1995

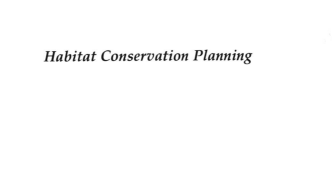

Habitat Conservation Planning

HABITAT CONSERVATION PLANNING

Endangered Species and Urban Growth

Timothy Beatley

UNIVERSITY OF TEXAS PRESS

AUSTIN

First edition, 1994

Requests for permission to reproduce material from this work should
be sent to Permissions, University of Texas Press, Box 7819, Austin,
TX 78713-7819.

∞The paper used in this publication meets the minimum requirements of American National Standard for Information Sciences—
Permanence of Paper for Printed Library Materials, ANSI Z39.48-1984.

Library of Congress Cataloging-in-Publication Data

Beatley, Timothy, date
    Habitat conservation planning : endangered species and urban
growth / Timothy Beatley. — 1st ed.
        p.   cm.
    Includes bibliographical references (p.   ) and index.
    ISBN 0-292-70799-1. — ISBN 0-292-70806-8 (pbk.)
    1. Habitat conservation—Planning. 2. City planning—
Environmental aspects. 3. Endangered species. 4. Biological
diversity conservation. I. Title.
QH75.B43   1994
333.95'416—dc20   93-22810

Contents

Preface

This book is a direct outgrowth of my long-standing belief that urban development and human settlement patterns can be managed to minimize environmental impacts. This interest has led me in a number of directions, including natural hazards mitigation, coastal planning, and urban growth management policy. In a sense, habitat conservation planning is simply one more extension of this professional focus.

It has become for me, however, a deeper and more serious issue. The magnitude of global biodiversity loss is daunting and perhaps the most significant environmental issue of our time. I am at once both discouraged by the pace of destruction, and encouraged by recent concern about the problem and by practical efforts to address it. In the American context, habitat conservation plans represent one such promising approach—one worthy of careful examination, and perhaps emulation, in other environmental policy areas here in the United States, as well as in other countries.

What follows is a study which examines the success to date of habitat conservation plans, and the political and practical issues and constraints which emerge from these experiences. While I do briefly discuss rationale for preserving biodiversity, this is not a philosophy text. I do, however, believe that the issue before us is ultimately a question of ethics. It seems to me that whether we are able to successfully balance the needs of development and species protection will in the long run depend on the ability of *Homo sapiens* to embrace a new ethical conviction toward the other forms of life that inhabit our planet, and toward the broader ecosystems which provide habitat for all. What is perhaps ultimately required is an ethic which truly views humans as members of a larger community of life. As members of this community we should be seen to hold clear obligations to protect the habitats and ecosystems of other lifeforms as well as our own. Aldo Leopold, more than forty years ago, articulated such an ethic when he discussed the need to move from an ethical position of conquerors of the environment to being "plain citizens" of it. To Leopold we are but equal members of a complex and interconnected network of life.

And if we are serious as a society about sharing our small planet and maintaining an ethic of respect for other species, the long-term implications are profound. They suggest a substantial rethinking of our lifestyles and our consumption patterns. For urban planners and policymakers, there are fundamental changes implied in the types of human settlement patterns and strategies that are appropriate and permissible. Perhaps the most basic change is the rejection of unnecessary land consumption. Sharing the planet implies a responsibility to minimize our "footprint" and a responsibility not to squander the limited common habitat. Among the specific land use and planning policies that seem required by such an ethic are: higher urban and suburban densities, and more compact and contiguous development patterns; the redirection of growth back into existing urban centers and the revitalization of declining areas; infilling and utilizing already degraded and committed lands for new developments before encroaching on environmentally sensitive habitat areas; and restricting the extent to which second homes and other less essential forms of development are subsidized or permitted at all.

The vision of a shared planet may also call for other changes in lifestyle that extend beyond the amount of land we directly consume for development. For example, a number of contemporary threats to species in this country involve water projects (e.g., dams, reservoirs, diversion systems). The vision of a shared planet may necessitate sharply curtailing the extent to which we wastefully consume a scarce resource such as water—particularly in the western United States. The same could be said about energy consumption, the consequences of which can severely and irreparably damage the habitat of endangered and non-endangered species (e.g., the destruction of a riparian ecosystem as a result of a hydro-electric project, the creation of acid deposition as a result of coal-burning power plants, and the damage done by recent oil spills). Human-induced global warming is a particularly serious threat in that many species will be unable to adapt to new climatic conditions largely as a result of human settlement patterns. There are many ways in which being a "plain citizen" may require rethinking basic lifestyle and consumption patterns. And, perhaps more fundamentally, the notion of sharing the planet will require serious efforts on a global scale to control population growth. Such strategies as higher densities, urban infilling, and energy conservation can do only so much to reduce the human impact when the quantity of people, activities, and resource demands are expanding at exponential rates.

At the very least, we must, as a species, enter a period of reflection about our position here on Earth and the responsibilities we have to its other inhabitants, as well as to our own descendants.

It should be emphasized that many of the habitat conservation plans (HCPs) examined in this book are still very much in development and any conclusions about their success must be tentative. The HCP process and tool is still very much in its infancy and in many ways it is much too early to conclude that such an approach will or will not ultimately work. Many of these plans are "moving targets" and will require many years of monitoring and evaluation before conclusions can be reached. Furthermore, several of the plans discussed in detail here have not yet been completed and as such may look quite different later from the snap shot presented here. It is extremely useful, however, even where plans have not yet been completed to take stock of the process and strategy being pursued in them. Improvements in our programs and policies to protect species and biodiversity in this country simply cannot wait until all of these plans have been completed. HCPs are being increasingly utilized throughout the country and now is an extremely opportune time to extract whatever lessons and constructive reservations might come out of our experiences to date.

Many individuals have assisted this work along the way. David Brower at the University of North Carolina at Chapel Hill initially roused my interest in the mechanism of habitat conservation plans, by relating his experiences chairing the executive committee for the North Key Largo Habitat Conservation Plan. Numerous individuals have spent many hours talking with me about habitat conservation plans and their perceptions of the benefits and limitations of them. These generous individuals have included: Kent Butler, Paul Selzer, Gail Kobitich, Jim Bartel, Tom Reid, Jim Movius, Paul Fromer, Bill Mayhew, David Brower, Al Muth, Keith Downs, Chuck Sexton, and others. At the University of Virginia, Bettie Hall has provided her usual cheerful and extremely competent typing.

Special thanks are owed to the staff at the University of Texas Press for their enthusiasm and strong support of this project.

T.B.

CHARLOTTESVILLE, VA

Habitat Conservation Planning

CHAPTER

ONE

Land Development
and Endangered Species:
Emerging Conflicts

Conflicts between Development and Species Protection

Public awareness and concern about the extinction of species have undoubtedly increased in recent years. Environmental groups like the World Wildlife Fund and the Audubon Society have been quite successful in elevating concern about the anthropogenic impacts on our great storehouse of flora and fauna. The loss of biological diversity, or "biodiversity," has been added prominently to the list of major environmental problems facing the planet. Even ten years ago the term *biodiversity* would have had little meaning even to many environmentalists or conservationists, and still less to the average person on the street. The writings of such scientists as Paul Erhlich and Edward O. Wilson have done much recently to popularize the concerns about the loss of biodiversity.[1]

Yet citizens and public officials in this country tend to see the biodiversity problem, if they see one at all, as primarily occurring in other countries. Species are facing extinction, in the minds of many, primarily as a result of tropical deforestation in countries such as Brazil and of illegal poaching in Africa and elsewhere. While these are in fact major threats to global biodiversity, there is sometimes a tendency to de-emphasize threats to biodiversity in this country, or in our own backyards. This book is principally focused on the conflicts which have been emerging between the need and desire to develop land and the need to protect endangered species and biodiversity.

It is useful and entirely appropriate to place the U.S. problem in the context of the larger global problem. Globally, species and habitat are threatened by numerous activities, including destroying habitat, overharvesting/over-exploiting, and invasive species disturbing habitat. In recent years habitat loss has become the primary threat to biodiversity as the extent of human settlements continues to grow.

In many parts of the globe this is clearly the direct result of dramatic rises in population levels and the attendant demands placed on the land to feed and shelter these populations. There has been an incredible rise in the global human population from a little over 1 billion at the turn of the century to around 5.4 billion today. A recent United Nations' report predicts that global population levels may rise as high as 12 billion before stabilizing.[2]

Estimating current rates of global extinction, and predicting future rates, are tenuous at best. There is little certainty about the total number of species on Earth, but estimates put the number between 10 million and 30 million. Wilson has estimated that if current rates of deforestation continue, extinction rates may exceed the loss of seventeen thousand species per year.[3] Others have concluded that as much as 25% of our existing species may become extinct by the beginning of the next century. While the predictions vary there is general agreement that the rates are very high and a large segment of the world biota stock is at risk.[4]

In the United States, the causes of habitat loss are more complex than simple population growth. Clearly population levels have risen substantially here, as well. However, compared with those in other nations around the world, the amounts of land and space per capita are quite large in the United States. The problem, it seems, in recent years has been the inefficient and wasteful nature of our land usage. The dominance of the automobile, the impact of federal subsidies provided for home ownership, major federal investments in a national highway system, and equal neglect of mass transit, among other factors, have led to the sprawling land-intensive patterns of development common in the United States.

It is important to note in this initial chapter that while biological diversity is the greatest in tropical regions, biological diversity in the continental United States is quite impressive (see Table 1.1). The 1970s, 1980s, and the early years of the 1990s have witnessed the emergence of serious and dramatic conflicts and confrontations between the forces of development and the advocates of protection of this biodiversity. For many, the enactment by Congress of the federal Endangered Species Act (ESA) in 1973 signaled a new concern about species conservation and spurred much of the conflict in recent years. As shown below, the habitat conservation planning process owes its origin to ESA.

Table 1.1. *Species Diversity in the United States (Known Species)*

Mammals[a]	466
Birds[a]	1,090
Reptiles[a]	368
Amphibians[a]	222
Fishes[a]	2,640
Insects[b]	88,090
Plants[a]	20,000

[a] U.S. Congress, Office of Technology Assessment, *Technologies to Maintain Biological Diversity* (Washington, D.C.: Government Printing Office, 1987).
[b] D. J. Borror, *Introduction to the Study of Insects* (Philadelphia: CBS College Publishing, 1981).

The conflicts between species protection and urban growth and development appear all around us, and virtually in every part of the country. Not surprisingly, conflicts are more frequent where the number of rare and endangered species are greatest and where population and development pressures are most severe. Much of the conflict, then, has focused on high-diversity and high-growth states like California, Texas, and Florida (see Figures 1.1 and 1.2). But, as the figures illustrate, there is diversity in every state and some degree of development and changes as well—thus, the potential for species/development conflicts.

Furthermore, environmental degradation in this country has gradually whittled away at these biological resources. The number of endangered or threatened species listed on the Endangered Species Act continues to climb and is currently well in excess of seven hundred. As well, thousands of additional species have been classified as candidates for listing and could be listed at some point in the future. The trends in biodiversity loss appear to move entirely in one direction—species become listed and remain on the list because they rarely recover sufficiently to be removed from it. Notable exceptions are the American Bald Eagle (in the continental United States) and the American alligator.

These increasing conflicts typically pit environmentalists and supporters of biodiversity conservation against developers and supporters of community development and growth. In addition, there are typically a variety of different stakeholder groups involved in these conflicts and in the preparation of habitat conservation plans, and all have varying perspectives and points of view on the issue, which may or may not fall on this conservation/development continuum.

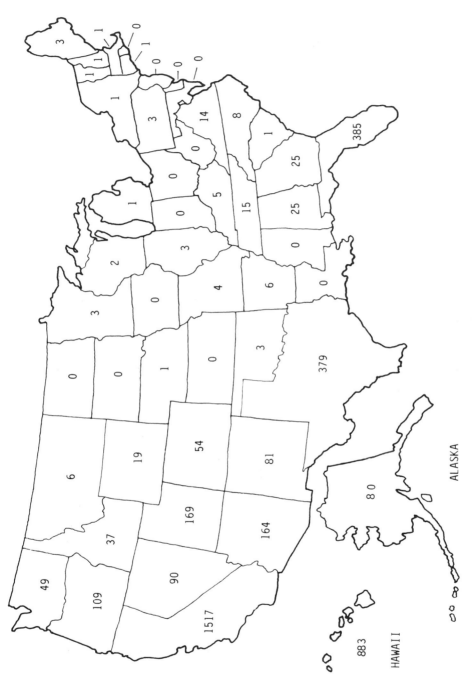

Figure 1.1. Number of Endemic Plants by State (Adapted from A. H. Gentry, "Endemism in Tropical versus Temperate Plant Communities," in Michael E. Soule, ed., *Conservation Biology*, 1986, by permission of Sinauer Associates, Inc., Publishers)

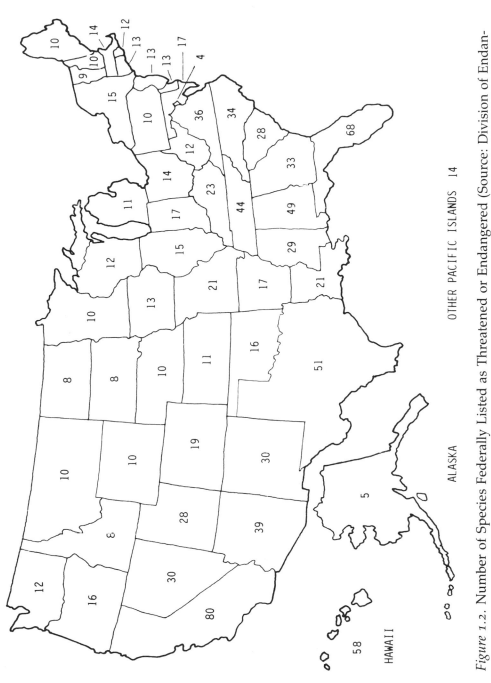

Figure 1.2. Number of Species Federally Listed as Threatened or Endangered (Source: Division of Endangered Species and Habitat Conservation, U.S. Fish and Wildlife Service, 1988)

Justification/Rationale for Protecting Endangered Species[5]

As the following cases illustrate, protection of biodiversity and endangered species often conflicts with demands for housing, economic development, and other social and individual objectives. To many these conflicts suggest that those advocating biodiversity must put forth good reasons why such societal sacrifices should be made. Why should we be concerned with the loss of biodiversity in the first place?

There are a number of arguments for protecting endangered species, and more broadly, biodiversity, and they range from utilitarian and instrumental views to views which support protection based on the intrinsic value and inherent worth of other forms of life. Before proceeding to a discussion of habitat conservation plans, it will be useful to briefly review these different positions.

Many have argued that species and biodiversity should be protected by humans because they produce, or will produce, numerous direct benefits for human society. These benefits may be medicinal in nature, for example, in that the globe's existing stock of flora and fauna represents an immense and largely untapped pharmaceutical storehouse. A large portion of commercial pharmaceutical products are derived directly from wild plants and animals.[6] These medicinal benefits are illustrated well by recent discoveries of the importance of the yew tree, indigenous to the forests of the northwest United States. The bark of the yew tree has been found to be a highly effective treatment for certain types of cancer. It has been estimated, however, that only 5% of all plant species have been examined for their potential pharmaceutical benefits.

Biodiversity may advance important research, from which scientific, medical, and anthropological knowledge can be formed. As John A. Murray notes:

> Bats and dolphins have given science insight into sonar. Physiologists study the metabolism of the black bear for insights into the problems of cholesterol and kidney disease. The bear's ability to enter a deep sleep resembling true hibernation also intrigues researchers, and could one day help science replicate the same state of suspended animation in human astronauts. The desert pupfish tolerates extremes of salinity and temperature that could have implications for our treatment of human kidney disease. It has recently been discovered that molluscs—clams, snails, mussels—rarely, if ever, get cancer.
> . . . who knows which of the threatened or endangered species, from the lowliest and least known to the most commonplace and familiar, might be of use to us in the future?[7]

Protecting biodiversity also holds the potential for numerous other economic and commercial benefits, such as the discovery of new disease-resistant crops or crops that may adjust better to changing climatic conditions (e.g., the buffalo gourd, which requires little water). As another example, a plant native to Central Africa (the kenof) is currently thought to be a much cheaper and less environmentally harmful source of pulp and paper fibers than trees.[8]

Perhaps more fundamentally, conservation of biodiversity is essential to protecting the viability of the larger ecosystem upon which all species depend. Endangered and threatened species are important indicators of how healthy and sustainable our planet really is. The loss of the Least Bell's Vireo or other songbirds may have little direct impact on people, yet may be indicative of the occurrence of broader environmental degradation as well as being a harbinger of more severe environmental calamities to come. Biologists Paul and Anne Ehrlich describe species extinction with the vivid analogy of rivets popping out of the wing of an airplane. With each popped rivet (loss of a species) the structural integrity of the airplane (Earth) is further undermined, until it reaches a point where the plane will no longer fly.[9]

Moreover, humans simply do not understand the intricate ways in which the loss of a single species will affect other species and in turn themselves. A basic and undeniable environmental axiom is that everything is connected to everything else. Each species is the result of centuries of evolving, speciating, and filling an ecological niche. The loss of one species may have long-term "cascading" effects, setting off an ecological chain reaction. (Examples of these ecological interactions are numerous; consider, for instance, the classic example of the American alligator that digs holes with its tail providing important watering and nesting areas in the Everglades for birds and other wildlife during periods of drought.)

While there is considerable truth to this line of argument, it is often difficult, over a short period of time, to discern any dramatic impacts of species extinction. It may take many years to detect the ripple effects on humans of the loss of, for example, the Northern Spotted Owl in the west and northwest United States. It often appears easier to argue that the loss of the habitat, not the species, may be of greatest consequence (e.g., advocating the preservation of Brazilian rainforests because they help stabilize global climate, rather than because they serve as habitat for the endangered golden-lion tamarin).

Protection of endangered species and biodiversity provides, or could provide, substantial recreational and aesthetic benefits for humans. This is apparent to anyone who has witnessed the flight of a peregrine falcon or the fishing behavior of a grizzly bear. Even less awe-inspiring species offer rewarding recreational and visual benefits; the behavior and life processes of invertebrates have for many a "fascination value" (to use the Ehrlichs' terms). One can envision a time in which people might refocus their curiosity and sense of intrigue away from material things and toward the many other forms of life inhabiting our planet. The increasing popularity of eco-tourism and wildlife-oriented activities, from bird watching to whale watching, suggests the growing importance of preserving biodiversity for these purposes. The importance of these types of activities is likely to continue to increase dramatically in the years ahead.

Biodiversity is also important in a deeper emotional sense. It seems that humans do value the existence and qualities of other forms of life as is seen in the names of automobiles and other product lines, the images in advertising and business affairs, and the animal symbols representing important societal and governmental institutions. The loss of each species diminishes our lives in important ways. The prospect of an increasingly empty planet in terms of the number and diversity of species is a depressing one. Species extinction represents innumerable lost opportunities for human enrichment.

While these arguments are convincing in their own right, is the existence of a species justified only if it holds some instrumental value or benefit to humans? This attitude, many writers and ethicists believe, epitomizes humans' arrogance as a species (what some have called "speciesism") by failing to perceive the intrinsic value of other forms of life. Over forty years ago in *Sand County Almanac*, which has become a classic environmental treatise, Aldo Leopold argued for a new ethical posture toward the environment and life forms inhabiting it.[10] Leopold argued for a vision of the environment as a community of life, of which *Homo sapiens* is but a single member. As members of this community, humans have certain obligations to it. Fundamentally, Leopold advocates a more modest view of humans' importance in the world—proposing a view of the human species as a co-inhabitor of the world and a "plain citizen" of it. Such a view ". . . implies respect for . . . fellow members, and also respect for the community as such . . . . The land ethic simply enlarges the boundaries of the community to include soils, waters, plants, and animals, or collectively: the land."[11]

Leopold's "land ethic" remains the clear starting point for much contemporary thought about a more expansive set of environmental obligations. While the detail of the Leopoldian land ethic is modest, it eloquently states a new non-anthropocentric view of how land and non-human members of the life community should be treated.[12]

Others have similarly questioned the arrogance of this species that has little hesitation in extinguishing other forms of life forever. In support of such views, David Erhenfeld has put forth the "Noah Principle," which holds that all species have the right to exist: "They should be conserved because they exist and because this existence is itself but the present expression of a continued historical process of immense antiquity and majesty. Long-standing existence in nature is deemed to carry with it the unimpeachable right to continued existence."[13]

Other environmental ethicists have sought to refine and expand the basis for the intrinsic value and inherent worth of nature. Particular emphasis in recent years has been given to biocentric and ecocentric perspectives which question the inherent moral superiority of the human species, and hold that nature has inherent worth and intrinsic value, irrespective of the instrumental values placed on them by human beings.[14]

There are, of course, competing perspectives which question many of these arguments. Some critics of species conservation efforts question the cost of these efforts and whether species loss will have any appreciable impact on human beings. While the loss of a Coachella Valley fringe-toed lizard or Northern Spotted Owl may be unfortunate, it is felt that their loss will not have very direct or discernible impacts on human life, and furthermore the loss of jobs, tax base, etc., is clearly not justified by any real or significant benefits provided. Some critics have suggested that while preservation of biodiversity would be nice, other things being equal, there are almost always more pressing needs for limited public funds, such as affordable housing, health care, and education. For most Americans, moreover, anthropocentric thinking continues to dominate, and the concept of species' right to exist or the intrinsic value of nature remain foreign.

There are, nevertheless, a number of strong arguments for protecting species and biodiversity, some utilitarian and anthropocentric, others more biocentric or non-anthropocentric in nature. Together these arguments do suggest the possibility of a new and different attitude toward other species and a solemn duty to minimize, to the extent possible, the species-threatening impacts of human actions. Such a view will not be an easy one for planners and policymakers to implement, as the case examples and discussion below will indicate.

Central Policy Questions

The following discussion of habitat conservation plans raises a number of serious policy questions, many of which will remain unresolved. Together, the HCP experiences documented here do shed significant light on the nature of environmental disputes in the U.S. policy context, and are equally applicable to many other emerging environmental policy areas, including wetlands' protection, forest management, control of non-point source water pollutants, and national parks' and public lands' management. While the specific actors may be different, and the geographic location and jurisdictional scale may be different, these disputes have many common attributes and raise many of the same policy questions. One of the more important of these questions arising from the HCP experiences is whether a balance between conservation and development can be achieved.

In many respects the HCP experiences documented here represent individual examples of the larger conflicts between different public policy objectives. These cases inherently represent political and value clashes between different groups. Some groups place high priority on protecting species or biodiversity, for the reasons cited above. Environmental groups have played, and will continue to play, an important role in championing this perspective. Other groups place less importance on protecting species or the environment, and are more concerned with allowing or promoting development, which in turn will lead, they believe, to more jobs, a larger tax base, and greater economic prosperity. While there are typically a host of other individuals and groups with varying perspectives involved in HCPs, the environment versus development dichotomy is always present. Habitat conservation plans, then, represent tangible examples of how this dichotomy has evolved and more importantly how practical compromises have been reached which accommodate both interests. The distinctive feature of HCPs is the ability to protect species and species habitat, while at the same time allowing a significant degree of development.

Habitat conservation plans, moreover, are prepared and implemented under the framework of the federal Endangered Species Act (ESA)—perhaps the strictest environmental protection statute in the world, and one which has become increasingly criticized as a rigid and inflexible law. An examination of the HCP experiences in the United States serves to test the ESA approach—an approach in which the federal government attaches unprecedented protection to listed species and stipulates stringent conservation standards for HCPs, but largely leaves states and local governments (along with developers, landowners, and other private parties) to work out actual plans and compromises. While many problems exist in this arrangement, it has functioned reasonably well in encouraging and permitting conservation/development compromises.

For each HCP experience, there are a number of specific technical and policy questions which must be addressed. One of the more central of these is what the level of habitat protection must or should be. While certain standards are specified by ESA and the U.S. Fish and Wildlife Service (USFWS), there are necessarily differences of opinion about what is required. Should only the bare minimum be protected, or should much larger habitats be set aside to ensure species survival? What types of recovery actions are necessary to ensure long-term survival and recovery, and what level of habitat rehabilitation is needed? Despite the desire for clear and definitive scientific answers to these questions, the HCPs described here illustrate the judgmental and speculative responses to many of these important questions.

Questions also arise about the best strategy for maximizing conservation dollars. Must habitat be protected where the destructive pressures are most evident (i.e., areas subject to urban growth) or should conservation efforts be focused in areas where greater amounts of habitat can be protected for less cost, and where the long-term ecological viability of the habitat is perhaps more secure?

There is as well in the HCP experiences the common tension between protecting the habitat for a single species, and protecting the integrity of larger systems of which that species may be a part. Reminiscent of the debate over the Northern Spotted Owl is the increasing belief that larger ecosystem integrity is more important, and that efforts should be made to protect habitat for multiple species of concern, not just a single species. In the most recent wave of HCPs, there are clearly lessons for the best way to take into account and protect these larger patterns of biodiversity.

The HCP experience also vividly illustrates a common policy dilemma in many other environmental areas—namely the question of who should bear the burden for conservation efforts. Whether it's the loss of logging jobs in the habitat of the Northern Spotted Owl, or the diminution of land value under wetlands regulations, distribution of conservation program costs is an important policy question. While each HCP committee has approached it somewhat differently, they all illustrate the ability to put together funding packages which distribute costs over a number of different sources, including development mitigation fees, federal and state conservation funding, and local bond referenda. Determining the precise package is another major topic in HCP deliberations and inevitably the result of a mixture of compromise and political reality.

Nevertheless, the costs of habitat conservation are typically very high, and the debate about who should pay the lion's share—which jurisdictional levels, which groups in society—remains unresolved. Some believe, for instance, that because the ESA is a federal law, the larger national public ought to accept a sizeable portion of the costs. Others believe that local governments and private developers, who tend to benefit from urban development, ought to pay the most. Considerable concern has been expressed in recent years about the financial impact of endangered species and other environmental laws on private landowners. Opponents of such regulations are quick to claim that they amount to unconstitutional "takings" of private property. If the public wants the benefit of protecting endangered species' habitats or wetlands or other environmental goods, should it not be required to pay for them? critics ask.

CHAPTER

TWO

The Federal Endangered Species Act: Key Provisions and Implications for Land Development

Introduction

Federal intervention to protect endangered and threatened wildlife is a relatively recent phenomenon. Historically, major federal intervention for wildlife dates back to the turn of the century, marked by the passage of the Lacey Act, which placed restrictions on interstate trade and transport of wildlife. Congress began to intervene in the management of endangered species in the 1960s, passing endangered species preservation acts in 1966 and 1969. While these acts were largely policy directives to federal agencies to protect endangered species, and contained few regulatory teeth, they did mandate establishment of a list of endangered species, and generally laid a policy framework for the subsequent congressional efforts.[1]

In 1973 Congress enacted a new Endangered Species Act which substantially expanded the powers of the federal government in this area and created authority almost unprecedented in previous environmental legislation. It has been described as a "prohibitive" law, because of the major and significant restrictions it placed on government agencies and private citizens regarding listed species. The stated purposes of the act "are to provide a means whereby the ecosystems upon which endangered species and threatened species depend may be conserved, to provide for a program for the conservation of such endangered species and threatened species, and to take such steps as may be appropriate to achieve the purposes of the treaties and conventions set forth [in the Act] . . . ."[2]

Since its original enactment in 1973, ESA has been reauthorized three times (most recently in 1988). Most political observers believe that despite the many development/species conflicts which have arisen since its enactment, political and popular support of the act has grown with each reauthorization.

Understanding the HCP process and the legal, political, and other dynamics of development/species conflicts requires some basic understanding of the key provisions of the act. While not an exhaustive review of it, several key components are described below: the species listing process; the Section 9 prohibition on the take of listed species; the Section 7 consultation requirements; and Section 10(a) incidental take provisions.

Key Provisions and Requirements
of the Endangered Species Act

Listing Endangered Species

The regulatory provisions of ESA apply to those species which have been placed on the federal list of endangered and threatened species. An endangered species refers to "any species which is in danger of extinction throughout all or a significant portion of its range" while a threatened species is "any species which is likely to become an endangered species within the foreseeable future throughout all or a significant portion of its range."[3]

Species can be placed on the federal list in several ways. They can be proposed for listing by the U.S. Fish and Wildlife Service (USFWS) or the National Marine Fisheries Service (NMFS), which share responsibility for enforcement and implementation of ESA (NMFS is generally responsible for marine species, USFWS for all others). Species may also be proposed for listing by citizens and private organizations. The listing process for the Northern Spotted Owl, for example, was initiated by a private environmental organization.[4]

The act mandates that biological factors are to be the sole basis for determining whether or not to list a species. In particular, economic factors are not to be considered. The act also requires that, where possible, critical habitat for the species of concern be designated at the same time. Critical habitat is defined in the laws as those specific areas which contain "physical or biological features (I) essential to the conservation of the species, and (II) which may require special management considerations or protection."[5] Amendments to ESA in 1978 do allow the consideration of economic factors in the designation of critical habitat. As a result, proposed critical habitats have often been substantially reduced as a result of protected economic effects and the political pressures generated by them. Politics, as we will see later, clearly has an influence on both the listing process and designation of critical habitat. There has been considerable debate about the benefits of designating critical habitat, with some arguing that it is unnecessary or even undesirable in some cases. Populations of species can also be listed; for instance, the continental population of the American Bald Eagle is listed as endangered even though this species is plentiful in its Alaskan range.

Species can also be classified as candidate species, usually while awaiting a listing determination. Currently more than thirty-six hundred candidate species are listed, representing a serious backlog. Candidate species are classified as either Category I or Category II. Category I species are those for which USFWS has sufficient information to warrant listing, but lacks the resources to undertake the listing process. Category II species are those that may warrant listing, but for which USFWS lacks sufficient information to make a determination. The great majority of candidate species (about thirty-two hundred) fall into this second category.

Theoretically, species can also be removed from the endangered species list when numbers have recovered sufficiently. Over the history of the act few species have recovered enough to have been removed. Proposals have recently been made to "delist" the continental population of the American Bald Eagle, but critics believe it is premature to conclude that the species is no longer in jeopardy of extinction. A species can also be taken off the list if believed to be completely extinct. The Dusky Seaside Sparrow, for example, was recently delisted because it is believed there are no more of this species in existence.

Section 7 Consultation

Once a species is listed, a series of protective standards and provisions are put into play. One of the most important of these is contained in Section 7 of the act, requiring federal agencies to consult with the USFWS or NMFS when projects, permits, or other federal actions will affect a listed species or its critical habitat. Both informal and formal consultation processes are utilized.[6] Typically, the process begins through informal consultation between the agency and USFWS. USFWS informs an agency when a listed species—or its critical habitat—may be present in a project area and if so, that the agency must prepare a biological assessment. If no impact on species or habitat is likely, the process stops here. However, if through the biological assessment it is determined that a listed species or critical habitat may be affected by a proposed project, a formal consultation process is then required.

During formal consultation USFWS must prepare its own opinion determining the extent to which the proposal will biologically affect the species or its habitat. ESA specifically prohibits such federal actions where they would jeopardize the continued existence of the species or adversely modify its critical habitat. Federal projects or actions can proceed only when USFWS (or NMFS) reaches a so-called "no-jeopardy" opinion.[7] Frequently, projects are allowed to proceed where appropriate mitigation components are incorporated to lessen impacts on species and habitats.

Historically, Section 7 has generated the most controversy under ESA. The most notable Section 7 controversy was the now-famous conflict over the completion of the Tellico Dam in Tennessee and its potential impact on the snail darter. Authorized by Congress in 1966, much of the Tellico Dam had been completed when the snail darter issue arose.[8] When the snail darter was listed as an endangered species in 1975, suits were filed under Section 7 by environmental groups seeking to enjoin the dam's completion and claiming that the flooding of lands behind the dam would completely destroy the species' known habitat. It was debated whether the act was intended to apply to such projects already underway, and whether the economic costs of saving the species could be taken into consideration. This legal confrontation reached the U.S. Supreme Court, and led to the famous opinion in *Tennessee Valley Authority v. Hill*.[9] The Supreme Court strongly sided with the prohibitive features of ESA and concluded that Congress had not intended for economic factors to enter into such decisions.

To many in Congress and elsewhere, the snail darter case represented the unreasonable extremes to which ESA could be taken. Amendments to the act in 1978 created a special appeal procedure designed to allow greater flexibility in these types of disputes and to allow for balancing into the equation the economic costs of a jeopardy opinion. Specifically, the amendments created the Endangered Species Committee (often referred to as the "God Committee" or the "God Squad") to which jeopardy opinions could be appealed. This committee is composed of the Secretary of Agriculture, the Secretary of the Army, the Chairman of the Council of Economic Advisors, the Administrator of EPA, the Secretary of the Interior, the Administrator of NOAA, and a member representing each state affected by the proposed project.

Ironically, the Tellico Dam project was appealed to the committee and rejected. (Congress later exempted the project from ESA.) Since its creation in 1978, only a handful of appeals have been made to the committee. The option of appeal to the God Committee has, although frequently discussed, been infrequently used. The Bureau of Land Management (BLM) has recently activated the committee in an effort to overcome restrictions to timber sales as a consequence of the listing of the Northern Spotted Owl. In May 1992 it partially approved this appeal, allowing logging on seventeen hundred acres of BLM land.[10]

Section 9 Prohibition on Take

One of the strongest provisions of ESA is found in Section 9, which prohibits the "taking" of species listed as endangered. The term "take" is defined broadly in the act, including: "to harass, harm, pursue, hunt, shoot, wound, kill, trap, capture, or collect, or attempt to engage in any such conduct."[11] The Section 9 prohibition applies to all parties, public and private. For federal actions requiring Section 7 consultation, "take" is permitted through USFWS's issuance of an "incidental take statement" (as part of its biological opinion), which must stipulate, among other things, "reasonable and prudent measures to minimize the impact."[12]

For threatened species the prohibition on take is not automatic under ESA. USFWS is authorized under 4(d) of the act to apply the ban on take to threatened as well as endangered species, and has done so in most cases.

The Section 9 prohibition on take has been particularly problematic (as we will see) for private landowners and developers who could be subject to criminal and civil penalties for undertaking grading, land clearance, and other construction-related activities which might harm or kill listed species. On the other hand, it is often difficult at best for USFWS to prosecute under Section 9.

There has been considerable debate and confusion over the types of actions that actually constitute "take," and more specifically the definitions of "harm" and "harass"—words contained in the ESA definition. Especially controversial has been the question of whether habitat alteration amounts to "harm" and thus prohibited take. A court decision in 1979, *Palila v. Hawaii Department of Land and Natural Resources,*[13] highlighted the differences of opinion on this question. In this case environmental groups brought suit against the state of Hawaii for maintaining populations of feral sheep and goats in the remaining habitat areas of the endangered Palila bird (a member of the Hawaiian Honeycreeper family). The goats and sheep were maintained for hunting but their overbrowsing and destruction of certain trees upon which the Palila depends had caused a gradual decline in its habitat. The federal courts found in favor of the plaintiffs, concluding that the state's failure to curtail the feral sheep and goats was a violation of Section 9 of ESA. The Palila case served to expand the interpretation of "harm" to clearly include habitat alteration.

The implications of the Palila decision caused USFWS concern and led to their attempting to redefine "harm" in the early 1980s. After a series of redefinition attempts, USFWS returned to a definition which views harm rather broadly. Currently, USFWS regulations define harm, in the definition of take in ESA, as "an act which actually kills or injures wildlife. Such act may include significant habitat modification or degradation where it actually kills or injures wildlife by significantly impairing essential behavioral patterns, including breeding, feeding, or sheltering."[14] A second Palila decision issued in 1985 reaffirmed and further expanded the court's interpretation that harm includes habitat alteration. This case involved a different type of sheep—mouflon sheep—that had similar effects on Palila habitat. The federal district court (affirmed by the Ninth Circuit Court of Appeals) concluded that even actions that merely prevented the recovery of the listed species could amount to a take.[15] The practical definition of take remains controversial and will likely be the subject of future litigation. Clearly, however, definition of "harm" includes habitat destruction or modification which can be shown to lead to death or injury, interference with essential behavioral patterns, or the impedance of recovery of the species.

Plants have not received the same extent of protection under Section 9. The 1988 reauthorization did, however, extend some protection. Specifically, take of endangered plant species is prohibited on federal lands or where take of plants is prohibited under state law.

Recovery Plans

The Endangered Species Act requires USFWS to prepare a recovery plan for each listed species. These plans are typically authored by a scientific committee with biological expertise on the species addressed. Among other things, recovery plans typically evaluate the status of the species, its life history, threats to its existence, and its habitat requirements. Each plan also outlines recovery goals and identifies actions needed to promote recovery of the species. The plans typically include detailed implementation schedules which prioritize recovery tasks, identify their likely cost and duration, and identify agencies responsible for undertaking them. Recovery plans have served as important biological foundations for several of the habitat conservation plans discussed in this book and remain a critical tool in promoting recovery of listed species.

The use of recovery plans has not been entirely successful, however. A recent General Accounting Office (GAO) report found that no plans have been prepared by USFWS for a significant percentage of listed species.[16] Moreover, for those species where plans have been prepared, frequently many of the proposed recovery actions are never undertaken. Also, recovery plans are in theory to be updated on a periodic basis but for many species such updates are infrequent. Lack of recovery plans, or updated plans, is often cited as an impedance to more effective habitat conservation planning.

Section 10 Incidental Take

As noted earlier, it is the prohibition of take under Section 9 that has generated the greatest concern for private landowners and developers. These parties would be subject to civil and criminal penalties if listed species were taken through such activities as grading, land clearance, and housing construction. On the other hand, enforcement and prosecution under these provisions are difficult, and the stopping of all development in habitat areas is seen as unfair and political.

To provide some degree of flexibility under ESA, the law was amended in 1982 to allow the U.S. Fish and Wildlife Service to issue an incidental take permit, under Section 10(a) of the act, in situations where developers and landowners have prepared satisfactory "habitat conservation plans." The actual idea of the HCP came out of a unique planning effort in San Bruno Mountain, California in the late 1970s and early 1980s, where development was halted because of its potential impact on several species of butterfly, including the federally listed mission blue butterfly. A special planning process was undertaken, involving both environmental and development communities, and eventually a special management plan was prepared that allowed some take of butterflies, but also set aside large portions of the mountain as protected habitat. The plan also incorporated provisions for long-term habitat management and restoration, and for a continuous funding source.[17] The plan itself was preceded by a series of biological studies which identified certain habitat types on the mountain necessary for the survival of the butterflies. Although the plan was experimental, USFWS gave its approval, and on the merits of the San Bruno experience, ESA was amended in 1982 to officially permit the use of this mechanism in other similar circumstances.

The Endangered Species Act establishes certain basic requirements for the preparation of HCPs and certain standards that plans must satisfy before USFWS can issue a Section 10(a) permit. Plans must at a minimum specify the following: the impact which will result from the taking; the steps that will be taken to minimize and mitigate such impacts, and the funding that will be available to implement these steps; the alternative actions to the taking considered by the applicant and the reasons why such alternatives were not chosen; and such other measures that the Secretary of the Interior may require as being necessary or appropriate for the purposes of the plan.[18] A Section 10(a) incidental take permit can only be issued if the following conditions are satisfied: the taking will be incidental to an otherwise lawful activity; the applicant will, to the maximum extent practicable, minimize and mitigate the impacts of such a taking; the applicant will ensure that adequate funding for the plan will be provided; and the taking will not appreciably reduce the likelihood of the survival and recovery of the species in the wild.[19]

The habitat conservation plan idea is clearly still in its infancy and USFWS has so far issued few Section 10(a) permits. More than fifty HCPs have been prepared or are in preparation (the majority in the latter category). The information to follow is primarily the result of extensive personal interviews conducted by the author with key participants involved in a number of HCPs. Because so few HCPs have been completed, and because most of the ongoing HCPs are "moving targets," what is presented here must be considered work-in-progress. It is far too early to reach any definitive conclusions about how well the HCP mechanism is working.

An initial distinction of some importance is between HCPs that are prepared for individual private projects and properties, and those which can be considered "regional" in nature (i.e., which involve multiple property owners and parcels, and usually multiple governmental units). These regional plans have been my primary research focus, and have been completed or are in progress in a number of locations around the country.

Most HCPs have followed fairly similar processes. Most have involved the appointment of a steering committee to oversee the preparation of the plan, usually comprised of representatives of the major stakeholder groups in the community or region (e.g., developers, environmentalists, local officials, representatives of federal and state resource management agencies). The committee is frequently chaired by a more neutral party, such as The Nature Conservancy (TNC). A biological or technical committee is also frequently convened to guide the preparation of necessary background studies and to offer advice on technical and biological issues. Usually a private consultant is hired to prepare the plan and any necessary background studies.

Most HCPs entail setting aside a certain amount of habitat acreage in the form of one or more habitat preserves. Preserve areas are generally secured either through fee-simple purchase or through land dedication by major landowners involved in the process. In addition to preserve acquisition, HCPs typically include a variety of other management techniques, including habitat restoration, predator control, and land use controls. Sources of funding, both for the initial preparation of the plan and its implementation (e.g., land acquisition) have been varied, but have generally involved a combination of federal, state, and local government funding, as well as some private funding (e.g., The Nature Conservancy). Most HCPs impose, through participating local governments, a mitigation fee on new development occurring in or near habitat areas (e.g., ranging from $250 to $1,950 per acre). Beyond these common features, there is considerable variation among the HCPs, including differences in the type and number of species addressed, the threats posed to species, the size of planning areas, the specific implementation and management techniques, and the specific funding combinations, among others.

State Endangered Species Programs

A number of states also have their own endangered species programs. Typically these programs include non-game management and reintroduction efforts (e.g., a number of states are attempting to reintroduce Peregrine Falcons), habitat acquisition, education, and funding sources (e.g., state income tax non-game check-off programs).

   Many states also maintain their own lists of rare and endangered species and have enacted restrictions against take which are similar to those found in ESA. The California Endangered Species Act, for example, is one of the strongest of these state acts. Under the California ESA, prohibitions on take apply not only to species listed as endangered or threatened but to candidate species, as well. The act requires a state agency to undertake consultation similar to Section 7 with the California Department of Fish and Game (CDFG) when proposed projects may impact a state-listed species. While the California law does not include provisions for incidental take per se, Section 2081 allows CDFG to enter into management agreements and permits, and HCPs can be approved where the agency reaches a no-jeopardy opinion. Typically, state wildlife officials work closely with USFWS during the preparation of HCPs, and HCPs are intended to satisfy the requirements of state ESAs, as well as the federal ESA.[20]

Conclusions

The Endangered Species Act represents the cornerstone of federal efforts to protect species and biodiversity. It is a powerful law according substantial protection to species once they are placed on the federal list of endangered and threatened species. Key provisions of ESA include the listing process and procedures, Section 7 interagency consultations, preparation and implementation of federal recovery plans, and Section 9 prohibitions on the take of listed species.

Section 9 prohibition on take has been particularly problematic for land developers, and has directly resulted in legal and political confrontations, often pitting environmentalists against developers and landowners. To provide flexibility in these circumstances ESA was amended in 1982 to allow, through Section 10(a), the issuance of an incidental take permit—permitting incidental take of a listed species where an acceptable habitat conservation plan (ensuring the survival and recovery of the species) was prepared.

Overview of Past and Ongoing Habitat Conservation Plans and Processes

Increasing Use of the HCP Mechanism

As the number of listed species continues to rise and urban growth and development increasingly infringe on habitat areas, it is not surprising that species/development conflicts increase. Furthermore, the use of HCPs as a mechanism for resolving these conflicts continues to increase as well.

This chapter provides an overview of the HCPs to date, and compares and contrasts them. In particular, approximately ten HCPs will receive special emphasis, and their characteristics are summarized in Table 3.1. The more specific histories, experiences, and management measures of many of these plans will be explored in subsequent chapters. The intent here is to provide a quick summary of the common features of most HCPs.

The first habitat conservation plan was prepared for San Bruno Mountain, California. One of the last remaining large tracts of open space in the San Francisco Bay Area, San Bruno was slated for development in the early 1970s by Visitacion Associates. Some eighty-five hundred residential units and 2 million square feet of office and commercial space were initially proposed for the mountain. After much opposition to the project emerged, a compromise was reached that substantially reduced the size of the project. In the meantime, the mountain was found to be the habitat of several species of rare butterflies, including the federally listed mission blue butterfly. Because development on the mountain would certainly have resulted in the loss of some butterflies, in one life-stage or another, environmentalists argued that such development was prohibited under ESA. The developers, also concerned about their liability under ESA, sought some mechanism that would permit development on the mountain to proceed, while ensuring long-term protection for the butterflies. The result was a unique management plan, developed after extensive biological study of the butterflies and their habitat needs, which identified areas of the mountain that would be set aside in perpetuity. The plan was developed jointly by the developers, environmentalists, local government officials, and others, and resulted in the setting aside of some 87% of the butterfly habitat. The U.S. Fish and Wildlife Service had agreed that if an acceptable conservation plan were prepared, it would issue an "incidental take permit" under Section 10, which allowed the taking of a portion of butterfly habitat in exchange for a program to enhance the propagation and survival of the species. Prior to San Bruno this permitting procedure had been used only to permit traditional research and wildlife enhancement activities. The San Bruno Mountain plan was viewed by those involved as such a successful process for resolving urban development/endangered species conflicts that the Endangered Species Act was amended in 1982 to specifically permit the preparation of such plans. The San Bruno Mountain plan was the first HCP to receive a permit under these provisions.

Since the San Bruno Mountain HCP was approved and the Endangered Species Act subsequently amended, a number of regional HCPs have been initiated. It will be useful to briefly compare and contrast these different HCP programs, according to both process and conservation elements, before attempting to assess their effectiveness. Table 3.1 presents brief profiles of ten of the regional HCPs completed or in progress, including the two long-term regional HCPs that have been approved by the USFWS, the Coachella Valley fringe-toed lizard HCP and the San Bruno Mountain HCP. This table provides a quick comparison of the differences and similarities between major regional HCPs.[1] The discussion which follows compares the HCPs according to certain features and characteristics, including the type and number of species addressed, the organization and structure of the HCP process, and the types of implementation and management measures incorporated.

Process and Methodology

Like those for San Bruno and Coachella Valley, many HCPs have gone through, or are going through, similar processes. Usually a steering committee, comprised of key stakeholders in the community or region, is formed to guide and oversee the preparation of the plan. HCP committees usually include representatives of the real estate and development communities, the environmental community, the local governments involved, and state and federal resource agencies (e.g., state wildlife agencies, USFWS, and the federal Bureau of Land Management). Table 3.1 lists the primary groups participating on HCP steering committees. In addition to the steering committee, which usually acts as the official policymaking body, HCPs often involve a technical or biological committee consisting of experts on the species of concern and other individuals who may have special technical expertise. Much of the background work on the HCP and the nuts and bolts of the conservation measures included in the HCP are undertaken by such technical committees. In addition, a private consultant is typically hired by the steering committee to collect necessary data, and to prepare the plan and the accompanying maps and environmental review documentation (e.g., state environmental impact reports and federal environmental impact statements). The bulk of the regional HCPs have been prepared by a small number of consultants (e.g., one consultant in California has prepared or is in the process of preparing at least six of the California HCPs, and another consultant is responsible for preparing three other HCPs currently in progress).

While each of the HCPs has gone through, or is going through, similar processes and methodologies, they differ in a number of respects. The HCPs vary, for instance, according to who is given responsibility for organizing and coordinating the process. In some instances, like the San Diego HCP, a regional government coordinates the process (San Diego Association of Governments or SANDAG); in other cases a single jurisdiction, such as a local planning department, coordinates it. And despite the general similarities in the types of groups and interests involved in HCPs (i.e., real estate and development interests, environmental and conservation interests, and local governments) substantial variation exists, depending on the specific local and regional circumstances. Because the individuals and groups having a stake in HCPs will tend to vary from place to place, the composition of HCP steering committees tends to vary as well. While oil and gas representatives have a special stake in the Kern County, California, HCP, this was not a group that had any interest at stake, for example, in the Coachella Valley or North Key Largo HCPs. Off-road vehicle (ORV) users have a clear interest in being involved in the Clark County, Nevada, desert tortoise HCP, and sand and gravel miners have a keen interest in the San Diego Least Bell's Vireo HCP (many of these operations are located in riparian areas; see Table 3.1).

Differences are also apparent in the methodologies of each HCP. The San Diego HCP, for instance, has employed a two-tiered approach, preparing a rangewide comprehensive species management plan, and

Table 3.1. *Overview of Selected Regional Habitat Conservation Plans Completed or in Progress*[a]

Selected Regional Habitat Conservation Plans	Status	Size of Study Area	Primary Species of Concern	Primary Conservation Tools/Strategy
1. San Bruno Mountain HCP (San Mateo County, CA)	Completed; 10(a) permit issued	3,800 acres	• Mission blue butterfly • Callippe silverspot butterfly	• Habitat set aside/ clustered development • Habitat restoration • Construction management
2. Coachella Valley HCP (Riverside County, CA)	Completed; 10(a) permit issued	250 sq. miles; 127 sq. miles of occupiable habitat	• Coachella Valley fringe-toed lizard	• Fee-simple acquisition of habitat • Three lizard preserves • Habitat restoration and management • Research program
3. North Key Largo HCP (Monroe County, FL)	Original plan never adopted; new versions under consideration	12,000-acre island; 12-mile segment of island; 2,100 acres of hardwood hammock	• Schaus swallowtail butterfly • Key Largo cottonmouse • Key Largo woodrat • American crocodile	• Zoning and TDR • Land acquisition (by state) • Development clustered into five development nodes • Restrictions on hammock clearance • Control and removal of exotic plants • Road removal and other habitat restoration

Development Mitigation Fee?	Other Funding Sources	Amount of Protected/ Conserved Habitat	Percentage of Existing Local Habitat Protected	Key Participants
Annual mitigation fee ($20 per year per unit for residential; $10 per 1000 sq. feet for commercial per year)	• Land donation as condition of development	2,700 acres	87%	• Visitacion and other landowners/developers • San Mateo County • Surrounding local governments (e.g., South San Francisco, Daly City, Brisbane) • Save San Bruno Mountain Committee
$600 per acre	• Federal Land and Water Conservation Fund • BLM Land Trades • The Nature Conservancy • California Wildlife Commission	17,000 acres in preserves (8,000 acres of blows- and habitat)	10%–15%	• Sunrise Development Corp. • California Nature Conservancy • Coachella Valley Association of Governments (CVAG)—nine cities • Coachella Valley Ecological Reserve Foundation • Bureau of Land Management
$2,500 per unit development fee; annual mitigation fee ($2.00 per overnight accommodations unit per night; $2.00 per week for residential units)	• Special $98,000 appropriation to fund preparation of HCP, with matching funds from private interests and state and local governments.	Projected 1,773 acres (hardwood hammock)	84%	• Florida Audubon Society • Landowners • Monroe County

Table 3.1. (*continued*)

Selected Regional Habitat Conservation Plans	Status	Size of Study Area	Primary Species of Concern	Primary Conservation Tools/Strategy
4. Metro-Bakersfield HCP (CA)	In progress	405 sq. miles	• San Joaquin kit fox • Blunt-nosed leopard lizard • Tipton kangaroo rat • San Joaquin antelope ground squirrel • Bakersfield beavertail cactus	• Restoration of state owned water bank (back to habitat) • Some additional fee-simple acquisition • Hand excavation of kit fox dens required
5. San Diego (CA) HCP	In progress	About 20,000 acres of riparian habitat in four river basins; about 5,000 acres of existing vireo habitat	• Least Bell's Vireo	• Land dedication/ habitat restoration through project-by-project mitigation • Habitat buffers and local land use controls (proposed HCP overlay zone) • Cowbird management • Habitat creation/ restoration
6. Balcones Canyonlands Conservation Plan (Austin, TX)	In progress	990 sq. miles in Travis County	• Black-capped Vireo • Golden-cheeked Warbler • Texas amorpha • Canyon mock orange • Bracted twist flower • Tooth Cave pseudo scorpion • Tooth Cave spider • Tooth Cave ground beetle • Kretschmarr Cave mold beetle • Bee Creek Cave harvestman	• Habitat acquisition; System of preserves • Land use controls through city's comprehensive watersheds ordinance • Cowbird control

Development Mitigation Fee?	Other Funding Sources	Amount of Protected/ Conserved Habitat	Percentage of Existing Local Habitat Protected	Key Participants
$680 per acre; proposed long-term fee of $1,000–$1,250 per acre		Projected 15,000 acres	Projected replacement of natural habitat: three acres for every one destroyed	• City of Bakersfield • Kern County • Major developers/Building Industry Association • The Nature Conservancy • Sierra Club
(None yet; mitigation requirements established on project-by-project basis)	• Matching funds from state legislature for HCP study • Possible special riparian assessment district to fund long-term management	Projected minimum of 9,000 acres of vireo habitat (15,000–22,000 acres of riparian habitat overall)	140% (Projected 40% increase in vireo habitat; small increase perhaps in riparian area, but main increase in vireo habitat through increasing ratio of vireo to riparian habitat)	• San Diego Association of Governments • Development Community • Sierra Club • Audubon Society • County League of Women Voters • U.S. Army Corps of Engineers
(None yet; proposed fee of $3,000 per acre of habitat; $300 per gross acre)	• Local band measure proposed • Utility surcharge • % of CIP improvements	Proposed 29,160 (minimum)	—	• Texas Nature Conservancy • Sierra Club • Audubon Society • Earth First! • City of Austin and Travis, Williamson, Hays, and Burnet Counties • Texas General Land Office • Texas Capital Area Builders Assoc.

Table 3.1. (*continued*)

Selected Regional Habitat Conservation Plans	Status	Size of Study Area	Primary Species of Concern	Primary Conservation Tools/Strategy
7. Clark County HCP (NV)	In progress	7,800 sq. miles; 5 million acres of tortoise habitat	• Mojave Desert tortoise	• Large blocks of BLM land will be set aside as tortoise preserves • Compensation will likely be needed for cattle grazers, miners and other users of these lands • 3 year short-term HCP approved
8. Eastern Riverside County (CA) HCP	In progress	Approx. 22,000 acres in ten study areas over an area of approx. 100,000 acres	• Stephens' kangaroo rat	• Short-term HCP approved • Land acquisition; system of preserves
9. Kern County Valley Floor HCP (CA)	In progress	3,200 sq. miles	• San Joaquin kit fox • Blunt-nosed leopard lizard • Giant kangaroo rat • Buena Vista Lake shrew	• System of protected land (otherwise too early in process)
10. Marina HCP (CA)	In progress	626 acres	• Smith's blue butterfly • Black legless lizard	• Development will be restricted to designated areas • Remaining conserved habitat will be deeded to a conservation group

[a]U.S. Fish and Wildlife Service has played or is playing a key role in each HCP and is consequently not listed here; the same applies to State Wildlife Departments.

Development Mitigation Fee?	Other Funding Sources	Amount of Protected/ Conserved Habitat	Percentage of Existing Local Habitat Protected	Key Participants
$250 per acre (additional $324 per acre in Las Vegas Valley under short-term HCP)	• Possibly proceeds of BLM land sales • Funds from several lawsuit settlements will be used for habitat acquisition and research • Revenue from state bond referendum	800,000 to 1 million acres of BLM land		• The Nature Conservancy • Bureau of Land Management • S. Nevada Homebuilders Assoc. • Clark County and cities • Resource users, including cattle ranchers, miners, and ORV users • Environmental Defense fund
• $1,950 per acre; maximum $1,000 per residential unit • Solid waste tipping fees		Estimated 10,000– 15,000 acres	Estimated 50%	• Riverside County and incorporated towns • Sierra Club • BLM • Building Industry Assoc. • The Nature Conservancy
(None yet, except those collected under metro-Bakersfield)	• California Division of Oil and Gas	(Too early in process)	(Too early in process)	• Oil and gas industry • Farm Bureau • The Nature Conservancy • Development Community • BLM California Energy Commission • Audubon Society
(None)	• California Coastal Conservancy and land owners split cost of HCP study • Room tax being considered to fund long-term habitat maintenance/ restoration	Projected 430 acres	78%	• Land owners (sand mining companies) • California Department of Parks • Regional Park Authority • Marina City

relying on a large thirty-member task force to oversee the preparation of the comprehensive species management plan. More detailed HCPs were prepared for four river basins, with individual advisory committees overseeing the preparation of the plans. Among other things, the comprehensive species management plan analyzes the rangewide needs of the vireo, and sets the goal of five thousand breeding pairs of vireos (there are currently as few as 350 breeding pairs) and at least nine thousand acres of vireo habitat (fifteen thousand to twenty thousand acres of riparian habitat overall). The river basin HCPs contain more specific plans for acquiring, regulating, and managing habitat areas, and generally achieving these broader breeding pair and habitat conservation goals. As another example, the Sand City and Marina HCPs are being prepared in combination with revisions to their LCPs—local coastal plans—required by law in California. This has necessitated consideration of issues not always germane to species conservation, such as coastal erosion, beach access, and coastal view protection, and has made the process more difficult in the minds of some.

Most HCPs are issued for a period of thirty years. The Section 10(a) permits for both the San Bruno Mountain and Coachella Valley HCPs were issued by USFWS for periods of thirty years, but are revocable if the plans are not successfully carried out. Some variation exists, however. The Metro-Bakersfield HCP, for instance, will only cover a twenty-year period.

Number and Type of Species Protected

The number and types of species addressed varies among the regional HCPs, as each plan involves different biological issues and resulting conservation strategies. Species of concern include reptiles, such as the threatened Coachella Valley fringe-toed lizard in the Coachella Valley HCP, the American crocodile in the North Key Largo HCP, the desert tortoise in the Clark County HCP, and the San Joaquin blunt-nosed leopard lizard in the Kern County HCP (see Table 3.1). Endangered rodents are heavily represented, including several species of kangaroo rat (the Stephens' kangaroo rat in Riverside County, the Morro Bay kangaroo rat, and the giant kangaroo rat in Kern County), the Key Largo woodrat and cottonmouse (North Key Largo HCP), the San Joaquin antelope ground squirrel (the Metro-Bakersfield and Kern County HCPs), and the Buena Vista lake shrew. Endangered butterflies have been a major focus of at least four regional HCPs (the mission blue and Callippe silverspot in San Bruno; the Smiths' blue butterfly in the Marina and Sand City HCPs; the Schaus swallowtail in North Key Largo). Several of the

major regional HCPs have focused heavily on endangered songbird species, including the Least Bell's Vireo (San Diego HCP) and the Black-
capped Vireo and Golden-cheeked Warbler (the Balcones Canyonlands
HCP). Only one regional HCP, the Balcones Canyonlands Conservation Plan, addresses non-butterfly invertebrates (specifically six cave-
adapted invertebrates). At least three regional HCPs are considering
plant species (the Balcones Canyonlands Conservation Plan and the
Metro-Bakersfield and Kern County HCPs). HCPs for larger mammals
have been fewer in number, although the endangered San Joaquin kit
fox is a primary focus of the Metro-Bakersfield HCP.

Different species of concern in turn imply different biological factors
and characteristics which will need to be considered. Some species like
the desert tortoise have wide ranges, while others have very narrow
ranges. Some species are migratory, such as the Least Bell's Vireo and
Golden-cheeked Warbler, while others are not. These different biological
characteristics in turn require different management and conservation
measures.

Types of Threats

All habitat conservation plans also vary by the types of threats presented
to species of concern. For instance, in Coachella Valley, the primary
threats are the direct loss of blowsand habitat (areas of unstable windblown sand) due to private urban and resort development (such as
the Palm Valley Country Club which in effect led to the initiation of the
HCP), and indirect degradation of habitat due to sand shielding. For the
desert tortoise, not only is direct loss of habitat from development a
problem, but a host of other threats must be addressed, including impacts on the species from a respiratory disease, off-road vehicles, over-
grazing, and raven predation. For the San Diego Least Bell's Vireo, the
primary threats have been from public projects such as state highways,
flood-control projects, bridges, and dams. San Bruno Mountain butterflies were endangered in large part because of the gradual replacement
of native grasslands (and host plants such as lupine) with brush and
other non-native vegetation.

Size of Planning Areas

Habitat conservation plans also differ by the size of their planning areas,
again in large degree a result of biological differences in the species of
concern. Planning areas range in size from the relatively small 550 acres
for the Marina Dunes HCP to fairly large areas, such as the several

hundred-square-mile planning area for the Metro-Bakersfield HCP, and the very large thirty-two hundred-square-mile valley floor HCP being prepared by Kern County (see Table 3.1). Some HCPs, such as the Kern County HCP, have sought to assume a larger, more regional scale while others have sought a more localized approach. Some HCPs address a number of different species of concern. The Kern County HCP and Balcones Canyonlands Conservation Plan, for example, are more regional in nature and seek to protect multiple species.

In general, HCPs have been limited in the number of species which they considered. The Coachella Valley HCP, for instance, was focused primarily on the habitat and conservation needs of a single species—the Coachella Valley fringe-toed lizard. The San Diego Least Bell's Vireo HCP is essentially a single-species approach. The same is generally true of the Clark County desert tortoise HCP. While these types of HCPs may serve to protect other species of concern and biodiversity in general, this is more by accident than design. Many of the more recently initiated HCPs, such as Kern County and the Balcones Canyonlands, are attempting to take a much more comprehensive biological focus, looking not just at federally listed species but also at state-listed species, federal candidate species, and other species of concern. There is an increasing recognition by those in both the conservation and the development communities that it makes sense, economically and technically, to deal with multiple species in a comprehensive management framework (e.g., looking at areas of overlapping habitat and comprehensive acquisition schemes).

Implementation and Management

The types of threats to species of concern, as well as other geographical, biological, and institutional factors, dictates the conservation and management strategies contained in HCPs. All of the HCPs share the basic and central strategy of identifying and protecting certain designated habitat conservation areas, as well as allowing some degree of urban development or non-conservation land uses to occur. The setting aside of habitat conservation areas has been accomplished in different ways. The Coachella Valley HCP, for instance, acquired, with the help of The Nature Conservancy, large privately owned lands. Three preserves were set up for the fringe-toed lizard, encompassing a total of more than sixteen thousand acres. The largest of these preserves is the Coachella Valley Preserve, encompassing approximately thirteen thousand acres, the bulk of which was purchased from a single private landowner, Cathton

Investments, Inc. The other two much smaller, satellite preserves were comprised primarily of Bureau of Land Management (BLM) property. The primary strategy of HCPs such as Coachella Valley, then, is to purchase fee-simple rights to habitat areas and essentially to set these areas aside in perpetuity as habitat preserves.

Other HCPs have taken different approaches to establishing habitat preserves. The original North Ley Largo HCP envisioned setting aside preserves of hardwood hammocks through a somewhat different means, relying heavily on the use of the local jurisdiction's zoning powers, in combination with a plan to allow the transfer of development rights to designated development nodes. While it incorporated a two-year waiting period that provided a window of time for the state to purchase habitat lands, after a certain date (August 1, 1988) the plan was to allow development only in designated development nodes, restricting by way of a conserved habitat zoning category any development outside of these areas (approximately 84% of the habitat). Under the plan a maximum of thirty-five hundred dwelling units would be permitted in the development nodes, with this maximum density achievable only through the transfer of density from the conserved habitat. Additional restrictions were also placed on the extent of hammock clearance permissible even in development nodes. Developers and landowners would not be permitted to clear more than 20% of the high quality hardwood hammock unless one of several mitigation actions were taken (e.g., preservation of two hundred acres of mangrove wetland for each additional acre cleared).

While the North Key Largo plan was never officially adopted (several more recent versions are currently being considered by Monroe County), in concept it would have relied in considerable degree on the protective elements of a local zoning ordinance. The state of Florida, through its Conservation and Recreational Lands (CARL) program, did utilize this two-year window to acquire the fee-simple rights to much of the hardwood hammock habitat, similar then to Coachella Valley. Coachella Valley–style, fee-simple habitat acquisition appears to be the most frequently employed conservation strategy.

In some cases, conserved habitat is established not through off-site purchases but by setting aside land already owned by developers or other parties to the HCP. For instance, in the San Bruno Mountain and the Marina Dunes HCPs, development was directed onto particular portions of a private site; that is, to cluster future development in ways which set aside in perpetuity conserved habitat areas. In the Marina Dunes HCP, the greater portion of the habitat of the Smith's blue butterfly is owned by three sand mining companies. The proposed plan would involve, much like San Bruno, restricting future development to certain designated development "bubbles," placing the remainder of the land (some 485 of the 626 acres) in conserved habitat. These conserved areas will then likely be deeded over to a public agency or a private conservation group.

HCPs also differ in the extent to which public land, usually federal, is involved and this in turn influences the strategy for conserving habitat. For instance, in the Clark County desert tortoise HCP approximately 90% of remaining habitat in the planning area is under federal ownership. Consequently, very little private land acquisition will be necessary there. What will likely be necessary, however, are actions which modify the uses of these publicly owned lands. Where necessary, compensation may need to be provided to individuals and groups who have certain rights or vested interests to use these areas (primarily miners, cattle grazers, and off-road vehicle enthusiasts). Other HCPs have attempted to find creative ways to utilize federal or state lands in setting up conserved habitat areas. For instance in Coachella Valley, a considerable portion of the land in the largest preserve was acquired through BLM land trades—that is, The Nature Conservancy (TNC) would first purchase preserve lands, and the BLM would then swap lands in other areas for these TNC-owned lands. The BLM would then become an owner of land in the preserve, while TNC would sell its newly acquired BLM land located outside the preserves to recoup its original acquisition costs. As another example of creative habitat conservation, the Metro-Bakersfield HCP is currently planning to restore kit fox habitat by converting existing agricultural lands back to native grasslands, in combination with a state water banking program. The State Department of Water Resources has recently purchased some twenty thousand acres of farmland southwest of the city which will become the Kern Water Bank, used to replenish regional groundwater supplies. The HCP may propose adding additional land to these, but envisions converting a significant acreage of agricultural land in the water bank back to grassland habitat. The Metro-Bakersfield HCP will also likely propose restoring and adding to city-owned acreage located along the Kern River which flows through the city. This river habitat will serve as an important migration corridor linking north and south kit fox populations. Thus while HCPs tend to share the common general strategy of setting aside a certain amount of conserved habitat, the specifics of how this is done vary, depending upon local circumstances.

In addition to setting aside habitat, each HCP typically includes a variety of other implementation actions. Most HCPs, for instance, involve a program for habitat management and restoration, as well as additional biological research and monitoring. Certain threats to species of concern may require special conservation techniques beyond habitat preserves. For instance, in the case of the San Diego HCP, an important component of long-term management may be programs to control the Brown-headed Cowbird, a species with a parasitic effect on the Least Bell's Vireo (depositing its eggs in vireo nests which displaces young vireos). A cowbird control program is already underway in Austin, Texas, and will likely be an important management strategy in the Austin HCP. Similar programs to control the expansion and propagation of raven populations, which prey on young desert tortoises, may prove to be an important component of any desert tortoise conservation program. In other HCPs, however, control of such competitor and predator species may be unnecessary.

Habitat conservation plans may include a variety of habitat restoration and management activities. In the North Key Largo HCP, for example, restoration and management activities involve controlling and removing exotic plants and domestic pets, eliminating aerial application of insecticides (for mosquito control), removal of roads and bridges to restore historic water regimes and to minimize human intrusion (e.g., closing and roadbed removal for state road 905), introducing host species (e.g., periodic burns to promote torchwood and wildlime—plants upon which female Schaus swallowtail butterflies lay their eggs), and modifying canal banks to provide nesting sites and habitat for the American crocodile. As another example, a major component of the restoration and management of butterfly habitat at the San Bruno Mountains was strict management of construction practices for development which occurs on the mountain (fencing of habitat areas, close monitoring of grading, and other construction activities) and restoring and replanting native grasslands.

An important consideration in any HCP process is the delegation of responsibility for implementing the resulting plans. While this is a question which has not yet been resolved for many HCPs, those completed have varied solutions. In the case of the Coachella Valley HCP, The Nature Conservancy administers and manages the funds generated by the mitigation fees collected by the local governments and assumes the primary habitat management responsibilities for the preserve system (under a management agreement between TNC, BLM, USFWS, and the state of California). In San Bruno Mountain, the San Mateo County planning department takes the lead on these types of implementation and long-term management responsibilities. Choosing an implementation and management arrangement depends heavily on the existing framework and may need to be adapted to the unique circumstances of each HCP.

Funding of HCPs

Another way in which to compare the HCPs is in terms of their funding schemes. The HCP mechanism requires funding at several points: initially, to undertake the necessary biological and planning studies and to conduct the HCP process, and later to prepare the plan and resulting environmental review documentation (e.g., environmental impact reports). In most cases, however, the major funding requirements are related to the acquisition and setting aside of habitat areas. Finally, funds are needed to undertake the various long-term management and restoration activities. Experiences to date indicate that most of the HCPs are employing some combination of federal, state, local, and private funding. The combination of funding for the Coachella Valley HCP is illustrative of these types of funding combinations (see Chapter 6). Approximately $10 million from the federal Land and Water Conservation Fund was secured to purchase preserve lands at Coachella Valley. State funding has also been important. The California Division of Oil and Gas, for instance, has put up much of the money to fund the Kern County HCP. As a further example, the California Coastal Conservancy has provided funds, on a fifty/fifty cost-sharing basis, for the Marina Dunes and Sand City HCPs. Private funding, both for the planning and process activities and for acquisition and management, has also been important. The Nature Conservancy in particular has played an instrumental role in this regard in several of the HCPs. TNC has funded much of the initial start-up cost and biological background work for the Balcones Canyonlands Conservation Plan.

Most HCPs have used or are using some form of development mitigation fee assessed on new development occurring in habitat areas. These one-time assessments are a form of impact fee assessed on a per-acre basis and are usually collected at the time a parcel is graded. Fees are normally tied to some delineated habitat area or mitigation fee zone. In the case of the Coachella Valley HCP a mitigation fee zone was delineated to roughly correspond to the range of the fringe-toed lizard.

In most cases these mitigation fees are first established on an interim basis even before an actual HCP is completed, with the funds collected early on to pay for biological and planning studies and to fund the HCP process itself. Once the HCP is adopted, the fee becomes a steady source of long-term funding for future management and acquisition. The fees range from $250 per acre in Clark County Nevada (desert tortoise HCP) to $1,950 in Riverside County for the Stephens' kangaroo rat HCP. At least one HCP, San Bruno Mountain, currently employs an annual mitigation fee ($20 per dwelling unit per year for residential; $10 per one thousand square feet per year for commercial) and the North Key Largo HCP envisioned a similar annual fee ($2 per week per residential unit; $2 per overnight accommodation unit per night), though such a fee has not yet been adopted. So far, development mitigation fees have been the major source of local funding and there have been few attempts to collect funds through broader community-wide taxation or revenues (e.g., a jurisdiction-wide sales tax or *ad valorem* assessment). The Riverside County Stephens' kangaroo rat HCP, however, does receive some of its funding from county landfill tipping fees. The San Diego Least Bell's Vireo HCP has sought special legislation to create a special habitat conservation assessment district, which would impose a $25-per-year assessment on property owners within a mile of riparian areas.

The imposition of development fees is generally deemed to be an equitable way to raise funds for HCPs, since development in habitat areas is creating the need for conservation measures in the first place. Critics of the impact fees argue that past development also causes the need for HCPs; thus the entire community should help foot the bill, for example through property taxes. Mitigation fees, however, are clearly supported because it is seen as more politically acceptable to pass these costs along to future homeowners and residents.[2]

Conclusions

This chapter has provided a brief overview of the major habitat conservation plans completed or currently underway. Most habitat conservation plans have as a major strategy the establishment of one or more habitat preserves, usually secured through fee-simple acquisition or developer dedication. Basic similarities also exist in the types of process used to prepare the HCP and the interest groups typically involved in their preparation. Similar patterns exist for funding HCPs, with most plans, for example, utilizing a development mitigation fee. While there are basic similarities in the processes, methodologies, and actors involved, there are also significant differences among the plans. These plans address different types of species, involve different study area sizes, and incorporate different conservation and protection strategies.

CHAPTER

FOUR

The Politics of
Habitat Conservation Planning:
Key Actors and Perspectives

Politics and Habitat Conservation Planning

The resolution of endangered species development conflicts, and the preparation of HCPs, are inherently political activities. As the more detailed case studies illustrate, these planning processes involve, indeed must involve, a variety of individuals and interest groups. I will refer to these collectively as "stakeholders," and a brief identification of these stakeholders and their typical perspectives is the primary objective of this chapter. Different stakeholders and stakeholder groups typically hold vastly different views of the habitat conservation planning process, as well as often fundamentally different perspectives of land, endangered species, and other issues. The conflicts which almost inevitably arise in the habitat conservation planning process are often the result of clashes between these different perspectives, and effective HCPs in the future will require an acknowledgement and understanding of these different viewpoints.

While the number of completed HCPs remains rather small, the experiences of San Bruno Mountain, Coachella Valley, and others suggest that practical compromises can be reached, and that participants do have certain interests which keep them at the table and involved in the process.

Actors and Stakeholders

While it is difficult to generalize across the more than fifty HCPs completed or in progress, given the similar nature of the conflicts involved, certain actors and stakeholders tend to be commonly involved in and

Table 4.1. *Stakeholders Typically Involved in the HCP Process and Their Perspectives*

	Level of Environ- mental concern	Value Placed on Endangered Species	Perceived Legitimacy of Land Regulation	Interest in Quick Resolution
Developers	−	− −	−	+ +
Landowners/ propertyowners	−	− −	− −	+
Environmentalists	+ +	+ +	+ +	− −
Local govern- ments	+ / −	+ / −	+	+
Federal and state resource agencies	+	+	+	+ / −
Recreational land users (e.g., ORV enthusiasts)	−	−	−	+

+ + = very high; + = high; − − = very low; − = low; + / − = neutral or substantial variation.

are concerned with the outcome of the HCP. Among the more promi-nent stakeholders in the HCP are land developers and the development community, environmentalists and the environmental community (e.g., The Nature Conservancy, Sierra Club), landowners, representatives of local government (e.g., elected officials, city and county planners), state and federal wildlife agencies (e.g., state departments of fish and game, the U.S. Fish and Wildlife Service), and state and federal land manage-ment agencies (e.g., the federal Bureau of Land Management).

Table 4.1 summarizes the key stakeholder groups involved in HCPs and contrasts the typical differences in their perspectives and outlooks on the issue.

Developers

The HCPs presented in these pages were typically initiated in response to a tangible conflict between land developers and others (e.g., local, state, federal agencies; environmental groups) over a project or proposal that might jeopardize a species of concern. Very often these conflicts stem directly from regulatory review of a specific project or develop-ment proposal which acts as a kind of catalyst. For example, it was a confrontation over a specific resort project in the Coachella Valley—the Palm Valley Country Club—that led to the initiation of the fringe-toed lizard HCP there.

The perspective of land developers is typically one of frustration and disdain, as they are often forced to halt or postpone their projects in response to the restrictions of the Endangered Species Act. Participating in an HCP is usually seen by the development community as a necessary evil—as a way to take care of a problem or an obstacle. If resource agencies, such as the USFWS appear determined to stringently implement the law, the HCPs may seem the only viable alternative to ensure their projects are allowed to proceed.

Developers talk of other alternatives, however. One alternative is the legal suit. A major segment of the development community was able, for instance, in the Clark County desert tortoise case to successfully press legal action to obtain a pre-HCP settlement. Another alternative frequently discussed is foregoing participation in a regional HCP and seeking individual Section 10(a) or Section 7 permits.

Also, the development community can threaten—sometimes explicitly, sometimes more subtlely—that if the species restrictions are enforced too stringently or inflexibly, political influence will be exercised in order to gut the Endangered Species Act, or to severely diminish its power.

In interviewing participants from the development community, I found that they tended to be very skeptical of the environmentalists' arguments about the need to protect species and biodiversity. Often they are quick to criticize the expenditure or potential expenditure of millions to acquire habitat for a single species of lizard or rat or songbird.

Those in the land development community often view the endangered species issue as a form of subterfuge and manipulation by environmentalists and others who are not as interested in protecting the species as in stopping growth altogether. If a rare lizard or rodent can be discovered in the path of a shopping center or highway so much the better. The view is, simply put, that environmentalists are fuzzy-headed idealists who are using the endangered species issue to promote an unrealistic no-growth or slow-growth vision.

Landowners

Other landowners besides developers also may have a stake in the species/development conflict. Landowners in agricultural and farming regions, for instance, are frequently concerned that endangered species restrictions will interfere with normal farming practices and often express a direct fear that such programs will interfere with their liveli-hoods. Farmers along the San Luis Rey River in San Diego County, for instance, have expressed considerable fear that protection of habitat for the endangered Least Bell's Vireo (which relies on willow riparian habi-tat) will interfere with their ability to draw water from the river for agri-cultural irrigation.

As well, most landowners, whether farmers, ranchers, or speculators, express a common concern about restrictions that may lower the value of their land, and its marketability for development or other uses. The common expression "scratch a farmer, find a developer" applies in many cases, as such owners of land see it and its gradual appreciating value (especially in metropolitan regions) as a nest egg, upon which to retire. Moreover, for many farmers and ranchers these appreciated land values serve as important collateral, against which funds can be bor-rowed for farm equipment, additional land purchases, etc.

An important subset of this stakeholder group, particularly in the west, are those who hold certain rights to use public lands—or public resources—including grazing rights, water rights, and mining rights. While underlying ownership, for instance in the case of grazing allot-ments, remains in the public's hands, rights holders frequently view them in the same proprietary manner that a fee-simple owner of land does. Habitat conservation efforts are often seen as a threat to these rights, and these individuals and groups tend to vehemently resist such protective efforts.

In recent years a number of private property rights advocacy groups, and groups which advocate development and use of public lands, have emerged in the United States. Often described under the label of the "wise use" movement, these organizations actively object to efforts to further restrict the use of land, whether public or private.[1] These groups have been vocal critics of efforts to further restrict development or use in wetlands, endangered species habitat, or other sensitive environmen-tal areas. They have been especially critical and suspicious of certain federal resource agencies, especially the U.S. Park Service, which they believe conspires to take away private lands. A number of grass-roots organizations have formed around the country in recent years, including such organizations as the Center for the Defense of Free Enterprise, the National Inholders Association, and the Wilderness Impact Research Foundation, among others. More mainstream national organizations, such as the American Farm Bureau, have also joined in support of this perspective.

A central view of many landowners, and landowner advocacy groups, is that government regulations on the use of land amount to unconstitutional "takings." Under the Fifth Amendment of the U.S. Constitution, government is forbidden to take private land for public purposes without providing just compensation. Many landowners affected by wetlands or other regulations are quick to claim that land use regulations *amount* to such takings and must either be judged as unconstitutional, or be accompanied by public compensation. The "takings issue" has become a centerpiece of the political and philosophical platform of many landowner groups.

Environmentalists

Environmentalists and representatives of environmental groups have played an important role in the initiation and formulation of HCPs. Very often it is the direct complaints to USFWS and other resource agencies, and the initiation of legal proceedings, or the threat of legal action by these groups that result in the initiation of HCPs. The North Key Largo HCP, for instance, was initiated by two lawsuits by the Florida Audubon Society claiming violations of ESA. The San Bruno Mountain HCP was also precipitated by the threat of legal action by the environmental group Save San Bruno Mountain, claiming that the major development proposed there would violate ESA. The activities of the Coachella Valley Ecological Reserve Society, and demands that developers fully mitigate for proposed habitat losses, set the stage for the fringe-toed lizard HCP there.

HCPs have involved a variety of environmental groups, with a variety of philosophies and orientations. So far, the following national organizations, or their local equivalents, have been represented in HCP processes: The Nature Conservancy, Sierra Club, Audubon Society, Defenders of Wildlife, Environmental Defense Fund, and Earth First! In addition to representation of national organizations, HCPs have also involved more specific localized groups, such as those like Save San Bruno Mountain and Friends of the Everglades.

The various philosophical orientations of these different environmental groups lead them to play varying roles. The Nature Conservancy, more than any other environmental organization, has played a major role in a number of HCPs. Their role has been a combination of behind-the-scenes leadership and promotion of agreement among parties. The TNC, for instance, chaired and shepherded the Coachella Valley fringe-toed lizard HCP and is doing the same in the case of the Clark County desert tortoise HCP and the Balcones Canyonlands Conservation Plan. This has been an effective role for TNC because they hold credibility in the eyes of both the development and environmental communities. The developers, in particular, see TNC as more reasonable and pragmatic in their approach to environmental conservation. TNC has also been able to play a unique and important role in actually purchasing habitat areas, even before an HCP has been completed. In the case of the Coachella Valley HCP, for example, TNC representatives had options on the key tract of land for the largest fringe-toed lizard preserve (the Coachella Valley preserve) well before the HCP had been completed and approved by USFWS.

In contrast to the conservative TNC are environmental groups that are more strident and uncompromising. Some groups are so pro-conservation in their outlooks that they see the HCP process as illegal and primarily a circumvention of the ESA. Friends of the Everglades held this view with respect to the North Key Largo HCP and saw their primary role as one of disrupting or undermining the process. Earth First! is another strident environmental group, and has been heavily involved in species protection issues in Austin, Texas (Balcones Canyonlands Conservation Plan). Earth First! members have waged a fairly effective media campaign there, staging protests of habitat destruction and calling for habitat protection efforts. In the fall of 1989, members of Earth First! occupied a series of karst caves for several days to bring attention to proposals to build on and around these unique habitats. This event resulted in national as well as local media attention, and the Earth First! actions are credited by some with expediting the emergency listing of five cave-adapted invertebrates inhabiting these cave ecosystems. The Austin Earth First! group has been instrumental in monitoring development and habitat alteration in the region (partly by aerial view) and providing USFWS with this information.

Resource Agencies

Several key resource agencies are usually involved in the initiation and preparation of HCPs. The U.S. Fish and Wildlife Service, along with the National Marine Fisheries Service, has primary responsibility for implementing the federal Endangered Species Act and consequently is a key player. The USFWS typically wears several hats in the HCP process, but their regulatory authorities and responsibilities may have the most significant effect. It is enforcement actions, and threats of enforcement by USFWS, which often bring actors to the bargaining table in the first place and create an atmosphere in which otherwise opposing factions see some mutual benefit to the process. A fear that USFWS would institute actions to close down development in Coachella Valley to protect the threatened fringe-toed lizard initiated the development community's participation in that HCP. The threat of enforcement, however, is often only that, and USFWS has seldom taken such extreme actions. Indeed, it has difficulty even imposing civil and criminal penalties for illegal takes, and such penalties are relatively infrequent.

Staff-level USFWS personnel tends to reflect a genuine high level of concern for wildlife and species conservation. Many have backgrounds or training in wildlife biology or other environmental sciences. USFWS has approached its mission in recent years in a highly politicized fashion. Perhaps not surprisingly, its policies and conservation decisions have been heavily influenced by the political tone set by political appointees and upper-level administrators. The last two national administrations have expressed concerns about the stringency of the Endangered Species Act and its economic costs. This has been epitomized in the Bush administration by Secretary of Interior Manuel Lujan, vocally criticizing the inflexibility of the act, and questioning the need to preserve every species at all costs. In a recent interview Lujan has been quoted as saying:

> Do we have to save every subspecies? The red squirrel is the best example. Nobody's told me the difference between a red squirrel, a black one, or a brown one.[2]

The political influence on USFWS has been illustrated recently by the agency action concerning the Northern Spotted Owl and the Mt. Graham Observatory proposal, both of which received considerable media attention.[3]

The USFWS wears other hats in the HCP process, as well. Staff scientists and wildlife biologists often have much to contribute in biological discussions. The USFWS recovery team established for the fringe-toed lizard had much influence on discussions about the minimum size and configuration necessary for habitat preserves. While not exclusively USFWS staff, these recovery teams (required to be established for every listed species) and their recovery plans have had a significant impact on habitat conservation planning.

While the USFWS in its enforcement of ESA creates strong reason for undertaking an HCP, and while it is generally involved in the meetings at various stages of the preparation of the HCP, when it comes to actual decisions about the scope and content of plans, its involvement declines. Its position is that USFWS will ultimately review and approve or disapprove the plan, and as such should give relatively little guidance in the formulation process itself. In interviews with HCP participants, USFWS is frequently criticized for failing to tell locals what constitutes an acceptable plan. In the words of one fundamental local planner, "Their view is that they will know a good plan when the see it." It has only been since the spring of 1990 that USFWS has prepared and made available draft HCP guidelines, and even these are quite vague. USFWS argues in response that much of the specifics of any particular HCP will depend on the biology of the specie or species involved and that it is difficult to establish clear, uniform conservation standards that would apply to all HCPs.

Other federal resource agencies are also often involved in HCPs. Most notable among them is the Bureau of Land Management (BLM). The BLM has been nicknamed by critics as the "Bureau of Livestock and Mining" because of its strong orientation toward those resource users. The BLM has been described also as a classic "captured" agency, in that it has tended to favor the interests of those users whose behavior it was intended to regulate. In recent years, the BLM has been forced by Congress to expand its mission and to consider, among other things, protection of wildlife and endangered species. The philosophy of BLM has changed markedly in recent years. In 1990 for example, it prepared a comprehensive wildlife management plan for its holdings. There are also notable examples of unpopular BLM actions taken in response to species protection needs. For example, following the emergency listing of the Mojave Desert tortoise in the fall of 1989, it closed down the popular Barstow-to-Vegas motorcycle race, an action which met with considerable anger on the part of off-road vehicle (ORV) groups. Despite these changes, most indications are that wildlife interests continue to be a secondary priority and that the interests of miners, cattle ranchers, and ORV enthusiasts will continue to be a dominant concern. Because of the large acreage of BLM land in the west, they will likely be even more significantly involved in HCPs in the future.

Different Values of Stakeholder Groups

Perspectives on Land and Regulation of Private Property

It is clear that dramatically different views of land are frequently at the heart of endangered species/development conflicts. Those in the land development community, for instance, frequently view land as primarily an economic commodity, and while there is great variation in the attitudes of landowners, many, especially those holding land for speculative purposes, have similar views.

Those in the environmental community tend to view land in more biological and collective terms. Land is not an economic commodity but an integral element of a larger ecosystem and home to numerous and assorted forms of life. They tend to hold views more consistent with Aldo Leopold's notion of land as a community which requires special ethical obligations. Moreover, land ownership is not absolute or inviolable. Rather, land ownership is a temporary privilege, which ultimately must be constrained by the rights and interests of the larger public, including future generations. Ownership implies certain obligations to nurture and protect the land and to be a good *steward.*

These different attitudes about land, in turn, correspond to attitudes about government regulations and restrictions regarding land. Those who view land as primarily an economic commodity believe land use regulations deplete their profit margins. Moreover, preventing land development to protect a species or a wetland or some other important environmental characteristic or component is seen as an attempt by government to procure public benefits without paying for them. Those whose development is restricted argue that a government "takings" has occurred and compensation is required. In a recent commentary Walter E. Williams verbalized these attitudes and how environmental restrictions can lead to the end of personal freedoms:

> Much of what's done under the pretext of environmentalism is an egregious violation of Fifth Amendment prohibitions against taking private property and represents violation of the principle of the "rule of law."
>
> Americans are well on their way to totalitarianism by ignoring and even promoting the steady erosion of constitutional principles and the rule of law. It's easy to ignore what the government is doing to people . . . We're busy trying to raise kids, pay bills, and keep body and soul together. But if nobody cries out about the injustices against these little people, when it becomes our turn to become victimized by our government, who will have the freedom to cry out for us?[4]

Environmentalists and others with more collectivist notions of land see these issues quite differently. Regulations on the use of land—whether preventing a landowner from filling a wetland, building too close to a wetland, or destroying sensitive forest habitat—are entirely legitimate and seen as preventing the creation of public harms and destruction of the larger public's collective heritage.

Special conflicts also exist with respect to *public* lands, typically federal lands. The BLM alone owns more than 330 million acres of land and many species/development conflicts arise on these lands. Who really owns these lands and how should they be controlled? Much of this land is under the direct control of private individuals through livestock grazing and mining leases. Others have become accustomed to using these lands for such activities as off-road vehicle use or hunting. There is frequently great resistance to changing the use of these public lands and excluding activities formerly permitted, particularly to protect wildlife or biodiversity. Efforts to take away or modify grazing allotments, for example, are vehemently opposed, and seen as a form of private land confiscation.[5] These differing attitudes about land—public and private—helped shape many species/development conflicts.

Perspectives on Species and Biodiversity

The different actors and interest groups also generally have varying opinions about endangered species and biodiversity, and the importance of protecting them. Not surprisingly, environmental representatives hold all species in reverence and believe strongly in the need to protect and conserve them. Depending on the environmental groups, the arguments are sometimes anthropocentric and utilitarian (i.e., humans need to protect biodiversity to protect themselves) and sometimes based on biocentric views or notions of the inherent right of species to exist, irrespective of their instrumental value to human beings. Protection of species, then, is often couched in terms of ethics and ethical obligations. Environmental representatives tend to place great importance on protection of biodiversity and all species, from panther to kangaroo rat, from Peregine Falcon to cave beetle.

While the general public has become increasingly concerned about environmental problems generally, the sense of concern about species extinction clearly varies depending on the species. Stephen Kellert's survey work strongly supports this view. In one survey, Kellert gave respondents a list of different animal and plant species and asked them which they would favor protecting if it resulted in higher energy costs. While 89% favored protecting the Bald Eagle, only 43% favored protecting the eastern indigo snake and an even smaller 34% favored protecting the Kanai wolf spider.[6]

The attitudes and positions of elected officials also tend to reflect some of this skepticism about the need to protect *every single species*, even invertebrates and plants. Land developers, property owners, and resources users as well, tend to be more skeptical about the need to protect all species.

Local officials are also often very concerned about the impact of protection efforts on the local tax base and on the ability of their communities to grow. They often view endangered species as an obstacle to be overcome and the ESA as the common enemy to be confronted. For instance, a number of local officials expressed open hostility towards the endangered lizard issue in Coachella Valley. In the beginning several local governments considered suing USFWS over the issue. The then mayor of Palm Springs, Frank Bogart, was one of the most incensed over the lizard issue. In his words:

> It is the biggest racket ever perpetrated on this valley . . . I say racket because the biologists in this area want to get a piece of our land for all the little animals and take it away from people who have been paying taxes for years and years.[7]

The then mayor of Rancho Mirage, Bill Wilson, expressed similar sentiments, calling it "ridiculous" to "stop progress because of a lizard."[8]

Arguments by biologists and environmentalists about the uniqueness and importance of particular species are, again, difficult to sell to many public officials. Despite the many arguments about how unique and specially adapted the fringe-toed lizard is, many local officials were simply not very convinced about the importance of spending large amounts of public funds to preserve this small reptile. Such an idea, to many, was preposterous. Consider the comments of one Rancho Mirage councilman:

> I don't get extremely emotional about the fringe-toed lizard. I really don't care if it stays or leaves . . . . I don't know whether it's endangered or not. I wear lizard boots, so there . . . .[9]

Particularly controversial is whether sub-species ought to be preserved, especially when the public and private costs are very high. While most scientists believe that the Coachella Valley fringe-toed lizard is a separate species, many people wonder whether the cost of the HCP—approximately $25 million—was justified considering that other very similar species of fringe-toed lizards exist. Most lay persons, moreover, would have difficulty distinguishing between them.

Attitudes about Funding

Stakeholder groups and participants in HCPs often have dramatically different views regarding responsibility for paying for conservation measures. Much of the debate and discussion in HCP steering committees frequently centers around this cost distribution question.

Those in environmental and conservation communities generally believe that developers should pay a lion's share of these costs, since their activities are causing the harm and the principle of culpability supports the argument for a large contribution on their part. Those in the development community, on the other hand, resent this exclusive blame. They argue that a species becomes endangered from a long-term pattern of habitat losses, implicating past development and the larger community, and that it is a federal law—the Endangered Species Act—which is causing the expenditures in the first place and thus, the costs should be spread to the larger public.

Dynamics of the HCP Process

While it is difficult to generalize about the political dynamics of the HCP process certain common observations can be made. Despite important differences among HCPs they tend to follow common procedural and methodological patterns.

Habitat conservation plans are initiated in many different ways, but frequently there are clear triggering events. Typically, HCPs are a reaction to one or more projects where an endangered species is confronted. The Coachella Valley HCP was triggered by a conflict over a proposed four hundred-acre resort development that threatened fringe-toed lizard habitat. (Until this project the question of the threatened lizard had remained largely dormant for several years.) The Metro-Bakersfield HCP was initiated largely in response to a proposed golf course (concession) on habitat of the endangered San Joaquin kit fox.

Frequently, these triggering events involve actual or threatened legal action. The North Key Largo HCP was triggered in large degree by two lawsuits against a large proposed housing development and federal water project that constituted violations of ESA. The threat of lawsuits, especially on the environmental side, explains why land developers, local officials, and others remain at the bargaining table.

The crafting of habitat conservation plans usually involves a delicate political balance. Some have described a necessary condition of a successful HCP as being a "balance of terror." Developers and environmentalists alike share liability if they choose not to participate. Developers on the one hand, risk delays for their projects or a complete inability to build. The very real threat existed that without an HCP the USFWS could essentially close down development in the Coachella Valley. On the other hand, many in the environmental community recognize the legal and political problems faced by USFWS in taking such actions.

Moreover, development interests frequently threaten to press for congressional changes ("gutting") in ESA if there is not some degree of compromise or flexibility in its application. USFWS staff frequently acknowledge their fear of the political (and personal and professional) ramifications of taking severe actions such as halting development entirely. Those representing environmental interests also frequently view the HCP as an opportunity to marshall resources—financial and political—for the protection of biodiversity, that would otherwise simply not be available. And in some cases it is clear, as in the San Bruno Mountain case, that the species of concern would be in greater danger without the HCP, and without some degree of habitat development and the funds generated from it.

The actual crafting of the HCP strategy happens through a negotiated process, typically involving a degree of compromise on all sides. Participants tend to negotiate from positions which further reflect their different perspectives and values. Among the central topics focused upon during the HCP process and on which negotiation and compromise occur, are the type and level of habitat conservation, the source of funding and the relative distribution of these costs, and the assignment of long-term management responsibilities.

Debate and negotiation concerning each of these issues tend to reflect the different stakeholder values. Those in the development community, for instance, tend to argue for modest mitigation fees, believing that fairness requires a greater contribution by the larger public, especially the federal government. Those in the environmental community tend to support larger mitigation fees. Determination of development mitigation fees is as much a result of political compromise, as technical analysis of funding needs.

The resulting HCP, then, is usually a collective product—the result of a series of negotiated compromises. While it must ultimately satisfy the Section 10(a) standards, there is considerable room for subjective interpretation of adequate fulfillment of these standards, the appropriate strategies for accomplishing plan objectives, the compromise of development and habitat protection, and so on. As is often the case with negotiated processes, few individuals or groups are entirely satisfied with the results (e.g., environmental groups typically feel that too little habitat will be protected; developers typically think too much has been preserved). And, the exact negotiated result will tend to depend on the particular political standing and resources that different stakeholders are able to command. It is evident, for example, that when HCPs are developed in areas where environmental organizations hold less clout (e.g.,

Coachella Valley), the resulting compromise may concede more to development interests than might otherwise be the case.

Conclusions

Habitat conservation, at least in the U.S. context, is inherently political in nature. The process by which HCPs are developed and implemented must necessarily involve a range of stakeholder groups, including land development interests, environmental groups, local governments, and resource agencies. These different stakeholder groups tend to hold different, sometimes opposing, views on key issues involved in HCPs, including the legitimacy of land use regulations, the importance of protecting biodiversity, and what constitutes a fair and equitable distribution of the costs of habitat conservation. While experience with HCPs suggests that practical compromises can be reached, participants in the HCP process, and those seeking to facilitate and promote habitat protection, must acknowledge and take into account these different perspectives.

CHAPTER

FIVE

Habitat Conservation Plans to Protect Butterflies and Other Invertebrate Species: San Bruno Mountain and Beyond

San Bruno Mountain and the Beginnings of Habitat Conservation Planning

While species/development conflicts were certainly not new, those which emerged over development on San Bruno Mountain (California) gave rise to important changes in the Endangered Species Act.

San Bruno Mountain is located south of the city of San Francisco in San Mateo County, and it is surrounded by the cities of South San Francisco, Brisbane, and Daly City. The history of San Bruno Mountain is an interesting one. The mountain, approximately thirty-five hundred acres in size, is one of the last remaining large areas of open space in the San Francisco area. Controversy over the mountain dates back to the 1960s when proposals were made to mine major portions of the mountain to provide materials for building the San Francisco International Airport. The conflict is credited with spurring the establishment of the "Save the Bay" Association, and later with the creation of the San Francisco Bay Conservation and Development Commission.[1]

More recently the mountain has been eyed by developers as a major development site. The bulk of the mountain was purchased by Visitacion Associates in 1970, and in 1975 they proposed to build eighty-five hundred units of residential development and 2 million square feet of office space. This proposal was itself extremely controversial and generated substantial opposition, especially from neighboring communities. To obtain development approval the developers had to receive approval of a plan amendment from the county. Eventually, in response to vocal concerns about the size and impact of the proposal, an agreement was reached which substantially reduced the size of the project. Instead of eighty-five hundred residential units, the development would be allowed to build only 2,235 units. As part of this arrangement, Visitacion agreed to donate and sell about two thousand acres of the mountain to become public open space and parkland.

It is interesting that the endangered species issue did not emerge until later, after this initial agreement, and resulting plan amendment, had been reached. The mission blue butterfly (*Plebejus icariodides missionensis*) had originally been placed on the endangered species list in June 1975. San Bruno Mountain supported the largest remaining population of the mission blue, estimated to be 85% of the species (two other smaller populations were also known).

It was not until proposals surfaced by the U.S. Fish and Wildlife Service to list another butterfly species—the Callippe silverspot (*Spegeria callippe callippe*) that the full significance of the mountain habitat for the mission blue, and other species, was recognized. The USFWS proposed in July 1978 not only to list the Callippe silverspot but, more importantly from the view of the developers and landowners, proposed to designate major portions of the mountain as "critical habitat." When Congress passed amendments to the ESA in 1978 it changed its definition of critical habitat (see Chapter 2), causing USFWS to withdraw its listing and critical habitat designations in many places around the country, including San Bruno. It reproposed the listing and designation in 1980, however.

For those wishing to develop on San Bruno, the proposed listing and habitat designation represented major obstacles. Moreover, during this period local environmental groups, the Committee to Save San Bruno Mountain in particular, as well as the USFWS, seemed to concur that development of the mountain would result in take of the already listed mission blue in one of its life stages, thus violating the ESA.

In an effort to resolve the impasse and to prevent protracted legal and political battle over the mountain's fate, and at the suggestion of a San Mateo County Supervisor (Ed Bacciocco), a series of meetings were held to explore possible management options and alternatives to such a standoff. Visitacion sought to convince USFWS to postpone the endangered listing and critical habitat designation for the Callippe silverspot, and proposed the preparation of what it referred to as a habitat conservation plan. Opponents of development, principally the Committee to Save San Bruno, also agreed to cooperate on some form of compromise plan. The USFWS reaction was understandable, believing they did not have the authority to participate in the development of such a plan and would not ultimately have the power to issue a permit to allow take once the plan had been developed. If, on the other hand, a federal project or permit were involved, it could participate through a Section 7 consultation, but no such "federal handle" existed in the San Bruno case. USFWS later changed its position, seeing merit in a compromise solution. And, USFWS did defer listing and critical habitat designation of the Callippe silverspot, although it based this decision on the fact that the range and habitat of the silverspot and the already listed mission blue were so close that additional protection was not necessary.

Development of the habitat conservation plan was guided by a steering committee representing the different interest groups having a stake in the outcome. The committee consisted of representatives of USFWS, California Department of Fish and Game (CDFG), San Mateo County, Visitacion and other landowners, the cities surrounding the mountain (Daly City, Brisbane, South San Francisco), and the environmental community, including the Committee to Save San Bruno Mountain. From the beginning the committee agreed to the importance of a plan based on a strong biological and scientific foundation. An initial and significant step in developing the HCP was to conduct basic scientific studies of the mountain, with particular emphasis on identifying essential habitat needs of the butterflies. The county hired a group of biological consultants to prepare the background study, and Visitacion agreed to pay the cost of the study. While Visitacion agreed to cover the expense of scientific study it also agreed not to interfere in any way with the study or seek to sway the findings. Thomas Reid and Associates were hired to prepare the study. In the end, the resulting biological report represents an exhaustive analysis of the butterflies, and their habitat needs, leading one commentator to remark that it "probably represents the most in-depth study to date of the population of a federally listed insect species."[2]

In particular, four types of studies were undertaken as part of this analysis: a mark-release-recapture study, a distribution study, a dispersal study, and a study of habitat needs. Together these analyses provided a fairly thorough picture of the current status of the butterfly populations on the mountain, and the habitat conditions needed to ensure their long-term survival.

The population study was of one single population of the mission blue butterflies on the mountain that had been divided into two primary clusters or "colonies" as a consequence of land use change. The same conclusion was reached for the Callippe silverspot. Interaction between the two colonies of butterflies was important to ensure genetic health. The larger colony was located along the southeast ridge; the other was located north of Guadalupe Hills. It was estimated that the larger colony was home to 60% of the mission blues and 75% of Callippe silverspot.[3] (Several other much smaller colonies of the mission blue were also found). The population studies found that there were approximately eighteen thousand flying adults of mission blue in 1981 and about eight thousand adult Callippe silverspots in the same year.

The biological study indicated that the mission blue and Callippe silverspot require a diversity of habitat conditions, and conditions that are not necessarily completely coterminous. In general, the studies concluded that a variety of habitat types and conditions are needed for the butterflies. The mission blue is highly dependent on three species of lupine, its larval food plant, which tend to be located in areas of rocky outcrops, poor soils, and disturbance. The larval food plant of the Callippe silverspot, violet, is found in grassland openings and locations not overgrown by larger brushy plants or dense grass. Mating and other behavioral requirements also translate into habitat needs. The male Callippe silverspots patrol hilltops; females fly up the hilltops to mate then back down to lay their eggs. The management plan, then, had to be responsive to protecting important elements of the mountain habitat for food sources and mating purposes.

It is important to understand vegetation patterns on the mountain and how these have changed over the years. The original vegetation on the mountain was a perennial bunch grassland. Settlement of the region led to the replacement of this native grassland with European annual grassland, followed by many years of livestock grazing. It is interesting that this livestock grazing tended to favor the butterfly species—the disturbed areas created by grazing favored the larval foods of the mission blue, lupines and nector plants (thistles). The grazing did not disturb the larger plants, and tended to keep out the invasion of brush and gorse and other exotic species (see Table 5.1). Over time, as livestock grazing was ended on the mountain, the brush species have gradually expanded, jeopardizing those grassland species upon which the butterflies survive. In addition, illegal off-road vehicle use has resulted in habitat degradation and significant damage to host plants.

Several other species of fauna were also considered in the plan. Two additional species of butterflies; the San Bruno elfin (*Callophrys mossii bayensis*) and the bay checkerspot (*Euphydryas editha bayensis*) are also found on the mountain. The San Bruno elfin had been listed as endangered and the bay checkerspot had been proposed for listing. Nine distinct colonies of the San Bruno elfin were identified and mapped and included in the HCP. The bay checkerspot occupies a much smaller portion of the mountain, and generally not areas where urban development

Table 5.1. *Change in Extent of Vegetation Types, 1932–1981*

	1932 (Acres)	Urbanized since 1932 (Acres)	1981 (Acres)	Change (Acres)	Change (%)
Gorse	52	52	334	+282	+545
Brush	600	50	1,141	+541	+90
Eucalyptus	124	46	206	+82	+65
Woodland	32	—	72	+40	+125
Cultivated	95[a]		0	−95	
Total, non-grassland	808	148	1,753	+945	+117
Total, grassland	4,047[b]	1,238	1,811	−2,331	−55
Total SBM	4,950	1,386	3,564.5	−1,386	

[a]Left out of the non-grassland sum since it was not natural land in 1932.
[b]The area of contiguous grassland in 1932 which is larger than the present study area of 3564.5 acres.
Source: San Bruno Mountain Habitat Conservation Plan prepared by Thomas Reid Associates. County of San Mateo, 1982.

would be possible. A final species receiving some specific attention was the endangered San Francisco garter snake. A herpetologist (Professor Ted Papenfuss) was hired to search for the snake on the mountain and to identify habitat locations. No active snakes were found, but the consultant was able to identify a small number of areas where the species might be encountered.

In addition to establishing baseline biological information on the population and habitat needs of the butterflies, a set of broader ecological principles for the mountain were generated. In this way, the plan—while emphasizing and focusing on protection of butterflies—also promotes protection and management of the mountain as an ecological unit, in turn resulting in conservation of other flora and fauna. As Marsh and Thornton note:

> In the end, although the habitat conservation plan continued to focus on the butterflies, it did so in the context of preserving the ecological vitality of the mountain as a whole.[4]

The conclusions of the extensive biological study were critical in shaping the content of the HCP. Moreover, the biological study was subjected to a peer review process by noted conservation biologists, including Paul Erhlich, which served to enhance the credibility of the findings.

In the following section the key provisions of the San Bruno plan are discussed.

Provisions of the San Bruno Plan

Together these inventories and biological studies were used in crafting a habitat conservation plan. The plan has a number of components, but a major strategy is setting aside large blocks of land as "conserved habitat" and the designation of other areas for development. Of the approximately thirty-six hundred acres of land on the mountain, about eighteen hundred had already been protected in public parkland. The HCP called for donation by developers of an additional eight hundred acres of land, to be added to the publicly owned habitat. On the other hand the HCP would allow the development of 368 acres of land—development which would be subject to both a one-time development fee as well as annual development fees to finance long-term mitigation and management. Also, a portion (about 25%) of the developed land would be restored to habitat after it was developed. Areas of conserved habitat and areas where development is permissible are indicated in figure 5.1. Some private land owners on the mountain were also not covered ("unplanned areas") and would likely be prevented from building under Section 9 of ESA (without their own individual 10[a] permit). The plan protects a relatively high percentage of the butterfly habitat on San Bruno, specifically, 87% of the mission blue's habitat, and 93% of the Callippe silverspot's habitat. Consistent with an underlying principle of the biological study, the plan protects a diversity of habitat types, essential for the survival of the butterflies. These different habitats include hilltops and valleys, north- and south-facing slopes, grasslands, etc.

Long-term enhancement and restoration are also key components of the San Bruno plan. The plan divides the mountain into four areas: Guadalupe Hills, Southeast Ridge, Radio Ridge, and Saddle. For each of these areas the plan describes the particular land use and habitat changes occurring there, and future actions needed to enhance and restore habitat (in different time phases). A number of enhancement activities and actions are envisioned in the plan, including the eradication of gorse and brush, seeding of host plants, and fire control. The plan provides detailed guidelines for specific management areas within each of these broader planning areas. Long-term research and monitoring are also important components.

An annual fee of $20 per dwelling unit for residential development and $10 per 1000 square feet for commercial office space (each adjusted

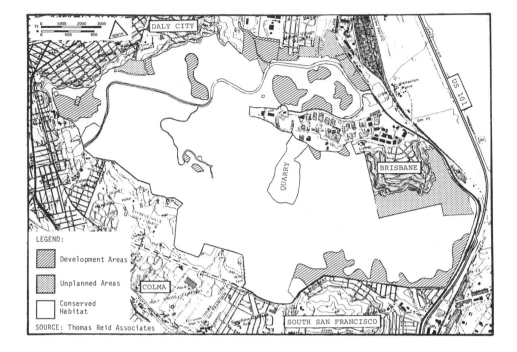

Figure 5.1. Areas to Be Developed and Conserved under the San Bruno Mountain Habitat Conservation Plan (Courtesy Thomas Reid Associates)

for inflation) is also assessed. These monies are placed in a special trust fund managed by San Mateo County, and are used to pay for habitat enhancement and management activities on the mountain. There is currently over $400,000 in the trust fund. In addition, developers must cover the costs incurred by the county in overseeing and monitoring construction activities. Developers must also cover the costs of habitat restoration and reclamation on their sites.

The HCP also incorporates a process for allowing plan amendments over time. Several types of amendments are allowed, including minor boundary adjustments, equivalent exchange amendments (i.e., exchanging lands designated as conserved habitat with land designated for development), and three-year amendments. Any substantial changes must generally go through the third type of amendment process, and must be approved by the local community, the county, and USFWS. Three-year amendments typically require the preparation of a biological study (showing the action will not interfere with long-term survival of the species). Several amendments have been approved since the HCP was approved. Such changes have included an amendment to allow a development company to repair several landslides upslope of its development project, an amendment to permit an accelerated grading schedule for a project, and an amendment allowing a portion of county parkland on the mountain to be used for an adjacent landfill (with extensive mitigation).

Under the plan, the Section 10(a) permit application was submitted by the county of San Mateo, and the cities of Brisbane, Daly City, and South San Francisco. The county of San Mateo was designated the "plan operator" and has been given primary plan implementation and enforcement responsibilities (county planning department, specifically).

Success of San Bruno

The San Bruno Mountain plan has been largely implemented as intended. The allowable development has occurred largely as predicted with about half the total allowed acreage already developed.

Ultimately the virtues of the HCP will be seen in its effects on the species of concern, the butterflies. The plan concludes that because habitat alteration will be small, the impact of limited take will be equally small. Under the HCP, development is to be limited to only 14% of the mission blue habitat and 8% of the Callippe silverspot (of which about 25% will be restored to habitat). This degree of habitat loss "is not likely to cause abrupt decline in their populations."[5] This amount of habitat loss, the plan concludes, should result in only a 2% to 5% increase in the likelihood of extinction for the mission blue and 1% to 3% for the Callippe silverspot.

Yearly monitoring reports offer some insight into how butterfly species have so far been affected. Recent reports show high population levels for both the mission blue and Callippe silverspot (although population estimates are dubious at best). Scientific observers believe the butterfly populations have stabilized, even though they are apparently very susceptible to climatic conditions (e.g., possible decline in numbers due to the drought).[6] Also, four additional mission blue colonies have been discovered in the bay area (reducing the San Bruno population of total population from 97% to about 70–75%).

Furthermore, it is clear that in the San Bruno case not allowing any development to proceed on the mountain might have been worse. A hands-off approach would likely result in a continuation of the gradual conversion of native grasslands to non-native species with a concomitant reduction in butterfly habitat. Limited development, as in the San

Bruno case, has resulted in a steady source of funds and a plan and organizational structure for bringing about substantial habitat restoration. This offers strong support that the San Bruno Mountain HCP helped preserve the threatened species.

Implementation of the San Bruno plan has not been without controversy, however, and was not uniformly embraced by all parties. A major legal challenge to the plan was presented in 1983 when a group called Friends of Endangered Species, Inc. sued in federal court claiming that the issuance of the San Bruno permit violated ESA by jeopardizing the continued existence of the listed mission blue. The suit also argued that USFWS violated the provisions of the National Environmental Policy Act (NEPA) for failing to prepare a complete environmental impact statement on the issuance of the permit. In *Friends of Endangered Species v. Jantzen*,[7] the U.S. District Court for the district of northern California rejected these claims and denied a motion for a temporary injunction.[8] More than a year later this decision was affirmed by the Ninth Circuit Court of Appeals. In both decisions the biological foundation of the plan appears to have played an important role in sustaining the plan. The fact that biological findings were supported through scientific peer review was also important. The courts seem also to have been impressed with the amount of habitat to be permanently protected and the provisions for habitat restoration and enhancement.

Political controversy has also developed over several of the amendment proposals, including the proposal by the W. W. Dean Company to build retaining walls above its property to protect against landslides, and a proposal by Pacific Gas and Electric to move and rebuild a gas line running through eastern San Bruno Mountain. The former case was eventually allowed by amendment, while the latter was resolved by rerouting the line.[9]

One of the most politically contentious issues to develop since the plan's approval involved development plans on the northwest ridge of the mountain. Here Southwest Diversified Company had planned to construct a 1,250-unit condominium project. As a result of political changes in Brisbane, where the project land was located, efforts were made to impose additional growth management controls on this development. The developers objected and saw these new anti-growth efforts as violations of the HCP agreements. Southwest Diversified took legal action against the city and eventually a compromise agreement was reached, resulting in a significantly reduced project (589 units). While this development plan was approved by the city council, a petition drive was mounted to recall the decision, subjecting it to a local referendum. The developers were successfully able to challenge this action in court, claiming that referenda were not legally permitted in this particular type of local action. Opponents of the project also mounted their own legal action claiming, among other things, that an inadequate environmental impact report had been prepared under the California Environmental Quality Act. All of these suits have been dismissed and ground has been broken on the project. (The developers have also applied for an equivalent exchange amendment to allow for a plan boundary modification.)

Despite these political controversies the basic elements of the plan have been maintained, and the San Bruno experience has been a positive one. A number of factors have been identified by participants and commentators as key elements to the success of the plan. Marsh and Thornton (1986) include among them, the following: the creation of a trusted forum by the county of San Mateo; the exercising of leadership by particular individuals which kept the process going when it could have been derailed (and the work of one county supervisor in particular); the importance of credible scientific and technical expertise; commitment on all sides to making the process work (i.e., the environmentalists and developers); and a recognition of "the value of solving the process in this fashion rather than resorting to litigation or to Congress."[10]

The HCP has received considerable support from the development community and the San Bruno case illustrates some of the important benefits that can be derived from such habitat protection efforts. While the overall level of development permitted on the mountain has been reduced, developers indicate that the units that are built will be in high demand. What will result are islands of development, surrounded by protected habitat and open space—areas that homeowners can be assured will never be developed. Although difficult to quantify, there is a strong belief that there is a substantial unique amenity value in these areas (compared with other similar developments in the bay area) and that this translates into greater desirability and marketability and higher unit prices. Securing these habitat areas is seen to confer significant economic benefits on developers in the area.

The San Bruno experience was seen by many involved in the process, and by outside observers, as a very rational and sensible mechanism for reconciling endangered species/development conflicts. Based on sound scientific study and principles, it appears to have ensured protection of the butterflies, while allowing some degree of urban development on the mountain. In part to promote and tout the San Bruno model as useable in other similar conflicts and to solidify the legal underpinning of a USFWS take permit (clearly at that time Section 10 take permits were intended primarily to apply to cases of traditional research and species enhancement activities) efforts were made to amend the Endangered

Species Act to allow for such planning processes to occur. Convinced of the benefits of the San Bruno model, the 1982 amendments did include the Section 10(a) provisions that today serve as the legal foundation for other HCPs. The San Bruno Mountain HCP received the first such 10(a) incidental take permit issued by USFWS on March 4, 1983.

Sand City HCP

Sand City, California, is a small, scenic, coastal town located north of Monterey. For several years it has been in the process of preparing an HCP for the federally listed Smith's blue butterfly (*Euphilotes enoptes smithi*). A major portion of the city's remaining undeveloped dune area is prime habitat for the butterfly, and its primary host plant, the buckwheat. A steering committee has been appointed by the city council to oversee the process, including representatives of developers and landowners, USFWS, CDFG, Caltrans, and environmental interests such as the Sierra Club and Native Plants Society. A consultant has been hired to prepare the HCP and background biological studies. Funding for the plan has been split between landowner contributions and the California Coastal Conservancy, with each providing $50,000.

The prime butterfly habitat in the city is located in dune areas seaward of the coastal highway (Highway 101). The largest remaining block of habitat is in an area known as the East Dunes. Much of the steering committee's discussion has centered on plans for this area. To developers and city officials, prohibiting all development in this area would be unreasonable in that it comprises such a large percentage of the remaining buildable land in the city, which is very small to begin with. In addition, this area is already heavily parcelized with some 250 existing lots. Buying these lands would be extremely expensive since small lots, even without public facilities, are selling for as much as $25,000. A number of alternative development concepts have been considered, including clustering development in the center of the area, with large areas of conserved habitat around the edges. Even under this type of arrangement it is unclear to city officials how the problem of existing lots will be addressed and how acquisition of the conserved habitat (if acquired outright) will be paid for. The steering committee has also been considering the establishment of a butterfly corridor to run adjacent to Highway 101.

Local officials have expressed considerable frustration about the HCP process. Despite repeated attempts to learn from USFWS what an acceptable habitat conservation scheme would consist of, they feel that they have been given little or no direction. Rather, they feel USFWS has adopted the attitude that "once we see the plan we'll tell you whether or not it's adequate." Officials have also been critical about the lack of federal or state funds to pay for habitat acquisition. In their case, the habitat in question is very expensive and represents a large percentage of the city's remaining potentially buildable land. Thus, there is no large development base over which to distribute the costs of conservation (e.g., by way of a mitigation fee), as there was in Coachella Valley and many of the other HCPs. Also, because areas such as the east dunes are some of the few last remaining areas to develop, the city's ability to expand its tax base is in jeopardy. City officials have also expressed concern that these are the last potential areas for affordable housing (at least relative to development in the Monterey region as a whole).

Marina Dunes HCP

Marina, California, is a coastal jurisdiction north of Monterey. The primary endangered species of concern there is the endangered Smith's blue butterfly. Several other species are also considered in the plan including certain rare plants, and the black legless lizard (*Anniella pulchra nigra*), a candidate for federal listing. Marina is jointly preparing an HCP for the butterfly and a new local coastal plan (LCP), together generally referred to as the Marina Dunes Plan. Funding for the plans has been split between local landowners and the California Coastal Conservancy, each providing $60,000. The process was originally initiated as a result of a lawsuit filed by the Sierra Club. A steering committee, consisting of the landowners involved, environmentalists, resource agency representatives, and local officials, has been meeting since 1986. Because of the joint HCP/LCP effort, the Marina committee has been considering a much larger set of management issues than just the butterfly, including such things as shoreline erosion, view protection, and public beach access. One consultant has been involved in preparing both of these components.

The primary butterfly habitat in Marina is located along a 626-acre continuous tract of beachfront, beginning just north of the Marina Point State Park. The Marina Dunes HCP has been made easier by existing landownership patterns (in contrast to Sand City). The habitat areas are essentially owned by three landowners: Lonestar Company, Granite Rock, and Monterey Sand. All three companies currently use the land as part of sand mining operations. The Lonestar Company is the largest of the three, owning about 370 acres of the habitat. In contrast to the experience of Sand City, the Marina steering committee has had an easier time reaching general consensus about the management strategy. The consultant has performed detailed analyses of the extent of land and vegetation disturbance, and the committee has made the general assumption that any future development should occur in areas owned by these companies. The committee has agreed that future development should be restricted to designated "bubbles," which will allow substantial density, but which will then allow large remaining areas to be set aside as conserved habitat. According to the draft plan completed in March 1991, of the 626 acres in the area, development will be permitted on about 141 acres. The remaining 485 acres have been designated as habitat, buffer, restoration, and other space/habitat uses. It does not appear that any land acquisition will be needed, as the conserved habitat will simply be protected by deed restrictions preventing any future development.

Among the habitat areas set aside and off-limits, certain lands have been identified for restoration. It will be the responsibility of the landowner to undertake this restoration, and a restoration plan will be required to be submitted to the city prior to development. Certain areas are also designated as habitat corridors. These are strips of land, ranging from fifty to two hundred feet wide, that provide connection and continuity between major habitat blocks. Within the acreage designated for development, a fifty-foot buffer is established around all development parcels, and no structures (except for boardwalks) are to be permitted in these areas. The draft HCP also specifies in more detail, on a parcel-by-parcel basis, permissible uses and intensities. The plan also sets forth certain pre-development planning, construction practices, and post-development activities which landowners must undertake (e.g., grading restrictions, fencing requirements, restrictions on pesticide use).

While there appears to be general agreement on the conservation strategy, a number of specific implementation issues have not yet been resolved. It is not clear who will be given management responsibilities for the conserved habitat areas once they are set aside. Among the alternative management entities which have been under consideration are the regional park authority, the California Department of Parks and Recreation, and U.S. Fish and Wildlife Service. At this point, it is probable that the regional park authority will take over these management responsibilities. Extensive funding does not appear to be necessary for Marina. Each landowner will be responsible for undertaking certain initial habitat restoration activities (until conserved habitat areas achieve certain restoration standards), after which management responsibilities for conserved habitat areas will be turned over to the regional park authority or other designated agency. Initial funding for the plan will come from contributions from the three major landowners. Longer-term funding will be provided through occupancy fees (on a per-occupied room basis).

At this point in time an administrative draft of the LCP/HCP has been prepared and will soon be presented to the city council for approval. It is estimated that the additional environmental review documentation will take another eighteen to twenty-four months to complete. To local participants a distressing aspect of the Marina Dunes process has been the length of time it has taken—nearly five years already.

Conclusions

The HCPs described in this chapter involve a common concern of protecting endangered butterfly species and their habitat. While the Sand City and Marina Dunes HCPs are too early in the process to offer many conclusions, the San Bruno Mountain case has involved sufficient time and reached closure to allow some conclusions about the experience. San Bruno was the first HCP, initiated even before the 10(a) provisions explicitly allowed such plans. It was viewed by most involved in the process as a necessary and productive compromise between development interests and conservation/protection advocates. The San Bruno experience became a positive model from which supporters were able to achieve modifications to ESA to allow such processes to occur in other similar conflicts.

The San Bruno Mountain HCP represents a good model from which other HCPs can be designed. It resulted in a combination of development and conserved habitat favorable to the butterflies (protecting approximately 87% of the mission blue's habitat). Moreover, the plan has resulted in funding and an administrative framework in which habitat restoration is occurring and will continue to occur on the mountain. It is fairly convincing that a complete hands-off approach to San Bruno Mountain would be more detrimental to the butterflies, in light of gradual expansion of brush and other non-native vegetation, than the compromise implemented. The plan is also admirable in its effort to take an ecological approach and to consider potential impacts on other rare species (e.g., the San Francisco garter snake).

Several key elements can be identified in the success of the San Bruno process. As other commentators have noted, much of what was accomplished is the result of the willingness of key participants to be actively involved in the process and to be flexible in their demands. Participants were able to see the advantages of cooperating and negotiating, rather than engaging in protracted legal and political battles. The structuring of the process, and especially the centrality of the biological study, were important factors. An impartial and thorough analysis of the butter-flies—their current populations and habitat needs—was important for establishing the credibility and acceptability of the final plan. Moreover, the San Bruno HCP is so far the only HCP to be challenged in court, and its legal defense was helped greatly by the credible biological studies. In these and other ways San Bruno, at least at a micro-level, established some useful yardsticks against which to evaluate subsequent HCPs.

Conserving Habitat for a Threatened Desert Lizard: The Coachella Valley Habitat Conservation Plan

Introduction[1]

The second habitat conservation plan to be formally approved by the U.S. Fish and Wildlife Service was that prepared for the threatened Coachella Valley fringe-toed lizard. This plan has been profiled in such publications as *National Geographic* and *The New York Times* and on television shows such as the ABC "Nightly News," and it is widely heralded as a national model for resolving development/conservation conflicts. This chapter presents a detailed case study of the Coachella Valley HCP; its history, provisions, success to date, and implications for public policy. It begins by reviewing the types and magnitude of development pressures in the Coachella Valley which have given rise to this conflict.

Growth and Development in the Coachella Valley

The Coachella Valley lies approximately one hundred miles east of Los Angeles, and is a northern extension of the Colorado Desert. The valley is three hundred square miles in size and is bounded to the north by the Little San Bernardino Mountains and to the south and west by the Santa Rosa and San Jacinto mountains. San Gorgonio Pass is at the western end of the valley, and the Salton Sea lies at the extreme east. The valley consists largely of windblown sand and rocky alluvial deposits.

The southern portion of the valley was converted to agricultural uses in the 1940s, following the construction of Coachella Canal in 1948. This canal brought water to the valley and permitted, for the first time, large-scale agricultural activities, occurring especially in the southern end of the valley. Urban development in the post-war period was initially modest, with development occurring mainly south of the Whitewater River. As demand for land and housing has increased over the years, urban development has expanded into blowsand habitat areas. The expansion of roads and highways, and the invention of air conditioning have made the desert environment more accessible and attractive.

The valley has experienced tremendous growth in recent years. While its permanent population was only about twelve thousand in 1940, it rose to more than 130,000 in 1980, and is projected to increase to 311,000 by the year 2000.[2] Because much of the population in the valley is seasonal, population pressures are even greater than these estimates suggest. Several of the fastest growing cities in California are located in the valley, including Desert Hot Springs, Palm Desert, and Rancho Mirage (see Table 6.1). Much of the valley has developed as exclusive resort housing, and the area is home to numerous entertainers and celebrities such as the former president Gerald Ford, Frank Sinatra, Bob Hope, and others. As development pressures have expanded over the years, much of the natural desert environment has disappeared. This has in turn meant shrinking habitat for wildlife, both endangered and nonendangered, and an increasingly greater intrusion of man into the natural landscape.

Table 6.1. *Population Changes in the Coachella Valley* **(Permanent Population)**

	1970	*1980*	*1988*	*Projected 2000*
Palm Springs	21,497	32,366	40,925	65,601
Cathedral City	7,327	11,096	26,758	29,847
Desert Hot Springs	2,738	5,941	10,383	17,150
Rancho Mirage	2,767	6,281	8,525	16,077
Palm Desert	6,171	11,801	18,088	30,053
Indian Wells	760	1,394	2,443	6,348
Indio	14,459	21,611	33,068	47,945
La Quinta	1,190	3,328	9,274	17,908
Coachella	8,353	9,129	14,115	23,625
Coachella Valley (including unincorporated areas)	88,999	133,419	202,231	311,911

Sources: Coachella Valley Association of Governments, *Coachella Valley Area Growth Monitor* (Palm Desert, Calif., 1988); CVAG, *Regional Housing Needs Assessment* (Palm Desert, Calif., 1989).

The Coachella Valley Fringe-toed Lizard

The Coachella Valley fringe-toed lizard (*Uma inornata*) is a medium-sized lizard, averaging six to nine inches in length. Whitish or sand-colored, it exhibits a pattern of eye-like markings forming longitudinal stripes along its shoulder.[3] The lizard exhibits morphological features and behavioral patterns that are distinctly suited to life in the desert. In many ways, the lizard is the quintessential example of a successful evolutionary adaptation. Its most obvious features are its fringed toes—a row of scales on the bottom edge of the lizard's toes substantially increases the lizard's foot surface and allows it to "skate" along the sand at high speed. The lizard can also dive into sand and can move under sand for short distances—sometimes called "sand swimming." Other adaptations include smooth scales to reduce friction, an ability to partially close its nostrils to keep out sand, a U-shaped nasal passage which serves to trap sand and allows the lizard to easily blow out these trapped materials, and a wedge-shaped snout to facilitate sand diving. It also has fringed eyelids with a double seal, and a flap of skin which covers its ears when diving into sand. As well, its upper jaw overlaps its lower jaw which helps to prevent the entrance of sand when diving underground. Its behavior is also specially adapted to its desert environment.

The Coachella Valley fringe-toed lizard lives in areas of fine windblown sand, and thus relies heavily upon a natural uninterrupted blowsand environment. Sand materials originate in the mountain areas and are brought into the valley through periodic flooding. Strong winds pass through San Gorgonio Pass at the northwestern end of the valley and move in a southeastern direction, transporting materials deposited in alluvial fans down the valley. These strong winds from the northwest serve to sort the materials.

At one time the range of the Coachella Valley fringe-toed lizard extended throughout the valley. Its habitat has been slowly reduced since the turn of the century as a result of a combination of conversion of land to agricultural uses, the interruption of natural sand movement by buildings, railroad windbreaks, and other man-made improvements, and the direct loss of habitat to urban development (i.e., roads, houses, golf courses). Off-road vehicle use has also taken its toll on the lizards.

Of the original 267 square miles of habitat, it has been estimated that one-half of this historic range has been directly converted to other uses. As of the completion of the habitat conservation plan in 1985 it was estimated that the occupiable habitat of the lizard was approximately 127 square miles, or 81,500 acres.[4] Furthermore, much of this remaining occupiable habitat is currently undergoing degradation due to the disruption of natural sand transport needed to sustain the blowsand habitat. It has been estimated that as much as 50% of the remaining occupiable habitat is currently experiencing some degradation due to blowsand shielding. In addition to roads, buildings, and other forms of urban development, shielding has resulted from various blowsand control measures.

The Emergence of Concern over the Lizard

One of the first individuals in the local conservation community to become seriously concerned about the status of the lizard and the blowsand habitat it depended upon was Wilbur Mayhew, a professor of zoology at the University of California at Riverside. He became frustrated at having to continually find new field sites for his classes as urban development intruded on the lizard's habitat. These concerns led Mayhew and others to form the Coachella Valley Fringe-toed Lizard Advisory Committee in 1977. The committee, consisting largely of state wildlife biologists and resource managers, and chaired by Mayhew, pushed strongly to have the lizard placed on both the federal and state endangered species lists, and to have a local lizard preserve established. Mayhew and the committee were not only concerned about the lizard, but saw it as a possible means of protecting a portion of the larger blowsand habitat. Mayhew saw the lizard's federal and state classification as endangered as a way to gain access to federal and state monies for land acquisition. The lizard was a logical focus because of its uniqueness (the species was found only in Coachella Valley) and the extent of information that had been collected on it in comparison with other species.[5]

The first studies which sought to assess changes in the population and distribution of the lizards were conducted in the early and mid-1970s. The results of these studies showed substantial declines in lizard habitat and populations as a result of habitat loss due to a combination of factors, including urban development, conversion of land to agricultural uses, blowsand control programs, and the use of off-road vehicles.[6] One of the most extensive studies was prepared in 1975 for the California Department of Fish and Game by environmental consultants England and Nelson.[7] The study undertook an extensive analysis of the extent and condition of blowsand habitat, as well as population counts for a series of sample sites throughout the valley. While England and Nelson found the lizard population to be relatively abundant over its current range, they found that substantial reductions in its range and habitat had occurred.[8] An analysis of county and city general plans and land use regulations indicated that most habitat areas had been slated for future development. The consultants issued a strong warning that actions needed to be taken, including the establishment of a blowsand habitat preserve, to ensure the long-term survival of the lizard.

The idea of a desert preserve, suggested by Mayhew's committee and by the England-Nelson study, had also been proposed by the County Planning Department. Although not specifically intending to protect the lizard, the planning department issued a report entitled, "Desert Habitat Preserve: A Preliminary Study" in December 1973, identifying four possible sites for such a preserve, and recommending a site in an area north of Interstate 10 and east of the community of Thousand Palms.[9] This report was never formally presented to the County Planning Commission or Board of Supervisors and no actions were taken to secure the preserve.

The lizard controversy heated up in September of 1978 when the U.S. Fish and Wildlife Service proposed to list the lizard as threatened and to designate a critical habitat which included almost all remaining blowsand areas in the valley. The original area proposed for critical habitat designation encompassed some 170 square miles of land, including an area extending thirty-five miles east of Cabazon to near Indio, and including the communities of Palm Springs, Rancho Mirage, Palm Desert, and Indian Wells. As expected, the listing proposal generated a firestorm of opposition from business leaders and local government officials in the valley, who claimed that the listing and habitat designation would bring development there to a standstill. In the words of one local Chamber of Commerce official: "The construction industry will be stifled, growth will be constricted, and the value of property will plummet."[10]

The USFWS proposal was short-lived, however. As a result of changes in the language of the Endangered Species Act under its 1978 congressional reauthorization, the U.S. Fish and Wildlife Service withdrew its proposed habitat listing for the lizard, along with other pending proposals for habitat designations for other species around the country. While this was viewed as good news by the business community and by local officials, there was still the fear that USFWS would designate at some later point an equally large critical habitat.[11] In light of this possibility, serious discussions began in the spring of 1979 about the possibility of setting up some form of lizard preserve—as Mayhew's Advisory Committee had suggested earlier—in the general vicinity suggested earlier by the county planning department. The Coachella Valley Association of Governments (CVAG) took the lead on the issue, with its executive committee voting unanimously in March to approve the recommendation of the CVAG environmental committee to establish a five-square-mile lizard preserve. The concept of a lizard preserve was endorsed by many because it was thought that such an action might prevent the designation of critical habitat by USFWS.[12] Despite these endorsements, and the general agreement about the location of the preserve, there was little tangible action taken to pursue the proposal at that time.

The U.S. Fish and Wildlife Service proposed listing the lizard's critical habitat again in the spring of 1980, holding public hearings in May of that year. The state of California had also proposed to list the lizard as endangered under its own endangered species act. Once again substantial opposition was expressed. Local landowner and development interests had formed a group called Friends of the Fringe-toed Lizard in an effort to establish a desert preserve and to derail federal and state efforts to list the lizard. The group reported to the California Fish and Game Commission in June that they were attempting to negotiate a land swap between the Bureau of Land Management and Dart Industries, the major landowner in the Thousand Palms Canyon area, which would establish an eighteen-square mile ecological preserve. While the group was able to successfully negotiate a land trade with local and state BLM officials, the proposal was eventually rejected by BLM officials in Washington.

Despite the general opposition expressed by such groups as the Friends, the lizard was placed on both the federal and state lists. The USFWS critical habitat actually designated was a much smaller area than that originally proposed in 1978. Less than the proposed 170 square miles, the designated habitat included an area of approximately twenty square miles (11,920 acres of private land and 690 acres owned by BLM). Despite the large area of potentially occupiable habitat, and a wide distribution of recorded sightings of lizards, the USFWS chose to designate a relatively limited area of critical habitat. To many observers these boundaries were selected primarily to avoid areas slated for development and in direct response to the vociferous local opposition to the 1978 proposal.

Palm Valley Country Club Proposal: The Conflict Re-emerges

Between 1980, when efforts were made to prevent the federal and state listing of the species, and 1983, relatively little attention was given to the lizard issue locally. The U.S. Fish and Wildlife Service had withdrawn its proposal to list a large 170-square-mile critical habitat, deciding instead to designate a much smaller area, located where development pressures were not as great. Some further attempts were made by the California Department of Fish and Game (CDFG) to acquire lizard habitat. The CDFG in conjunction with the Desert Protective Council formed a new non-profit group, called the Coachella Valley Ecological Reserve Foundation (CVERF). Modeled after the highly successful Anza Borrega Foundation (instrumental in securing land for the Anza Borrega State Park), CVERF's objective was to raise funds to purchase land for a desert preserve. The foundation was not very successful, however, at soliciting funds. During this period the CDFG did manage to obtain sufficient funds from the state to purchase approximately three hundred acres of blowsand habitat in the general area proposed earlier for a preserve.

The endangered species issue came to a head once again, however, in 1983 when several major development projects were proposed involving lizard habitat. One project—the four-hundred-acre, eleven-hundred-unit Desert Falls development in Palm Desert—involved a federal (HUD) mortgage guarantee, yet failed to go through the necessary Section 7 consultation procedure required under the Endangered Species Act. The Coachella Valley Ecological Reserve Foundation, and its committed director, Allan Muth, began to play an increasingly important watchdog role during this period, alerting federal and state officials to such violations. Muth, director of the University of California's Boyd Deep Canyon Desert Research Center, was himself a lizard expert. Under his leadership, the CVERF became a significant advocate of habitat preservation in the valley and carefully monitored all development activities. The Desert Falls project was forced by these watchdog efforts to undertake a Section 7 consultation.

By far, the most significant triggering event for the habitat conservation plan was the proposal of the Palm Valley Country Club—a 433-acre, thirteen hundred-unit condominium project to be located in the county near Palm Desert. Much of the controversy focused on the project's initial assessment of its likely environmental impacts. Under the California Environmental Quality Act (CEQA), projects requiring local development approval must prepare an Environmental Impact Report (EIR) where a significant environmental impact is likely (similar to an Environmental Impact Statement under the National Environmental Policy Act). As part of this impact statement developers must prepare biological assessments which, among other things, must examine the potential impacts on endangered plant and animal species. The biological assessment prepared for Palm Valley Country Club was the source of considerable criticism from Al Muth. Muth strongly questioned the conclusions of the biological assessment that no fringe-toed lizards existed on the site, and that in any event the designation of critical habitat by the U.S. Fish & Wildlife Service had in effect taken care of the lizard problem. Muth wrote a scathing letter to the County Planning Department indicating that, quite to the contrary, there had been clear signs of the presence of fringe-toed lizards on-site (recent sightings and tracks), and that the project would also have a considerable off-site impact by blocking sand transport for a large area south of Country Club Road.[13]

This letter triggered a dialogue between the developer and the county concerning appropriate actions to mitigate these impacts. Muth suggested that the developer—the Sunrise Company—replace the habitat acreage that would be lost by the project on an acre-for-acre basis (i.e., purchase and set aside one acre of lizard habitat for every one acre lost because of the development). The developer estimated that this would cost some $2 million at prevailing land prices and strongly objected to this idea. Instead, Sunrise offered to contribute $25,000, which was equally unacceptable to Muth and the county.

In an effort to resolve the issue, Sunrise Co. officials arranged a meeting with Al Muth, to see whether there were opportunities to compromise on the project. To represent them, Sunrise hired a noted local attorney Paul Selzer, of Best, Best, and Krieger. When asked by Sunrise what it would take to satisfy the concerns of the foundation, Muth again reiterated the demand that an acre of habitat be set aside for every acre destroyed. Sunrise continued to balk, viewing such a contribution as excessive and unreasonable.

What emerged was a kind of Mexican standoff. Sunrise believed it could support considerable litigation for the amount of money requested in mitigation fees. Moreover, it was commonly believed that Bill Bone, chairman of the board of Sunrise Company, had friends in high places, and might successfully mount an assault on the Endangered Species Act itself—perhaps severely weakening its enforcement provisions. On the other hand, Muth and others in the environmental community believed that the U.S. Fish and Wildlife Service had the power to stop all development in habitat areas, where potential takes were possible, essentially bringing development in the valley to a complete standstill. While most believed that the Fish and Wildlife Service would not, for political reasons, take such an extreme action, it was nonetheless a real threat that Sunrise and others took seriously. Each side, then, faced a certain degree of risk—the "balance of terror."

In light of this mutual risk, both sides eventually compromised, agreeing to participate in a process that would ultimately lead to the establishment of a lizard preserve. Muth and Sunrise signed a memorandum of understanding agreeing to this process, and the county approved the project contingent on the good-faith participation of Sunrise.[14] Thus began the process of finding a long-term permanent solution to the "lizard problem."

Preparing the Habitat Conservation Plan: Key Actors and Issues

Al Muth and Paul Selzer took the lead in approaching individuals to participate in this process. The group called itself the "lizard club" and met informally for the next two years. It was soon recognized that a variety of interests and agencies should be involved in crafting a solution (see Table 6.2), including federal and state resource agencies, the development community, the environmental community, and local governments. The Nature Conservancy in California was also requested to be involved from the first stage, because they were already considering the acquisition of wetlands (palm oases) in the area of the proposed preserve.

The group initially focused on how to acquire land for a preserve, but it was October of 1983 before a proposal to prepare a habitat conservation plan under the Endangered Species Act was unveiled.[15] The preparation of such a plan for San Bruno Mountain had led to a successful resolution of endangered species and development interests there. It was suggested that if such a plan were prepared for the lizard, it might lead to the issuance—by U.S. Fish and Wildlife—of a Section 10(a) incidental take permit which would cover development throughout the lizard's habitat. A smaller HCP steering committee was formed to oversee the preparation of the plan which included most of the key lizard club members. The California Nature Conservancy was asked to chair the committee. A consultant in Palo Alto, California, Thomas Reid Associates, was hired to prepare the biological and other background ma-

Table 6.2. *Groups Participating in the Preparation of the Coachella Valley Habitat Conservation Plan*

Coachella Valley Association of Governments (CVAG)
Bureau of Land Management (BLM)
California Department of Fish and Game (CDFG)
U.S. Fish and Wildlife Service (USFWS)
Coachella Valley Water District (CVWD)
Riverside County Planning Department
Coachella Valley Ecological Reserve Foundation (CVERF)
Sunrise Development Company
Agua Caliente Indian Tribe
The California Nature Conservancy (TNC)

terials and to write the HCP report. The approximate $100,000 cost of the consultant was contributed by TNC.

To temporarily resolve the lizard issue for development purposes while the HCP was being prepared, the ten local governments agreed to impose an emergency mitigation fee of $750 per acre for new development in habitat areas. While the U.S. Fish and Wildlife Service did not officially endorse this temporary arrangement, it seemed that they tacitly agreed to it and chose not to interfere. In addition, to ensure that development activities in the critical habitat area did not jeopardize the eventual acquisition of the lizard preserve, the Riverside County Board of Supervisors enacted special modifications to its zoning ordinance restricting development in the area. While characterized by some as a development moratorium, the changes merely modified the types and densities of development permissible in this area.[16]

The lizard club met frequently over approximately a two-year period (on average every four to six weeks). During this period a number of different issues were confronted. The key management strategy pursued by the steering committee was essentially that which had been proposed earlier by Mayhew, the Fringe-toed Lizard Advisory Committee, and others—namely to acquire and protect undisturbed, off-site habitat areas. The concept of on-site mitigation was soon discarded, as the lizard's viability was so closely tied to the existence of a well functioning natural blowsand habitat. It was generally concluded that attempts to preserve small, scattered fragments of habitat would not be successful.

Much discussion centered around the number of preserves necessary, the size the preserves must be to ensure the long-term survival of the lizard, and their location. A USFWS recovery team had already been formed and had been meeting for several months prior to the formation of the lizard club. It helped particularly to answer these questions. Under the Endangered Species Act, USFWS must convene a recovery team for each species classified as endangered or threatened. This team, usually consisting of wildlife biologists, is to prepare a recovery plan which sets forth recommendations for programs and activities which will enhance the survival and recovery of the species. The recovery team served in effect as technical and scientific advisors to the HCP group. They presented their findings to the lizard club in August of 1983. The key recommendation of the recovery plan was the establishment of at least two habitat preserves, each at least one thousand acres in size.[17] The team also had definite opinions about the location and configuration of the preserves, believing that as much of the designated critical habitat as possible should be set aside.

There was general consensus, then, within the HCP group that the most logical place for a large lizard preserve was the area north of Highway 10, designated as critical habitat by USFWS. This was an area that had not yet received significant development pressures and where the natural blowsand system had not yet been disrupted. This was also a logical location in that TNC was already interested in securing land here (Thousand Palms Oases).

It was also decided that two other, much smaller preserves should be established: one in the Willow Hole/Edom Hill area and the other along the Whitewater floodplain. The concept of establishing three geographically separate preserves was deemed important from a biological perspective, and was strongly advocated in the USFWS recovery plan. While it was estimated that genetic transference between the populations would be frequent enough to ensure a healthy gene pool (it was estimated that at least one lizard must enter a different colony at least every five years), the geographical separation would prevent catastrophic loss of the entire species, such as from disease or a natural disaster.

A major source of conflict and debate among committee members was the extent to which the large preserve—the Coachella Valley Preserve should extend further westward into the Indio Hills area, consistent with the boundaries of the USFWS designated critical habitat. As mentioned, members of the USFWS recovery team argued that these lands should be included. Because of the west-to-east wind pattern in the valley, it was thought that securing these lands would be necessary to protect the primary source of sand for lizard habitat to the east. To better resolve disagreement about this issue a special study was commissioned to examine the actual sources of windblown sand for these habitat areas. The consultant concluded that a substantial portion of the sand materials were supplied from the Thousand Palms Canyon and other areas to the north, and that this supply would be sufficient to ensure the long-term viability of the habitat.

Another primary reason for this decision was that land in this western area had been heavily subdivided—there were hundreds of parcels with hundreds of different property owners. The general conclusion reached was that acquisition of this area would be difficult and very time-consuming. Secondly, most of these lands were located in floodplains, and without the construction of a major flood-control project significant development there would be unlikely. It was felt, then, that the loss of these lands, at least in the short run, was improbable.

Considerable discussion in the lizard club also centered around the future flood-control plans of the Coachella Valley Water District. The district had been contemplating plans for a number of years to implement stormwater protection for the community of Thousand Palms. Indeed, the district's early involvement in the fringe-toed lizard issue was largely spurred by the realization that the lizard might serve to obstruct such improvements. District representatives made presentations to the lizard club describing their proposals. The district's stormwater/flood-control plans could have a significant effect on the Coachella Valley Preserve, both by blocking the flow of blowsand from the north, and, depending upon the actual location of dikes and control devices, by directly flooding lizard habitat. No real resolution to this issue was reached by the lizard club and to some this is a serious deficiency in the resulting plan. The resulting HCP acknowledges only that flood control projects may be necessary in the future and that they may have significant effects on the preserve and the lizard population. However, the plan skirts this problem by stating that specific flood-control plans will be reviewed in the future and must generally be compatible with the HCP.

Much of the HCP committee debate centered around how the preserves would be paid for, and what constituted an equitable distribution of the costs. It was generally agreed that the costs of the preserves should be shared by the public and private sectors. The developers argued that because the Endangered Species Act was a federal statute it was only fair that the larger public bear a portion of the costs of the preserves. Two sources of federal contribution were pursued early on: land trades through BLM and acquisition monies from the federal Land and Water Conservation Fund.

Because earlier efforts had been made to set up a preserve through BLM land trades, it was natural that this idea would be resuscitated. Early on in the process, Paul Selzer and Steve McCormick, of the California Nature Conservancy, reinitiated talks with BLM about the possibility of such trades. BLM was initially asked to finance the entire preserve acquisition—the equivalent of $20 million in land trades. Selzer argued that this was not an unreasonable request because the lizard problem was the result of a federal law. Ed Hasty, California State Director of BLM, vehemently rejected such a large contribution, later agreeing to contribute land with a cash value of $5 million.

The land exchange represented an ingenious approach to securing preserve lands. Under the arrangement, The Nature Conservancy would purchase land within the Coachella Valley Preserve, then swap these lands for BLM lands in other locations. Once TNC was given title to BLM lands outside of the preserve, it would then sell these lands on the open market, using the proceeds to repay itself for the costs incurred in buying the preserve land.

Selzer and McCormick also sought, at the suggestion of the USFWS, to secure federal acquisition monies from the Land and Water Conservation Fund. Representative Al McCandless (R–Bermuda Dunes) and Senators Pete Wilson (R) and Alan Cranston (D) were supportive in getting the necessary congressional appropriations. Selzer, McCormick, and TNC congressional liaison Nat Williams made the rounds in Washington to garner support. Ultimately these efforts were successful, and Congress approved appropriations amounting to $10 million (over two fiscal years). The success at obtaining federal funds has been attributed in large part to the "shared funding" approach. It was not simply an attempt to solicit a congressional handout. Rather, other parties were also willing to make financial sacrifices, including developers, the state, and environmental groups like The Nature Conservancy.

The development community agreed to make a significant contribution in the form of mitigation fees. It was eventually decided that all future development occurring within a designated mitigation fee zone, roughly corresponding to the historic range of the lizard, would be required to pay the amount of $600 per acre until the sum of $7 million was collected, and then $100 per acre after that. Some committee members agreed with Al Muth's and the County Planning Department's support of larger developer contributions in the form of a one-for-one habitat replacement ratio. This would have required a landowner mitigation fee much larger than the $600 per acre ultimately agreed upon. Indeed, at that time, land in habitat areas was selling for $3,500 to $8,000 per acre—suggesting that landowners/developers were being required to replace habitat at about a one/fifth-to-one ratio at best (i.e., $600 providing enough to purchase only about 0.2 acres of habitat).[18] Selzer and the developers steadfastly held from the beginning that they would not tolerate such high contributions. Indeed, when the consultant recommended that the permanent mitigation fee remain at the $750 per acre, it was clear that even this was considered too high by the development community. Eventually a compromise was reached and the current $600-per-acre figure was adopted.

Much of the lizard club's work involved the technical and political process of establishing the boundaries of the mitigation fee zone. It was generally decided that the boundaries of the fee zone should correspond to the historic range of the lizard. It was also decided that the Whitewater River should comprise the western boundary of fee zone, as the lizards' habitat generally did not extend south or west of the river. However, the boundary did dip below the river in several areas where it was clear that potential habitat existed. The group received considerable pressure to modify the fee boundaries, usually to exclude certain lands.

The lizard club responded firmly to such attempts to alter the boundaries. A major argument made to the development community, with considerable effectiveness, was that the smaller the boundary was, the higher the per-acre mitigation fee would have to be. Maintaining a fairly large fee boundary meant that the costs would be distributed over a larger number of landowners and development projects. In addition, the question of whether the Section 10(a) permit would cover takes outside of the mitigation fee zone arose during the process, and USFWS indicated that it would not. This served as a further argument to landowners wanting to be excluded from the zone—if they later found lizards on their property they would not be covered under the HCP and would have to secure their own Section 10(a) permit. Maintaining the integrity of the boundary was also seen as important to protecting the legal and scientific soundness of the plan, and preventing arbitrary differences in the treatment of similarly situated landowners. Nevertheless certain concessions were made to local governments to keep them in the process.

The Nature Conservancy took the lead in purchasing the core lands in the Coachella Valley Preserve. It had funds available for local acquisition which it had obtained through a loan from the Richard King Mellon Foundation, and which were to be replaced through local fundraising. In November of 1983, TNC successfully reached an agreement on the purchase of the bulk of the Coachella Valley Preserve from Cathton Investments, Inc. (which had bought the land from Dart Industries). Under this multi-year agreement, TNC secured options to purchase 9,420 acres for a total price of $13 million, with all options to be exercised within roughly a two-year period.

For the plan to work, the ten local jurisdictions in Coachella Valley would also have to sign the HCP.[19] Throughout the HCP process, periodic presentations were made by steering committee members to local city councils. Generally, the local governments of Coachella Valley could be characterized as pro-growth and pro-development, and their attitude by and large has been one of either indifference or antagonism toward the lizard issue. There has been little or no concern expressed about preserving the species itself—rather the species was seen as a problem to be overcome. There was considerable hostility expressed towards the lizard issue by some local governments, and the USFWS was generally seen as a common enemy to be overcome.

A plea to stick together was frequently made by Lester Cleveland of CVAG—who directly represented the local governments in the process. If any one of the localities balked at the plan, he and others argued, it would jeopardize the entire solution. Despite the threats by several local governments to abandon ship along the way, they all eventually embraced the plan and signed the necessary implementing agreement. In the end, the arguments of people such as Cleveland seemed to be convincing, and each locality began to recognize that the alternative to the HCP might be a complete halting of development in the valley.

For most local elected officials this was not an issue of high importance to them or their constituents. There was certainly no groundswell of popular demand to save the lizard. As Supervisor Patricia ("Corky") Larson observed, she, like many, originally did not feel that saving a small lizard was very important. And, despite the arguments of Professor Mayhew and others about how unique and special the lizard was, she was still not convinced about the need to take such expensive actions to save it. To many local officials the whole idea of expending such a large amount of money to protect such a creature was preposterous (and it became the butt of many jokes).

But the attitudes of officials like Larson, Mayor Bogart of Palm Springs, and others did change markedly over time—not, however, as a result of any greater appreciation of the lizard. Rather, for local elected officials the more convincing arguments appeared to be those which stressed the importance of preserving the land and not the lizard. Mayhew and others frequently pointed out that the Coachella Valley Preserve would likely be viewed by residents in the future in the same way in which New York City residents affectionately view Central Park. As the valley continued to develop, it might be the last remaining sliver of open space. Elected officials like Larson eventually came to view the preserve as something important to be set aside for future generations.

As already mentioned, specific tensions arose over the mitigation fee boundaries. The city of Palm Springs threatened to leave the process if certain portions of the city south of the Whitewater River were not excluded. Other jurisdictions, including Desert Hot Springs and La Quinta, made similar objections. Eventually the lizard club agreed to modify the boundaries to exclude those areas. A dispute also arose in Palm Springs over the city's airport. Under the original delineation of boundaries of the zone, the airport was excluded. Later, USFWS argued that this area was indeed occupiable habitat and demanded that it be included. Palm Springs objected, but eventually agreed to a compromise which allowed the fees on these lands to be collected incrementally as actual construction occurred around the airport. (The greater percentage of the land is owned by the city and leased to private developers).

Other adjustments in the mitigation fee system were made to accommodate the concerns of the agricultural community. Farmers objected to paying the mitigation fee when they converted habitat to agricultural uses. Before a public hearing of the Riverside County Planning Commission, which was considering endorsement of the HCP, several farmers testified that agricultural operations were financially marginal to begin with and that such a mitigation fee would, in the words of one farmer, unfairly penalize him for "feeding the nation."[20] A compromise was reached which reduced the mitigation fee to $100 per acre in cases of conversion to agricultural uses, with the remaining $500 per acre to be paid when and if the land was converted to urban uses. Even this marginal $100 fee was eventually scrapped. If land is converted to agricultural uses, the owner pays nothing; only when the land is converted to urban development will the $600-per-acre change be enforced. It was also decided that land which had already been in agricultural use prior to August 4, 1982 and had remained in agricultural use would be exempt from the fee if later developed. This date was chosen primarily because aerial photos were available on that date and thus administration of the fee would be easier. This was also close to when the lizard was listed and thus it had an element of fairness to it.

The final draft of the HCP was reviewed and approved by the ten local governments in the late fall of 1984 and early spring of 1985. Once approved by each of the local governments the plan was sent to the U.S. Fish and Wildlife Service, which approved the plan in April 1986, issuing a thirty-year Section 10(a) permit. Thus, roughly three years after the Palm Valley Country Club conflict had initiated the process, a long-term conservation plan had been adopted. A detailed summary of the HCP, as ultimately approved, follows.

The Resulting Solution: The Coachella Valley Fringe-toed Lizard Habitat Conservation Plan

The key strategy of the HCP is the acquisition of off-site habitat contained in three habitat preserves. The total projected acreage and lizard habitat acreage for these three preserves is presented in Table 6.3. The largest of the three preserves—the Coachella Valley Preserve—is to eventually contain more than thirteen thousand acres. Located north of Interstate 10, in the Thousand Palms Canyon area, this preserve will contain approximately fifty-two hundred acres of fringe-toed lizard habitat.

Two other preserves were also identified in the plan and have since been secured, each with its own sand source: the Willow Hole/Edom Hill Preserve, and the Whitewater Floodplain Preserve. The lands in these two preserves were already partially under BLM ownership or

Table 6.3. *Amount of Lizard Habitat Protected in Preserves* (Projected Acquisition)

Preserves	Total Preserve Acreage	Amount of Habitat[a]	Percentage of Total Lizard Habitat in Coachella Valley[b]
1. Coachella Valley Preserve	13,030	5,201	6.4
2. Willow Hole/Edom Hill Preserve	2,469	1,407	1.7
3. Whitewater Floodplain Preserve	1,230	1,230	1.5
Total	16,729	7,838	9.6

[a] Potentially occupiable habitat; this acreage is not necessarily currently occupied by fringe-toed lizards.

[b] Estimated total lizard habitat in the Valley in 1985 was 81,500 acres.

Source: Coachella Valley HCP Steering Committee, *Coachella Valley Habitat Conservation Plan,* prepared by Thomas Reid Associates, 1985.

control. The Whitewater Floodplain Reserve contains 1,230 acres, all of which are lizard habitat. This preserve was established in 1984 prior to the actual adoption of the HCP, as mitigation for a CVWD flood-control project, required under a Section 7 consultation.[21] While the land is technically owned by CVWD, it is under management control by the BLM. The Willow Hole/Edom Hill reserve is to contain 2,469 acres, of which 1,407 are lizard habitat. While a large portion of this land was already owned by BLM, the HCP envisions the acquisition of an additional 775 acres of adjacent private land. Additional BLM lands on which wind energy leases have been issued, will also be managed to protect lizard habitat. These BLM preserve lands are to be protected through their designation as "ACECs"—Areas of Critical Environmental Concern. This is a special protective BLM land use designation which prevents such activities as off-road vehicle use.[22]

Together these three preserves will encompass about seventeen thousand acres of protected land, including some 7,838 acres of occupiable habitat. It is estimated that this represents approximately 10% of the occupiable habitat that existed at the time the HCP was prepared, and some 16% of the amount of unshielded, natural blowsand habitat.

The Coachella Valley Preserve, in particular, contains a fairly large and impressive remnant of desert ecosystem. In addition to the fringe-toed lizard, the preserve is home to 180 other animal species including an extensive resident and migratory bird population, including burrowing owls, kestrels, and roadrunners. Some 120 different plant species are found on the preserve. It is also home to four other rare species: the flat-tailed horned lizard, the Coachella round-tailed ground squirrel, the giant red velvet mite, and the giant palm-boring beetle.

The total projected cost of establishing the preserves was $25 million, to be obtained from a combination of sources (see Table 6.4). The cost of acquiring land for the Coachella Valley Preserve was estimated at approximately $20 million, with approximately $2 million needed to acquire supplemental land for the Willow Hole/Edom Hill preserve.[23] In addition to the costs of acquisition, funds would be needed to maintain the preserves. The HCP estimated these reserve maintenance costs to be between $50,000 and $125,000 annually.[24] The HCP assumes that these annual reserve maintenance costs will be generated by a special trust fund established towards the end of the acquisition program, the principal of which would be approximately $2.5 million.

The total amount of mitigation fees to be collected from private development over the thirty-year plan period was estimated at approximately $10 million. Because much of this money would be obtained a number of years into the future, the present value of this total contribution was estimated at $7 million (see Table 6.4). The HCP assumed that, given the continuation of existing development trends, the mitigation fee would generate a yearly income of approximately $860,000. The boundaries of

Table 6.4. *Projected Distribution of Funding for Coachella Valley Fringe-toed Lizard Preserves*

Funding Sources	$ Million
Federal	
Land and Water Conservation Funds	10.0
BLM land exchange (cash value)	5.0
State Wildlife Conservation Board	1.0
Nature Conservancy	2.0
Developer Mitigation Fees	7.0
	$25.0

Source: Coachella Valley HCP Steering Committee, *Coachella Valley Habitat Conservation Plan,* prepared by Thomas Reid Associates, 1985.

the mitigation fee zone were drawn to roughly correspond to the lizard's historic range (see Figure 6.1). It was thought to be equitable to require all developers with projects in these areas to contribute to acquisition costs even if lizards did not currently exist in a specific area or on a particular parcel.

In addition to land protected through fee-simple acquisition, the HCP also envisioned that certain additional public lands would be managed so as to protect lizard habitat (specifically, land in the Indio Hills, south end of Dillon Road, and in East San Gorgonio Pass). When these "managed areas" are taken into consideration, the total area of conserved habitat increases to approximately 12,300 acres. This comprises approximately 15% of the remaining occupiable habitat, and approximately 26% of the remaining unshielded habitat. The HCP also envisioned that certain privately held lands, specifically those near and around the Coachella Valley Preserve, would be subject to land use controls which might provide additional protection for lizard habitat.

Once the HCP had been completed, the local governments of Coachella Valley became joint applicants to the U.S. Fish and Wildlife Service for a Section 10(a) incidental take permit. In April 1986, USFWS issued the 10(a) permit for a period of thirty years. The permit is revocable at any point during this period should USFWS feel the plan is not being implemented. The HCP is implemented through two sets of legal agreements, executed concurrently with the issuance of the Section 10(a) permit. The first agreement is between the local governments, the U.S. Fish and Wildlife Service, and The Nature Conservancy. It sets forth the obligations of local governments to collect the mitigation fees, and the obligations of The Nature Conservancy to manage and further acquire preserve lands. The second agreement is a preserve management agreement between TNC, BLM, California Department of Fish and Game, and USFWS, necessitated by the multiple ownership of the Coachella Preserve.

The basic land acquisition and funding proposals contained in the HCP have been largely implemented. The vast majority of the acreage planned for acquisition under the plan has been acquired; only an estimated five hundred acres remain to be purchased in the Coachella Valley Preserve. The costs of this acquisition appear to be close to original estimates.[25] While TNC acquired most of the land, it has conveyed the majority of acreage to the USFWS, BLM, and the state of California, retaining only 880 acres for itself (the core area of palm oases). The other two preserves have, as already mentioned, been established, but none of the additional private land planned for acquisition at the Willow Hole/

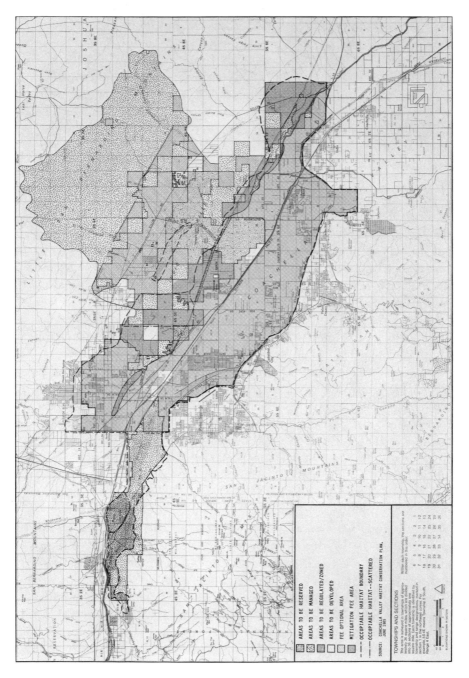

Figure 6.1. Coachella Valley HCP Land Status (Courtesy Thomas Reid Associates)

Edom Hill preserve (nearly eight hundred acres) has been secured. The BLM does still intend to acquire these additional lands when sufficient funds become available.

Funding for the HCP has occurred largely as planned, with each projected source providing revenue. As planned, Congress approved $10 million in funding from the Land and Water Conservation Fund ($5 million in each of fiscal years 1985 and 1986). These amounts were reduced somewhat as a result of across-the-board budget cuts, and the final amount secured by USFWS was approximately $9.6 million. While some of these funds were used by USFWS to cover administrative overhead, the majority were used for land acquisition (mostly to purchase land in the preserve from TNC).[26]

While the Bureau of Land Management originally agreed to a contribution of $5 million in the form of land swaps, the amount of their contribution was later increased to $6 million.[27] The Coachella Valley land swaps were temporarily suspended along with all other BLM trades in 1987 as a result of a National Wildlife Federation suit.[28] The suit alleged that the Reagan administration was selling and opening federal lands without going through certain required procedures. Representative McCandless was able to gain passage of a bill in Congress (with the National Wildlife Federation's blessing) which exempted the Coachella Valley trades from the pending suit. Also, the state of California has satisfied its $1 million contribution through acquisition of land in the preserve, and the Nature Conservancy has met its $2 million fundraising goal.

Some concerns have been expressed over the last several years that the mitigation fees were not being consistently collected by the ten local governments in Coachella Valley. As a result of these suspicions, USFWS undertook a monitoring study in January of 1989. Aerial photographs were compared with information about which projects had paid fees. USFWS found that, contrary to suspicions, the fees were being collected by localities.

The most serious problem with this segment of the funding has been a significant shortfall in the revenue generated from mitigation fees. As of June 30, 1989, $2,881,994 had been collected through the county and the nine cities. While the HCP projected annual revenues from the fees to be approximately $864,000, the amount collected has averaged only about $600,000 per year (although fiscal year 1989 was an improvement with $786,000 in fees collected).[29] The shortfall has been explained in several ways. It has been partly blamed on a depressed second-home market as a result of changes created by the 1985 Tax Reform Act (specifically the suspending of mortgage deductions for second homes). The market has picked up in the last several years, in part because of the restoration of these second-home subsidies. A second explanation of the fee shortfall has been that several of the development "hot spots" in the valley have actually been outside of the mitigation fee zone.

There has also been concern expressed recently that over time the purchasing power of collected funds has gone down (as the cost of habitat in Willow Hole/Edom Hill rises). One possibility being considered is to incorporate some sort of "inflator" provision which would allow adjustments in the mitigation fee to compensate for this.

The resulting preserve system is one in which ownership is divided between TNC, BLM, USFWS, and the state of California. The Nature Conservancy has overall responsibility for managing the preserve system, and has hired a full-time director. As mentioned earlier, management of the system is guided by a management agreement signed by each of these parties. A preserve advisory committee has also been formed to help oversee preserve management, and has been meeting regularly. A management plan has been prepared for the preserve to guide habitat management and enhancement activities. Many of the management and research activities identified in the biological program element of the HCP have already been undertaken (e.g., population monitoring, habitat enhancement, and restoration activities).

Success of the Coachella Valley Plan

The accomplishments of the Coachella Valley HCP are impressive to say the least. Eventually setting aside preserves of close to seventeen thousand acres is a significant environmental accomplishment. The Coachella case, moreover, illustrates again the tremendous benefits of constructive compromise between otherwise rivaling factions. Together environmental and development interests accomplished what individually would have been difficult. Virtually every participant interviewed for this study viewed the outcome as a "win-win" solution. There are few detractors and most seem to have developed feelings of pride and proprietorship about the plan. Indeed, the plan has received considerable publicity as an ideal model for resolving future conservation/development conflicts.

Several important ingredients to the Coachella Valley success ought to be highlighted. Much of the success of the experience is due to the reasonableness and willingness to compromise of certain key individuals. Moreover, the fact that each individual had tremendous respect and credibility in their respective professional communities did much to deflect any potential challenges to the plan and process. The role of The

Nature Conservancy, both in staffing the HCP process and in spearheading the acquisition of habitat, played a crucial role.

Landownership patterns also clearly facilitated the achievement of the off-site preserve system. Specifically, the greater part of the land in the Coachella Valley Preserve—the largest preserve—was under single ownership. The Nature Conservancy was able to save the bulk of the preserve in one step. In localities where habitat is fractured into numerous small parcels, with numerous owners, acquisition of such large preserve areas will be much more difficult.

The ultimate test of whether the Coachella Valley HCP is successful, of course, is whether the lizard's survival is assured. Most of the participants interviewed for this study admitted that the HCP was a gamble and that there was no assurance that the lizard would survive in the long term. The HCP itself acknowledges that the understanding of the biology of the lizard is quite limited. Particularly troubling are the dramatic population swings exhibited in the lizard population. Since 1986 an annual lizard count has been conducted in each of the three preserves. These data confirm that lizard populations are prone to "wild yearly fluctuations."[30] There is considerable uncertainty about the cause of these fluctuations. However, there is general consensus that much of it is due to fluctuations in rainfall. Lizard populations appear to decline following low rainfall years, as a result of the reduced amounts of vegetation and consequently diminished sources of food (while the lizard is omnivorous, it appears to rely heavily on insects, which are more numerous under conditions of greater vegetation). During the last two years, lizard numbers have been dramatically on the rise (in the Coachella Valley and Willow Hole/Edom Hill preserves); again it appears largely to correspond to increased precipitation levels.[31]

Interviews with members of the scientific community find guarded optimism and little confidence that the lizard's continued existence is assured. Most are quick to observe, however, that the chances of survival with the preserves are much greater than without them. This highlights a general problem which arises in development/species conflicts. While years of careful scientific research on a species and its habitat may ideally be needed to fully understand its conservation needs, the timeframe of the development community is a much shorter one. Their desires are to move ahead rapidly—and where problems such as endangered species arise, they seek to overcome the problem quickly. These perspectives are frequently in conflict.

Some have strongly criticized the Coachella Valley scheme as one which protects a relatively small portion of native habitat, while opening up vast portions of the valley for development. While close to seventeen thousand acres will eventually be acquired through the three preserves, this includes only about seventy-eight hundred acres of occupiable lizard habitat. One recent commentator has argued that the Coachella Valley HCP " . . . can only be described as doing, under the guise of an 'incidental take,' great violence to the concepts of recovery and survival."[32]

Others, including members of the steering committee, have been critical of the HCP strategy, because it signifies giving up on existing lizard populations in those areas outside of the preserves. This raises several policy questions. While there has certainly been degradation of habitat due to sandshielding, the sand transport system is poorly understood, and the actual extent of degradation due to windshielding is debatable. If development activities were curtailed or brought to a halt in these areas (e.g., south of Interstate 10) would sufficient sand be transported to permit long-term viability of lizard habitats? Moreover, could not much of the blowsand disruption be corrected through some fairly straightforward public actions? Because much of the disruption is a result of blowsand control along the Southern Pacific Railroad right-of-way (cited in the HCP as the major cause of disruption), dismantling this windbreak system, as suggested by one member of Lizard Club, would accomplish much. These possibilities were apparently never seriously considered by the group.

Others have continued to raise questions about the boundaries and design of the preserve system. The failure to secure the western portion of the critical habitat is still seen by some as a flaw. While a significant amount of the blowsand material for the Coachella Valley Preserve indeed comes from the north, between 50% and 75% may be blown into the preserve from the west—areas which could eventually be developed. Moreover, a portion of the materials coming into the preserve from the north ends up being blown into areas outside the preserve to the east. One member of the steering committee has argued that the configuration of the preserve should have been more east-west, rather than north-south, to better reflect these wind patterns. Several members of the Lizard Club also expressed concern about the failure to explicitly resolve the flood-control issues in the HCP. The potential impacts of a major flood-control project on the lizard population in Coachella Valley Preserve could be devastating and could negate the major protective features of the HCP.

Lack of adequate sand transport has been an especially serious problem in recent years in the Whitewater River satellite preserve. Lizard counts here have been very low, and sand has been increasingly blown off the preserve without adequate replacement (primarily it is believed because of no major flooding events to transport materials into that area of the valley). As a recognition of these sand transport problems and the generally low level of understanding about the sand transport system, the California Nature Conservancy will soon be funding a sand transport study. Among other things the study will identify potential obstacles to sand transport, and areas outside of the existing preserves that may need to be acquired to better protect sand sources.

The potential impacts of future flood-control projects, or other development activities that might adversely affect blowsand transport, is part of the general problem of adjacent uses. The Coachella Valley Preserve system is not unique in its vulnerability to such adjacent activities, and the long-term survival of the lizard may ultimately depend on the ability to control these uses. This problem was particularly highlighted by a recent proposal to build an auto racetrack on Indian Avenue, in close proximity to the Whitewater River satellite preserve. The scientific evidence suggests that the noise generated by such an adjacent activity, as well as the possible overflow of people into the preserve, could have potentially disastrous impacts on the lizard population there. The County Planning Commission eventually denied the proposed racetrack (although Palm Springs has indicated that it desires to see the project proceed, perhaps through annexation). The long-term viability of the fringe-toed lizard depends on an ability to exercise some degree of effective control over adjacent activities. The willingness of the cities in the Coachella Valley to exercise this management responsibility is questionable.

The fringe-toed lizard HCP also raised questions concerning whether society should seek to preserve *species* or *habitats.* Professor Mayhew and other members of the fringe-toed lizard committee unabashedly sought to use the lizard as a tool to preserve a portion of the larger desert ecosystem, and the larger set of flora and fauna contained within it. The fringe-toed lizard case illustrates, however, the great political benefits of focusing, where possible, on the ecosystem. Throughout the history of the lizard conflict most elected officials, developers, and average constituents did not generally support actions—particularly expensive actions—to preserve the lizard. To most it was akin to another snail darter. Had the species been more visually attractive or symbolically important, such as a Bald Eagle or a Florida panther, the concern might have been greater. This reaction is consistent with research showing that people tend to attach greater importance to protecting the larger, more attractive species, and less importance to species like snakes, insects, and plants. Rather, what was ultimately acceptable and justifiable in the eyes of Coachella Valley officials and constituents was the setting aside of a segment of the natural desert environment to be enjoyed by future generations.

There was ultimately considerable disagreement about who should pay for the costs of preserving endangered species. Many participants in the Coachella Valley HCP process seemed comfortable with the position that because the plan was necessitated by a federal mandate (the federal Endangered Species Act) the costs should be shared by the broader national citizenry. A major point of disagreement, however, was the amount of contribution required of developers. While some members of the lizard club lobbied for a higher level of compensation by new development, most participants seemed to take Attorney Selzer's word that the development community in Coachella Valley would not accept higher fees. The political and practical feasibility of higher developer fees aside, it could be argued that the development community got off rather cheaply. Its total contribution will amount to approximately $7 million, or about 28%, of the total $25 million. This could be considered relatively modest, considering that it is the very activities of these developers that are endangering the species in the first place. Moreover, given the considerable potential profits from development in the valley, the $600-per-acre fee seems rather low.

In considering the distribution of costs associated with preserve acquisition, it is interesting that local governments were not asked to contribute funds. This has been explained partly by the current financial status of local governments in California; as a result of Proposition 13 and other restrictions, most local governments in California are still financially straitened. The assumption of HCP participants was that financial contributions from the local governments would be difficult, and would not be popular. And technically, the fringe-toed lizard was not a problem the local governments were required to deal with—while most enlightened local officials saw the need to solve the problem, they could easily have left the issue entirely up to developers and landowners. Nevertheless, it could be argued that existing residents and property owners ought to contribute to solving the problem as well as new residents and property owners. Indeed, existing residents and property owners have been indirectly responsible for past habitat loss and thus ought to bear some of the burden.

The Coachella Valley experience also raised questions about whether, and the extent to which, listed species should be placed at risk prior to the formal approval of an HCP. In the case of Coachella Valley, USFWS tacitly agreed to allow take of the species, even though an HCP had not yet been developed. The basic dilemma faced by USFWS was a difficult one. They acknowledged the political and economic difficulties of imposing growth moratoria. Yet, to permit take prior to any tangible protective actions, such as in the case of Coachella Valley, is taking a significant risk, and would seem (at least to some) contrary to the specific requirements of the Endangered Species Act. This problem suggested the need to explore other forms of interim protection, and the current short HCPs in effect for the Stephens' kangaroo rat (in western Riverside County) and the desert tortoise (Clark County, Nevada) were responses to this problem.

Conclusions

The Coachella Valley HCP was the second HCP to officially receive a Section 10(a) permit from USFWS. The geographical, biological, and political issues confronted in Coachella Valley, however, were quite different from those confronted in San Bruno Mountain. The accomplishments of the Coachella Valley are impressive, including the long-term protection of some seventeen thousand acres of desert habitat. However, the Coachella Valley has raised numerous policy questions, including the extent of habitat loss or degradation allowable, the level of habitat protection and management actually required, the equitable distribution of the costs of habitat protection, and the extent to which a species ought to be placed at risk prior to approval of an HCP.

Habitat Conservation in the Florida Keys: The North Key Largo Habitat Conservation Plan

The Setting: The Florida Keys

The Florida Keys comprise a narrow string of islands approximately 100 miles in length, from just south of Miami to Key West on the western tip of the state. The keys are home to a diversity of flora and fauna, including endangered wildlife such as the key deer and the American crocodile. The coral reef system just off shore harbors a complex ecological system; extending 165 miles from south of Miami to the Dry Tortugas, it supports a diversity of fish and aquatic life and productivity which rivals many tropical rainforests. The International Union for the Conservation of Nature (IUCN) has declared this reef system one of the top five endangered habitats in the world.

The study area encompasses North Key Largo (the northern portion of Key Largo) and is approximately 12 miles in length, bordered to the east by the Atlantic Ocean and to the west by Card and Barnes Sounds. Landownership in North Key Largo is mixed. A substantial area is owned by USFWS as part of the Crocodile Lake National Wildlife Refuge (approximately 7,000 acres in size). State government holdings include the Pennekamp Coral Reef State Park. This park extends along the Atlantic coast for approximately three miles, from mean high water to three miles offshore. The Key Largo Coral Reef National Marine Sanctuary has for many years been contiguous with Pennekamp. Recently, Congress created a new much larger marine sanctuary encompassing the entire Florida Keys.

Development/Species Conflicts

Major development pressures on North Key Largo arose in the early 1970s. Proposals to extend water and electrical services to the area by the Florida Aqueduct Authority and the Florida Keys Electric Cooperative (with the Federal Housing Authority and Rural Electrification Administration funding) served to initiate the North Key Largo HCP. Florida Audubon filed suit claiming these proposals would result in the take of listed species and would thus violate ESA. The USFWS had similarly concluded that, as originally proposed, the projects and the growth that would follow would represent significant threats to the listed species.

Another primary proposal sparking controversy was the relatively large proposed Port Bouganville development. Plans for this project were originally submitted to and approved by the Monroe County Commission as early as 1973, but the project did not proceed at that time (with the exception of a clubhouse, a few condominiums, and several hundred boatslips) primarily because the financing failed. The project was later resurrected (under the name of Port Bouganville) after being sold to a Canadian investment company. The proposal encompassed more than four hundred acres, and was to be an "imitation Mediterranean coastal village," including residential units and a marina.[1] Opposition to the project was expressed from a number of quarters and centered around the potential impacts of the development, including the potential sewage and non-point source impacts on the surrounding water quality and the sensitive reef system. Specific concern was expressed about the potential impacts of the proposed marina and estimates suggested that some additional five hundred to one thousand boats would be used in the area, with an accompanying increase in bilge and chemical pollutants. Moreover it was feared that such an increase in marina capacity would lead to much greater direct visitation pressure on the reef system (e.g., increased diving and snorkling) in turn further damaging the reefs. Several law suits were filed in response to this potentially damaging project. The state of Florida filed suit against it, as did Florida Audubon on the grounds that it violated the federal Endangered Species Act.

The practical effect of these legal actions was to stop development in North Key Largo. In response, landowners approached USFWS and the state about finding a long-term resolution to the conflict. Accordingly, then-governor of Florida, Bob Graham, issued an executive order on September 4, 1984 creating the Habitat Conservation Plan Committee (HCPC), a special panel charged with preparing an HCP, roughly modeled after the San Bruno plan. The group was to consist of representatives of environmental groups, developers, and landowners, and local, state, and federal agencies. This group met periodically over a roughly two-year period, and the HCP was completed by the HCP committee in July 1986.

From an early stage it was considered important to have a chairman of the working group who was independent and perceived to be reasonably impartial. In the words of an early discussion outline, "He should be independent, of stature, and statesmanlike."[2] As a result, Governor Graham asked a respected planning academician, David J. Brower, from the University of North Carolina, to chair the HCP committee. Brower brought considerable credibility as an expert and experienced practitioner in the areas of growth management and land use planning.

At the time these species/development conflicts arose in North Key Largo, Monroe County was in the process of preparing a new countywide land use plan. In anticipation of this plan, in February of 1982, the county adopted a moratorium, which applied to North Key Largo as well, on all new development. A consultant had already been hired to prepare the county plan and it was believed that the efforts should be coordinated in some way. Consequently, the HCP for North Key Largo would be essentially the land use plan. The same consultant was hired to prepare this plan and the special HCP elements, and to serve a staff function for the HCP process itself.

Initial funding for the HCP came from the governor's office in the amount of $100,000. In addition, several of the larger landowners in the study area contributed funds to pay for biological studies of the several species of concern.

Species of Concern

North Key Largo is home to a diversity of plant and animal species. The HCP focused on protecting four listed species: The American crocodile (*Crocodylus acutus*), the Schaus swallowtail butterfly (*Papilio aristodemus ponceanus*), the Key Largo woodrat (*Neotoma floridana smalli*), and the Key Largo cottonmouse (*Peromyscus gossypinus allapaticola*). Several rare plant species were also addressed in the plan.

Certain background biological studies were undertaken as part of the process, including several population and distribution studies of the Key Largo woodrat and cottonmouse, as well as a study of the habitat needs of the Schaus swallowtail butterfly and the effects of insecticides on the butterfly. These studies were modest in scope and were viewed by many as an insufficient biological basis for the HCP.

Main Provisions of the Plan

The study area of the North Key Largo HCP consisted of a twelve-mile segment of the island. The area has an extensive interior of tropical hardwood hammock, with extensive mangrove wetlands along the shoreline. The Crocodile Lake National Wildlife Refuge is located to the immediate west.

From the beginning there were different perspectives of ideal results from the HCP. As noted, Florida Audubon and other environmentalists saw the most desirable outcome as one which left the remaining habitat undeveloped. The preferred option, then, from their point of view was some form of land acquisition, public or private. Moreover, this was not unacceptable to representatives of landowners in the areas, as long as they could be assured that they would receive fair compensation for their land.

As a result of the sentiment that acquisition was the preferred alternative, the plan incorporated an interesting provision extending the prohibition on new development for a two-year period of time—sufficient time, it was felt, to give the Florida state legislature an opportunity to allocate the funds to buy the land (allowing for two complete legislative cycles).

Should acquisition not have occurred by the end of this period, the provisions of the HCP would be activated. Under the HCP a major strategy was to protect a large percentage of existing hardwood hammock in a large block of conserved habitat, allowing development to take place in five designated development nodes (see Figure 7.1). (Note: The plan is sometimes described as including seven nodes, because the northern node incorporates three different non-contiguous parcels.) Under the plan this conserved habitat area would protect approximately 84% of the existing hardwood hammock.

Early on in the process it was determined that the North Key Largo planning area could accommodate a maximum build-out of thirty-five hundred dwelling units. This was largely based on analysis of the traffic capacity of the existing road system. The HCP sought to allow this level of development, but at the same time to protect the bulk of the existing habitat. The result was to restrict all future development to these five nodes.

Development could occur in the development nodes only under certain conditions and would be subject to mitigation requirements, such as restricting the extent of hammock clearance permissible even in development nodes. Developers and landowners would not be permitted

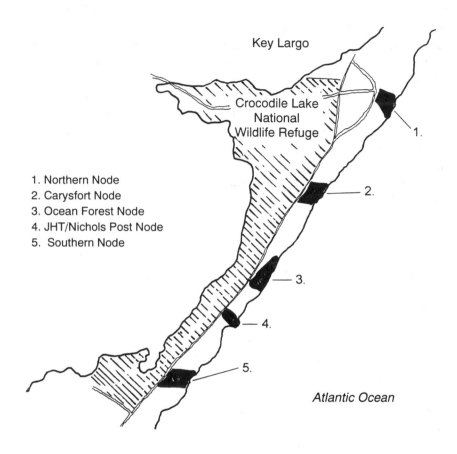

Figure 7.1. Development Nodes for North Key Largo (Map drawn by Betty Hall)

to clear more than 20% of high-quality hardwood hammock unless one of the following mitigation actions was taken:

1) Preservation in perpetuity through transfer to public ownership of two hundred acres of mangrove wetland in the conserved habitat for each additional acre cleared; or

2) Preservation in perpetuity through transfer to public ownership of four acres of hardwood hammock in the conserved habitat for each additional acre cleared, and the extinguishment of the development rights for eight dwelling units appurtenant to the land; or

3) Preservation in perpetuity and replanting of hardwood hammock on three acres of successional habitat (returning to hardwood hammock) for each additional acre cleared . . . ; or

4) Preservation in perpetuity, replanting of hardwood hammock, and provision of no less than three and no more than six rubble piles of four cubic yards of either rock or logs on two acres of scarified land for each additional acre cleared . . .[3]

In addition, trapping and relocation of cottonmice and woodrats for five consecutive days before land clearing would be required, as well as replacement of any torchwood or wild lime plants destroyed during the land clearance.

This development scheme, including restrictions on building in the conserved habitat, was to be implemented primarily through the Monroe County zoning ordinance, and this makes the North Key Largo HCP different from others.

Under the HCP, landowners within the designated conserved habitat would not be allowed to develop at all. They would, however, be given development credits which could be transferred or sold for use within the five development nodes or in other designated receiving zones in the county. Allocation of development credits would occur according to the type of land involved: hardwood hammocks—2.0 units per acre; transitional habitats—0.6 units per acre; scarified or disturbed lands—1.2 units per acre. Maximum build-out in the development node would be achievable only through the purchase of additional development rights thus creating a market of these rights. In this way those who were restricted in the conserved habitat would be allowed to realize some development potential, possibly approximating fair market value.

The placement of the development nodes was, and continues to be, controversial. In theory it was felt that nodes ought to be located in and around areas that had already been scarified, or where some degree of development or habitat degradation had already occurred. While this seems to have been the result for some of the nodes, others appear to have been designated in a more random fashion, or, as critics have charged, according to the wishes of those landowners involved in the process. There has been considerable criticism expressed from a number of quarters that the plan is not explicitly founded on the ecological and biological conditions of the study area.

Funding to implement the plan was to come from several sources. Protection of the conserved habitat area, as already mentioned, was in a sense to be funded by development in other areas, because the planners envisioned that developers in the nodes would buy the development rights of those in the conserved habitat areas. Long-term management and other activities would be funded through a combination of a one-time development impact fee, and an annual mitigation fee placed on development. To implement the financing provisions the plan envisioned creation of a special North Key Largo taxing district.

In addition to land-use controls and land acquisition, the HCP set forth a series of other actions which would be undertaken to promote recovery of the species. These included: actions to control and remove exotic plants and domestic pets; controlled use of insecticides; restoration of natural habitat, including the removal of roads and bridges to restore historic water regimes; introduction of host species (e.g., periodic burns to promote torchwood and wild lime, the plants upon which the female swallowtail lays her eggs); modification of canal banks to provide nesting sites and habitat for the American crocodile; trapping and relocation of endangered woodrats and cottonmice prior to development; captive breeding and reintroduction; education programs; and research and monitoring activities.

Success of the Plan

The original North Key Largo HCP was never adopted by Monroe County, nor submitted to USFWS for its review and approval. To many this has been a disappointing outcome of the long and arduous preparation process. However, from the beginning, the plan expressed the assumption that the preferred result was acquisition of the habitat in the study and much of this acquisition has occurred. Even though the plan has not been approved or implemented it has served as a strong catalyst for state land acquisition, specifically under the state's Conservation and Recreation Lands (CARL) program.

A factor in the North Key Largo HCP is the fact that at the time the plan was formulated the condominium market had become quite soft. A number of observers have cited this as one factor explaining the willingness of the development community to be involved in the compromise HCP. The land acquisition alternative preferred by Florida Audubon and others was acceptable to most landowners, provided a decent price was offered.

One concern for landowners was the appraisal process required under CARL, which they felt resulted in low offers. Two separate appraisals were required and the state could offer no more than 110% of the lower of the two estimates. In 1988, special legislation was enacted to change the appraisal standards and overcome this inflexibility. Under the new standards the state could offer up to 125% of the average of the two appraisal values. This has in fact led to an ability to offer higher prices and has resulted in more acceptable purchase offers to North Key Largo landowners.

The original plan was not uniformly accepted by all groups. Some environmental groups were especially critical of both the process by which it was prepared and its resulting provisions. Since the completion of the original plan, several efforts have sought to refine or modify it. When the plan was submitted to the Monroe County Board of Commissioners, the commission, reacting to criticisms, postponed action on it. In the spring and summer of 1987 the county directed its staff to rework the plan, specifically considering the potential impact of development on the reef.[4] Later the consulting firm of Dames and Moore was hired to revise the plan and to complete environmental documentation.

In interviews with participants and observers of the North Key Largo HCP process, concerns were expressed frequently about the fairness and objectivity of the process. Some described it as "sleazy" in nature. One newspaper article summarized this perception as a concern by many that the process was a "sham" which was "designed to slide potentially high-profit development projects through the briar patch of environmental legislation with the least damage."[5] Holding objections from the beginning, the group Friends of the Everglades expressed strong opposition to the plan's content. In the words of the group's attorney, Michael Chenoweth:

> The HCP is empty rhetoric—there is no conservation and there is no plan. It's just another "deal" and a way to keep most of us occupied while the landowners calculate how to wring the most profit out of the situation. There is no science . . . the so-called "plan" has gone ahead without the results of biological studies that were considered necessary at the beginning of the process, but are still incomplete or just ignored.[6]

Other national environmental groups also came out in opposition to the plan, including the Isaak Walton League of America and the Sierra Club. Representatives of the Sierra Club handed out a highly critical report on the HCP at the day of the final meeting. Concerns about the plan's content were also expressed by state and federal resource agencies. The Florida Department of Natural Resource expressed concerns about the loss of habitat in approved CARL project areas and the impacts on the acquisition price of these lands. Concerns were also expressed about the potential impacts of allowable development on the Pennekamp State Park and North Key Largo National Marine Sanctuary.

Representatives of the Florida Game and Fresh Water Fish Commission questioned, as did the Sierra Club and others, the logic by which development nodes were designated, and recommended eliminating two of the nodes. In the words of Bradley Hartman, director of Environmental Sciences:

> In the beginning of the process, we were looking at the establishment of conservation areas as a form of mitigation for allowing development in other areas. It is now apparent that there is much less of a direct relationship than we had hoped, and the nodes are being treated much more as individual developments than as a necessary part of the HCP.[7]

It is not clear to many why nodes were chosen where they were. There is the perception that nodes were selected primarily to cover the private parcels of those large landowners most active in the process, both publicly and behind the scenes. The Sierra Club report states bluntly that, "It appears that the proposed development nodes are concentrated on property owned by committee members. . . ."

Further, the Sierra Club report concludes that the HCP allows

> . . . extensive new development, above and beyond several subdivisions and a major resort area at the north end of the island. Its provisions do not provide the protection required by federal law for endangered species; are not fully supported by biological research; and amount to little more than a land use plan that promotes suburbanization of a unique, relatively undisturbed ecosystem . . . .[8]

In this process it appears that the interests of smaller landowners were not as effectively advanced. In the words of one landowner criticizing the plan before the Monroe County Board of Commissioners: "There was an arbitrary and capricious line drawn between what land is environmentally sensitive and what land is not."[9] Landowners such as this one whose land was outside the development nodes tended to oppose the plan, while those with land in the nodes, not surprisingly, tended to support the HCP.

As well, there is a general concern expressed about how this "allowable" development pattern was determined. It appears that the thirty-five-hundred-unit capacity was determined based on existing road capacity and had very little to do with the biological limits of the species of concern and their habitat. The number of development nodes selected appears similarly unsupported.

The former county biologist (now with The Nature Conservancy) is highly critical of the logic behind the selection of the development areas. He claims that a more ecologically sound approach would be to opt for a development pattern which would create larger blocks of untouched habitat. In particular, he suggests that development should be directed to the southern end of the study area where the hammock is the narrowest. It would be advisable to reserve the upper study area, where the hammock is wider, for conserved undeveloped area. On a parcel-by-parcel analysis the results of the HCP do not appear ecologically sound either. A prime example is a parcel in the northern portion of the study which the former county biologist describes as "perhaps the most ecologically significant parcel in the entire state." Number one on the CARL list, this parcel was, oddly to some, included in the northern development node. Again, this leads many to conclude that the HCP process heavily favored the large landowners who were actively involved in the proceedings, and indeed provided much of the money for it. A rational, ecological planning process, ignorant of property lines, would yield a different outcome. It has also been suggested that attempts to get land included in the development nodes are really efforts to enhance the market value of the land, such that the owner can obtain a higher price for the land when state acquisition is undertaken (common strategy in the keys).

Members of environmental groups were also very concerned about the TDR provisions which they viewed as a mechanism that would allow even greater levels of development in the designated nodes (up to 17,500 dwelling units, opponents claimed). Even though the plan does appear to solidly restrict density to thirty-five hundred units, there was considerable confusion about this.

The original plan has been heavily criticized for its failure to consider the impacts of development in the study area on the coral reefs. To many it is ironic that the plan would focus on four discrete species, but neglect one of the most biologically complex and productive systems anywhere. Margory Stoneman Douglas, founder of the Friends of the Everglades and author of the highly acclaimed book, *Rivers of Grass*, issued an eloquent plea to the Monroe County Commissioner in the spring of 1987: "I beg Monroe County to realize its great responsibility to protect this national and international treasure."[10] This highlights the limitations of a species-by-species approach, heavily driven by ESA. (More recent drafts of the HCP have sought to address this deficiency.)

Another concern raised by some conservation groups is that even if the plan were adopted there is no assurance that the land designated as conserved habitat will remain such. It would still remain in private hands (unless purchased under CARL or by TNC) and rely on local zoning. Some observers have expressed concern that ultimately attempts to develop in these areas would prevail—the county would eventually give in to development pressures. A rebuttal might be that if USFWS accepts the HCP it would not issue any Section 10(a) permits unless they were consistent with the plan. A proposal to develop in a conserved habitat area would be inconsistent with the HCP and would in theory be denied by USFWS. However, as with the county, some believe USFWS is vulnerable to buckling under development pressure as well (or perhaps allowing individual property owners to break from the park submitting their own mitigation plans). These concerns may suggest the need to gain a stronger legal assurance that areas designated for conservation/ no development would remain that way. Perhaps landowners in conservation areas would be required to donate easements (this would be an unpopular idea) restricting future development, before the plan is officially approved. For this to be an acceptable alternative some greater level of direct cooperation would probably be required, as well as a reverter clause that would provide that the right to develop would revert to the property owner under certain circumstances (e.g., that USFWS does not ultimately approve the plan). An equitable approach would require landowners in the development nodes to compensate those in the conservation zones.

In addition to its failure to consider the impacts of development on the reef, the plan also does not take a comprehensive view of other flora and fauna inhabiting the island.

Serious concerns about the adequacy of the biological studies have also been expressed—both on scientific and political grounds. From a political point of view, many believe that the studies conducted were focused on the property of the major landowners involved in the process. These are the landowners who paid for much of this analysis and there is a fear that the studies were intended to support the conclusion that their lands could be developed with little impact.

On more technical grounds, to some the use of species' density is an inappropriate measure of what to protect and what not to protect. As one observer noted, density studies are like snapshots of a moving parade. While the woodrat may be densely populating one parcel of land or portion of the study area now, it may not be in five, ten, or fifteen years. So many natural processes and events, from fires to hurricanes, could modify the natural environment, that existing species' densities have little relevance. In response to this fact the appropriate strategy would seem to be the protection and retention of large tracts of undisturbed habitat—ensuring the ability of the parade to march on, to continue with this analogy.

Even with extensive state acquisition of land in the study area, there are serious concerns about how these protected acquired lands will ultimately be used. As noted earlier the state has now purchased the Port Bouganville property. It has been suggested that this property be used as the site of a new headquarters for the John Pennecamp Coral Reef State Park. It is feared that this will further attract boaters, divers, and snorklers, and otherwise increase pressures on the reef.

Other concerns expressed by environmentalists and resource agencies included concerns about the plan's amendment process and the lack of clear provisions of plan implementation and enforcement.

Conclusions

While the North Key Largo HCP has not been officially adopted or submitted to USFWS, it has served as a catalyst for habitat acquisition, primarily by the state under its CARL program. And, while the North Key Largo plan exhibits a number of deficiencies and imperfections, including inadequate biological studies and serious questions about the influence of large landowners, it does offer some interesting proposals for habitat conservation which differ from most of the other HCPs reviewed in this study. The heavy reliance on a combination of county land use controls (zoning) and transfer of development rights make its approach unique. Such techniques may involve significantly greater amounts of uncertainty in the eyes of resource agencies such as USFWS, but—given the increasingly high cost of habitat acquisition—may represent promising tools for habitat acquisition in the future.

Protecting Migratory Songbirds: The Least Bell's Vireo Habitat Conservation Plan

The Least Bell's Vireo, a small grayish migratory songbird, once inhabited much of southern California. As a result of habitat loss and the gradual expansion of development this songbird has slowly dwindled in numbers. This chapter describes a regional habitat conservation effort spearheaded by the San Diego Association of Governments (SANDAG)—an effort to protect the last remaining riparian habitat areas upon which the bird relies. The Vireo HCP is unique in several respects, including the use of a two-tiered planning process, starting with a broad comprehensive management plan, and followed by more detailed HCPs for each of the rivers containing major habitat.

Like many of the HCPs discussed here, the SANDAG effort at protecting and managing habitat occurs in the face of tremendous population growth pressures. It is estimated that the San Diego region grows by seventy thousand to eighty thousand people per year. It has been predicted that the region will increase 1.5 million by the year 2015. This case illustrates the direct conflicts which exist between the needs of flora and fauna and the variety of facilities and projects that a growing population requires, from roads and highways to flood control and expanded sewage treatment. Conserving habitat in this context is difficult.

Primary Species of Concern: The Least Bell's Vireo

As noted above, the Least Bell's Vireo (*Vireo bellii pusillus*), a small grayish migratory songbird, once inhabited much of Southern California and northern Baja Mexico. The species has experienced tremendous reductions in population and range, primarily as a result of the gradual conversion of its natural riparian habitat (stream-side willow woodlands) to urban and agricultural uses. The expansion of the range and numbers of the Brown-headed Cowbird, a competitor and parasitic species, has also been responsible for shrinking numbers. The cowbird lays its eggs in vireo nests and because of the larger size and aggressiveness of the cowbird chicks, they tend to displace vireo chicks.

The vireo is a migratory bird which summers in southern California and winters in Baja, Mexico. The vireo typically arrives in California in March or April, and returns to Mexico around September. It is believed that the California population of Least Bell's Vireos has dropped to about 350 pairs. As a result of these dramatic declines, the vireo was placed on the California endangered species list in 1980, and on the federal list in 1986.

The HCP Process

Since 1986 the San Diego Association of Governments has coordinated an ambitious effort to prepare a regional habitat conservation plan for the vireo. The primary threat to vireo habitat comes from public improvements, such as highways, dams, and flood-control projects. The San Diego program is also organizationally more complicated than the other HCPs profiled. A two-level approach has been taken. To address conservation of the species on a rangewide basis, a Comprehensive Species Management Plan (CSMP) has been prepared. Among other things, the CSMP examines data on the existing number of vireo pairs and the extent of existing habitat in each riparian area, and sets quantitative targets for each specific river basin. Biological studies conducted as part of the CSMP have included field surveys, nest counts, cowbird studies, and vireo banding. The CSMP sets a goal of five thousand breeding pairs of vireos (as recommended in the USFWS recovery plan), and at least nine thousand acres of vireo habitat (fifteen thousand to twenty thousand acres of riparian habitat overall) (see Table 8.1).

Another level of planning was undertaken at the river basin level. More detailed HCPs were prepared for four river basins: the San Luis Rey River, the San Diego River, the Sweetwater River, and the Santa Ana River. These river basin HCPs were intended to contain more specific plans for acquiring, regulating, and managing habitat areas. Two other important river basins in the area were not included for more detailed HCP studies because they are primarily under the control of the federal government (the Santa Margarita River, which flows through Camp Pendleton Marine Corps Base, and the Santa Ynez River, which is under the jurisdiction of the U.S. Forest Service). The significance and

Table 8.1. Habitat Needs for Recovery (Acres)

Drainage	Existing Riparian Habitat	Existing Vireo Habitat	Recovery Goal (Pairs)	Existing Number (Pairs) (1987)	Capacity of Existing Vireo Habitat[a]	Capacity of Existing Riparian Habitat[b]	Vireo Habitat Needed	Existing Ratio of Vireo to Riparian Habitat	Needed Ratio of Vireo to Riparian Habitat[c]	Time[d] to Reach Capacity within Existing Vireo Habitat		Time[d] to Reach Goal, Assuming Habitat Is Available within Existing Vireo Habitat	
										2.0	2.5	2.0	2.5
Santa Ynez	1,200	800	200	20	200	300	0	0.667	0.667	28	12	28	12
Santa Clara	4,500	900	625	1	225	1,125	1,600	0.200	0.556	66	27	79	32
Santa Ana	7,633	200	265	21	50	1,500	880	0.026	0.139	11	4	31	13
Anza-Borrego	1,200	340	225	6	85	300	560	0.283	0.750	32	13	44	18
Santa Margarita	3,000	1,200	300	98	300	750	0	0.400	0.400	14	6	14	6
San Luis Rey	1,688	617	265	34	154	400	660	0.365	0.628	25	8	25	10
Jamul/Dulzura	50	40	38	6	10	12	112	0.800	3.040	6	3	23	9
Sweetwater	774	256	75	64	64	125	44	0.331	0.388	—	—	2	1
Tijuana	180	125	30	4	15	31	60	0.694	0.666	16	7	25	10
San Diego	802	385	150	21	96	225	350	0.480	0.748	19	8	24	10
San Dieguito	500	135	100	5	34	125	265	0.270	0.800	24	10	37	15
Salinas	1,000	500	300	0	125	250	700	0.500	1.200	59	24	70	29
Other	—	—	2,427	11	0	0	9,708			—	—	66	27
Total	22,527	5,498	5,000	291	1,358	5,143	14,939	0.244	0.456				

[a] Assuming ±4.0 acres per vireo pair.

[b] If all habitat were converted/managed for vireos.

[c] A ratio of 1.0 indicates that all riparian habitat is managed to be suitable for vireos; 0.4 to 0.6 is the assumed range for natural habitat; greater than 1.0 implies new habitat must be created.

[d] Time in years, at reproductive rates of 2.0 fledglings per year and 2.5 fledglings per year; mortality for both juveniles and adults assumed to be 0.457 per year and reproductive rate of 1.69 fledgling per year yields a stable population (Fromer, 1989 unpublished MS).

Source: Regional Environmental Consultants, *Comprehensive Species Management Plan for the Least Bell's Vireo*, prepared for the San Diego Association of Governments, San Diego, Calif., May 1989.

role of these habitat areas were considered in the CSMP. Because of strong landowner opposition to the San Luis Rey River HCP, plans to apply for a Section 10(a) permit for this river have been dropped. The Santa Ana River HCP will also probably not lead to a Section 10(a) permit application, but will be adopted as a policy document by the local governments involved.

Two sets of steering committees were formed to administrate the process. A thirty-member task force was established to oversee the entire program and to direct the preparation of the CSMP. Each of the individual river basins had its own separate advisory committee guiding and overseeing the preparation of each of these more detailed HCPs. Because the landownership patterns and development threats, as well as the status of the vireo, are somewhat different in each of the river basins, the content of the individual HCPs differ accordingly.

Funding for the preparation of the plan and background studies has come from a combination of state and local sources. Total cost of the planning process, including the cost of hiring consultants, has been approximately $650,000. The greater part of this, some $350,000, has been provided through state appropriations, on a matching share basis. Local governments contributed approximately $150,000. The bulk of the funds has been used to pay consultants to conduct the necessary biological studies, and to prepare the draft CSMP and HCPs.

Some have argued that an HCP for the Least Bell's Vireo was simply not needed because virtually all projects in riparian areas must go through a Section 7 consultation with the USFWS anyway (as a result of the need to obtain a Section 404 federal wetlands permit). In reply to this, supporters of the HCP process point to the value of taking a regional view, and of evaluating specific project-level proposals within the context of the broader rangewide needs of the species. The regional planning effort has already been influential in the design and review of several highway and bridge projects (including an extension of State Highway 52, which will cross the San Diego River).

Many of the key implementation issues in this HCP have yet to be resolved, including how the plan will be funded. A number of alternatives are being considered, including the creation of special riparian assessment districts. Unlike Coachella Valley and most of the other HCPs, little emphasis is being placed on fee-simple habitat acquisition; instead much of the implementation of the HCPs will continue through project-by-project mitigation (e.g., replacement of habitat lost with new habitat). The San Diego program has experienced significant opposition from some landowners, particularly farmers along the San Luis Rey who fear that the HCP may result in restrictions on their ability to extract water from the river (i.e., because of the potential impacts on streamside willows). It is because of this landowner opposition that the San Luis Rey River has been dropped from the regional plan.

The Comprehensive Species Management Plan and Individual Riparian HCPs

As already noted, the HCP process for the Least Bell's Vireo is considerably different in structure than other HCPs. The Comprehensive Species Management Plan was intended to "present a rangewide program designed to ensure the continued existence and recovery of the Least Bell's Vireo despite urbanization and use of the drainages in southern California."[1] This broader plan comprehensively analyzed and evaluated the rangewide threats to the bird and its habitat, and its population and biological attributes. The plan also establishes target numbers of vireo pairs to be supported in each of the riparian areas. The comprehensive plan also presented an analysis of the remaining habitat in each of the river basins and provided target acreage of habitat to be protected in each. The comprehensive HCP documented well the nature of threats to vireo habitat. While private land development is an important concern, public projects are a much greater direct threat to vireo habitat. The comprehensive species management plan identified some ninety major public projects that could impact the vireo and its riparian habitat. These projects included highway expansions, bridges, and flood-control projects, among others.

The goal of five thousand breeding pairs was established in the Comprehensive Species Management Plan. This number was suggested as a minimum viable population in the USFWS recovery plan. To reach this number, the Comprehensive Species Management Plan concluded that at least nine thousand acres of habitat for vireo would need to be protected, with fifteen thousand to twenty thousand acres of overall riparian habitat necessary. The conservation targets differed for each of the basins, depending on their particular circumstances. Moderate increases in overall riparian habitat and in the ratios of vireo habitat to other riparian land were viewed as necessary in the San Luis Rey and San Diego rivers, for example. In the Sweetwater River basin, however, recovery goals seemed achievable simply by maintaining existing habitats and vireo habitat ratios.

The Comprehensive Species Management Plan identified a number of potential conservation measures. Immediate measures included protecting current vireo habitat by excluding development from the areas (at least until permanent recommendations are implemented), designing public improvements to avoid important habitat area, and controlling cowbirds. Much of the CSMP was devoted to identifying long-term conservation measures. These potential measures included mitigation and habitat improvement through project review, management of existing habitat areas to protect important existing habitat conditions, inclusion of a riparian habitat conservation zone in local general plans and a special regulatory overlay zone in local zoning ordinances, acquisition of habitat areas through dedication, fee-simple acquisition or land trades, incentives for landowners to improve degraded habitat areas (e.g., tax credits, density bonuses, transferable development rights), and promotion of clustering new development away from habitat areas.

A central proposal was the provision of a riparian buffer zone along habitat areas. The CSMP suggested a buffer of 150 feet, with one hundred feet creating a biological buffer, and an additional fifty feet providing a planning buffer. The biological buffer was to be an extension of those areas used by vireos, and thus to be included in conserved habitat for foraging and protecting against encroachment. The planning zone was intended as a deterrent for development and other activities around the conserved habitat. The CSMP envisioned that these buffer zones would be included as an HCP overlay zone in local zoning ordinances.

The CSMP also addressed long-term management of conserved habitat areas. It proposed that a "management entity" be created to oversee and coordinate conservation efforts, to manage conserved habitat areas, and to coordinate review of projects in habitat areas. Several different options were identified for provision of these management responsibilities, including the expansion of responsibilities of the County Parks and Recreation Department, a joint powers agreement to establish a new management agency, establishment of permanent staff positions in USFWS or CDFG for this purpose, a management agreement with one or more non-profit organizations, incorporation of responsibilities into existing flood-control management, or formation of a special conservancy or management district.

The Comprehensive Species Management Plan identified several different approaches to providing long-term funding. Three options in particular were identified: 1) trust fund approach, 2) district approach, and 3) regional approach. Under the first option a trust fund would be created to provide operating and maintenance costs. Funds would be derived largely from contributions made by impacting projects in habitat areas. Potential contributors identified in the CSMP are County Water Authority, the California Department of Transportation (CALTRANS),

Sand Mining Companies, cities and the county, Corps of Engineers, sewer districts, and private development. The second approach would involve the establishment of some form of management district (perhaps a watershed maintenance district) which would have some degree of taxing authority (for example, there has been discussion of establishing riparian preservation assessment districts). The third option would rely on broader sources of funding including, perhaps, general obligation bonds and a regional development fee.

The Original River Basin Plans

The individual river basin HCPs represented detailed examinations of the habitat conservation issues and necessary strategies pertaining to each particular river basin. According to SANDAG, each plan was to:

document the historic and current distribution of the bird in the watershed;

examine the impact of existing and future land uses on the remaining birds and habitat;

map a focused planning area for conservation measures and local land use controls;

identify acreage to be conserved, restored, or reclaimed for vireo habitat;

identify conservation measures and permitted activities for land use categories and specific parcels;

assess the cumulative effects of proposed measures and land uses on the species; and

describe the agreements and institutional arrangements needed to implement the plan.[2]

More detailed HCPs were prepared for the Sweetwater River, the San Diego River, the San Luis Rey River, and the Santa Ana River basins. Plans had been completed for all four, although only two—the San Diego River and Sweetwater River HCPs—were submitted to USFWS for 10(a) permit approval (and then later revised into a single plan, as described below). In the case of the Santa Ana River HCP it was believed that a more appropriate approach would be to issue the plan as a set of policy guidelines, to be utilized by the various agencies and entities with management responsibilities along the river. The policy guidelines approach emerged from the realization that opportunities for future take would be limited, and the primary role of this particular HCP would be to help guide and coordinate local regulatory actions (e.g., buffer requirements) and to operate and manage responsibilities of agencies with land in the riparian area.

It will be helpful to briefly describe and summarize the steps undertaken and used in preparing these more detailed river basin HCPs, using the Sweetwater HCP as a case in point. The Sweetwater River is the southernmost of the four rivers and runs west forty miles from San Diego Bay to Rancho State Park. The watershed area contains approximately ninety-two hundred acres and is home to the largest number of vireos (about sixty-four pairs of vireos). In the process of preparing the basin HCPs a focused planning area was identified, based largely on the extent of riparian habitat and floodplains. This area includes the one-hundred-year floodplain plus a 150-foot buffer on either side (reflecting the buffer standard established in the CSMP). This area was then further divided into reaches. The HCP divided the Sweetwater River area into six reaches. In addition, the river basin HCPs identified administrative parcels, which represented major categories of use or landowners, and which then became the focus of much of the plan and its implementation provisions. Twenty administrative parcels were identified for the Sweetwater River.

These basin specific HCPs also classified land in the focused planning area based on important habitat categories. Four categories were used, based on the classification system used by USFWS in the vireo recovery plan: vireo riparian habitat (VR), riparian habitat presently suitable for vireos (R-1), riparian habitat presently not suitable for vireos (R-2), and land potentially reclaimable to riparian habitat (RECL).[3] The classifications for one stretch of the river are presented in Figure 8.1. Aerial photography and field surveys were used in mapping habitat. These river basin HCPs provided a detailed analysis not only of the extent and quality of vireo habitat, but also of the existing land uses and potential threats to habitat. Like other riparian habitat areas much of the future threat to vireo habitat is coming from public projects, especially transportation facilities (i.e., roads, bridges, etc.). Along the Sweetwater River there is also substantial potential for residential and other private development.

The initial Sweetwater River HCP laid out a conservation and management program which included habitat preservation, habitat management and reclamation, cowbird and predator control, and local regulation.[4] The plan proposed to protect and maintain 821 acres of existing riparian habitat as conserved habitat (which included presently occupied habitat, presently suitable habitat, and potentially suitable habitat,

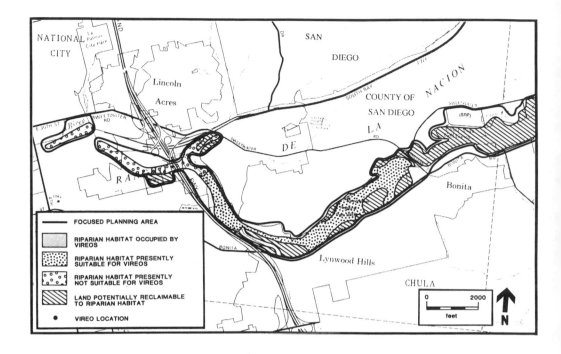

Figure 8.1. Existing Riparian Habitat and Vireo Locations for Sweetwater River (Courtesy Regional Environmental Consultants)

or classes VR, R-1 and R-2; see Figure 8.2). Conserved habitat lands were seen to be entirely in public ownership (requiring some amount of acquisition of private lands). This represented approximately 90% of the existing riparian habitat and was intended to ensure the protection of a fairly continuous block of riparian habitat. About fourteen hundred acres of land was identified as potentially reclaimable land, and would provide opportunities for expansion of conserved habitat and reclamation.

The plan assumed that local governments would modify their existing codes to create a special project review process for activities proposed within the focused planning area (FPA). Projects would be prohibited within conserved habitat areas (including biological buffers), unless they were determined to be unavoidable. If projects were allowed to proceed, mitigation would be required, with the extent and type specified in the HCP, varying according to the habitat class impacted. For activities affecting VR habitat, mitigation would be provided by creating new VR habitat of equal area and quality (prior to habitat destruction). The plan

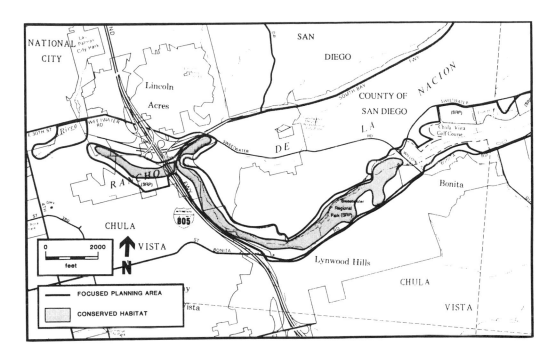

Figure 8.2. Conserved Habitat for Sweetwater River (Courtesy Regional Environmental Consultants)

stated that "in no case will a net loss of habitat quantity and quality occur." For R-1 habitats, concurrent removal of habitat was permitted, but was to be replaced at a rate of three to one.

Acquisition of private lands designated as conserved habitat was clearly envisioned in the original Sweetwater River HCP, although it was somewhat vague about how this acquisition was to occur, and according to what priority. It was suggested that the coordinating committee prepare a list for priority acquisition, although this was one of the least developed components of the HCP. Moreover, there was little explicit identification or programing in these initial basin plans of the costs that would be involved in acquisition of private lands.

The Sweetwater and San Diego River HCPs were submitted to USFWS, in September of 1991. During reviews of the plans, the USFWS expressed major concerns about whether the 1991–1992 status and distribution of the vireo had changed since the initial data was collected (1986–1988) and the original plans were prepared. Concerns were also expressed about whether the status and/or design of projects along the two rivers had changed since the plans were first drafted (specifically which projects would be covered by the permit).

Staff at SANDAG began redrafting the plans (along with the biological consultants) in the spring of 1992. A combined conservation plan for both rivers was resubmitted to USFWS in August 1992, and is currently under consideration. The combined plan is intended to supersede the earlier plans but builds on the earlier analysis and planning. The plan seeks two 10(a) permits—one for each of the two focused planning areas identified in the earlier HCPs. Each permit would cover a twenty-year period and would authorize take only after local governments (with land use authority) agreed to implement the plan, and adequate funding had been secured (to cover implementation for at least five years). The types of take anticipated have been more clearly and directly specified under the new plan, and include take due to habitat management (e.g., removal of exotic plant species), habitat removal less than or equal to five acres (take from individual projects would be limited to this amount, and conditioned on no net loss and mitigation of indirect effects), take due to indirect effects (adjacent development), and habitat removal of more than five acres (which could be authorized as amendments on a case-by-case basis).

The new combined HCP specifies a series of conservation and mitigation measures very similar to the initial river HCPs. The plan calls for local governments to designate Habitat Management Areas (HMAs) within FPAs where conservation and management efforts will be focused. These are areas where contiguous VR, R1, RS, and RECL habitat are found, and correspond (initially at least) to the areas delineated as conserved habitat under the initial plans. Individual HMA operating plans will more precisely delineate boundaries, and where possible will be expanded to cover other sensitive species and their habitats. Local governments will be expected to designate a habitat operator who will have day-to-day management responsibilities for the HMAs, and who will prepare an annual operating plan which will indicate specific management measures for each HMA: annual surveys and monitoring of vireo habitat and nest sites, cowbird control, and enhancement of degraded habitat and creation of new habitat. The new plan appears to retreat even more from the need to acquire additional private lands, either through fee simple or through easements. Rather, "The preservation strategy will focus on prescriptive habitat management, land use controls, monitoring measures, and cooperative agreements among agencies and with individual landowners."[5]

As in the initial river HCPs, the latest version relies heavily on a process of project review. All projects proposed within the FPA must be reviewed for consistency with the plan. Prior to a local government's issuance of a grading permit, it must reach one of these findings:

1. The project has no direct or indirect impacts on vireos, vireo habitat, or planned reclamation of habitat;
2. The project has avoided and minimized impacts to vireos, vireo habitat, or planned reclamation to the maximum extent practicable, does not directly affect more than five acres of vireo habitat, and has proposed mitigation consistent with CSMP guidelines; or
3. The project's impact on vireos, vireo habitat, and planned habitat reclamation has been authorized by USFWS and CDFG based on mitigation identified through the federal and state consultation process or, if not covered by "2" above, through an approved amendment to the permit and agreement.[6]

The plan also specifies detailed impact avoidance and mitigation requirements to be applied during this review process (and generally based on the CSMP guidelines). The standards vary somewhat according to the type of habitat involved, but generally require avoidance where possible, and minimizing and mitigating impacts to the maximum extent practicable where avoidance is not possible. No net loss is to be allowed, and habitat of equal area and quality to that to be removed must be created. These mitigation actions must occur prior to any removal or degradation. In the case of R1 and R2 lands, concurrent removal and replacement of habitat is allowed, as long as the replacement area is at least three times the size of habitat being removed. Also, no habitat removal is permitted during the vireo nesting season. Impacts from projects on adjacent lands will be reviewed as well, and appropriate development setbacks will be required (as included in the earlier versions of the plans), determined on a case-by-case basis.

Implementation of the plan will occur through a series of coordinating agreements (among local governments, SANDAG, USFWS, CDFG, etc.). A coordinating committee will be appointed to oversee implementation of the plan (a single committee for both FPAs). The coordinating committee will be assisted by a more broadly based advisory committee (e.g., consisting of representatives of environmental groups, civic groups, property owners). As mentioned, a habitat operator would be designated, and be responsible for day-to-day management of the HMAs. The plan also calls for a five-year comprehensive review of its implementation.

As in the original river HCP, the new plan estimates that annual operating costs will be approximately $400,000 per river. Funding remains uncertain, but as in the earlier drafts, a number of possible sources are identified, including appropriations from the federal Water Conservation Fund, appropriation for the California Environmental License Plate fund, local impact mitigation fees, general obligation bonds, and a special district assessment. The idea of a special habitat taxing district is one that has received considerable attention for several years.

Legislation to allow the creation of these special taxing districts has been enacted several times by the California legislature, only to face a governor's veto. In 1992, Governor Wilson vetoed the legislation primarily due to concerns that such taxing districts could be created, and their boundaries delineated quite broadly, without much clear connection to habitat and conservation requirements. Supporters of the bill believe they can correct these perceived problems (by tying the district more explicitly to HCPs) and there are plans to reintroduce the legislation in January of 1992. Among other things, the legislation could allow the creation of a district which would likely cover both the Sweetwater and San Diego rivers, including property within a mile on either side. The district would impose a yearly $25 fee on property.

Related Habitat Planning and Management Activities in the Region

As in the case of the Riverside County Stephens' kangaroo rat HCP, the Least Bell's Vireo HCP is being prepared in a quickly changing regional environment in which a number of related planning and wildlife conservation initiatives are under way. Many of these initiatives have developed within the last year. Some provide opportunities complementing the vireo HCP and most involve a recognition of the need to move toward a multi-species approach.

Considerable attention has been paid in recent months to one particular species—the California Gnatcatcher—which has been proposed for federal listing and, until recently, for listing under the state endangered species act as well. The gnatcatcher's primary habitat is coastal sage scrub and there is a large amount of this habitat type remaining in the San Diego region. It is estimated that the bird inhabits some 250,000 acres of land. Because of its location much of this land has been slated for development and the gnatcatcher issue has in recent months raised the political ire of the development community. It was predicted by the Building Industry Association of Southern California that the listing of the gnatcatcher could result in a loss of some 200,000 jobs over an eighteen-month period.[7] While it looks as though the USFWS will list the species, the California Fish and Game Commission recently chose not to place the species on the state list, at the specific request of Governor Wilson. Most observers saw this as a direct response to the opposition expressed by the development community. In place of the listing, Governor Wilson's administration has proposed that the gnatcatcher/coastal sage issue be addressed through a new state-level conservation initiative called the Natural Community Conservation Planning (NCCP) program.

Legislation was enacted in 1991 to allow the preparation of conservation plans for multiple species. Initial efforts under this program have been focused on the coastal sage scrub habitat issue. As a first step in this process, a special scientific panel has been appointed, comprised of notable conservation biologists who will advise how much and which areas of coastal scrub habitat ought to be protected. More detailed habitat analysis has proceeded through the designation of ten subregional focus areas. This program has considerable implications for San Diego, Orange, and Riverside counties where most coastal sage scrub is located.

Another large wildlife planning effort underway in San Diego County is a multi-species habitat plan being prepared under the county's Clean Water Program—a program designed, among other things, to expand regional wastewater treatment facilities. A study is currently being prepared in response to environmental review requirements under the California Environmental Quality Act (CEQA), specifically that, when evaluating wastewater service extension plans, analysis and consideration of secondary growth brought about as a result of such improvements is required. Most believe that a result of this program will be the acquisition and setting aside of major blocks of habitat in San Diego County based on the conclusions of the multi-species plan.

The San Diego circumstance also illustrates well the interconnection between habitat conservation and growth management. SANDAG has been involved for a number of years in encouraging regional growth management. It is currently developing a regional growth strategy which it hopes all jurisdictions in the region will be willing to embrace and implement. As part of this implementation process participating jurisdictions will be asked to adopt certain minimum planning and conservation standards. These standards will address, among other things, regional open space and management of sensitive lands. These elements of the regional growth strategy could result as well in habitat conservation.

SANDAG has been contemplating its possible role in the area of regional open space protection, and habitat protection could be a major focus. There is a precedent for this more aggressive regional government role in the area of transportation. SANDAG currently serves as the regional transportation commission, planning and coordinating regional transportation improvements. To fund this function it levies a $.01 regional sales tax. SANDAG staff have suggested that a similar regional role in the open space and habitat acquisition area would be feasible.

Implementation of San Diego's growth management program has also involved wildlife habitat issues. As part of the city effort to discourage inefficient sprawl and to promote more compact growth patterns it has—since the 1970s—designated an area as an urban reserve. This area, called "future urbanizing," was to be conserved for a period of twenty years. As the expiration of this period approaches, studies are underway to determine how to develop these areas. This urban reserve area contains sensitive habitat, including coastal sage scrub, and it is expected that the resulting plan for development will protect significant habitat areas and corridors.

A number of other smaller habitat protection initiatives are also underway in the region. A special management plan is in preparation for the San Dieguito River (under a joint powers agreement). The city of Carlsbad, in northern San Diego County, is currently preparing a habitat management plan. SANDAG has been attempting to encourage similar habitat conservation efforts by other North County jurisdictions through a series of meetings it calls the North County Wildlife Forum. It is hoped that this will result in an agreement between the North County jurisdictions to protect habitat in that area. Coordinating these different habitat, open space, and growth management initiatives will be a significant challenge for SANDAG in the future.

Potential Success

The Least Bell's Vireo process is unique in a number of respects. Unlike most of the other HCPs, initiative for the process has come largely from the public sector. Indeed, it is public projects that represent the major threat to the vireo and vireo habitat. Moreover, the structure of the process is unique—initially preparing a comprehensive species management plan, and then preparing more detailed HCPs for each of the four river basins.

As with all the HCPs, there has been considerable uncertainty about funding. Some progress has been made on devising funding arrangements for the plan, with the introduction of a legislation in the California legislature allowing the creation of Habitat Conservation Assessment Districts. Through a modest yearly fee, SANDAG estimates that most of the plan's operating expenses can be covered. This is an admirable effort to expand the traditional funding source for HCPs, and it may prove to be a useful tool with other HCPs. There is a certain amount of equity in placing such assessments on nearby property owners in that they will tend to benefit more than others (through higher property values, access to open space, etc.) from the riparian reserve system.

Some concerns have been expressed from the beginning about the real need for this HCP effort in light of the fact that most of the projects along the river already have a "federal handle"—largely because of the Section 404 federal wetlands provisions—and thus would already be required to go through a Section 7 consultation process. Proponents of the plan have argued that what is provided is a clearer and more comprehensive view of what needs to be accomplished to protect the species. Individual Section 7 consultations may provide some degree of mitigation, but by their very nature are project-specific, raising questions about their ability to provide any logical habitat conservation strategy.

It is clear that the HCP mechanism will serve as an important component in any project-specific decisions that occur in the future. Indeed, even before the planning process had been completed these plans have been useful in such decisionmaking. A case in point is the recent consultation over the State Route 52 crossover—a proposed bridge and crossover over the San Diego River. While the San Diego River HCP had not yet been finalized, its initial habitat mapping and analysis were influential in selecting a particular design option which ultimately minimized vireo impacts. In this way the HCP process has already had beneficial effects, and the rangewide and more detailed river basin analysis undertaken should definitely promote more informed future decisions about such projects and the mitigation required in connection with them.

The Least Bell's Vireo approach also has the political advantage of working out agreements in advance on habitat needs between important stakeholder groups and project sponsors. A major criticism of the existing process is that it invariably leads to a battle over each and every project or proposal involving vireo habitat. Because efforts have been made to include all major perspectives in the HCP process—at both the comprehensive species level and the river basin plan level—it is hoped that many of these protracted battles can be avoided in the future. The HCP approach, then, has the advantages of streamlining project review processes, reducing uncertainty about mitigation requirements, and potentially reducing the time and expense involved. For these reasons, developers in the area—of both public and private projects—have generally been very supportive of the HCP approach.

While the more detailed river basin HCP envisions the use of a combination of conservation tools, including land use controls, the plan does assume that project-by-project review and analysis will be a primary method by which vireo habitat is protected. Again, the plans will serve as guides in this review process, and in determining the appropriate type, extent, and location of habitat mitigation (i.e., like the Route 52 case). Consequently, unlike the Coachella Valley and most other HCPs, the Least Bell's Vireo HCP does not envision a major habitat purchasing program. Conserved habitat will be largely secured and protected through project-by-project mitigation. This strategy appears sensible in light of the relatively high level of public ownership of land in these riparian areas. It has also been observed that in the San Diego case there are few deep pockets to tap. Most of the state agencies and public entities sponsoring projects in habitat areas are already low on funds. Because there are relatively few private land developments there is less ability to use mitigation/impact fees to collect funds—for acquisition, for example.

The plans have also proven useful in modifying other development proposals near riparian areas. The San Diego plan was influential in modifying proposals by the Mission Trails Regional Task Force to construct new park facilities along the river. Specifically, equestrian trails were redesigned, buildings were sited to avoid habitat impacts, and certain maintenance procedures were agreed to for the equestrian center (to reduce cowbird attraction). Another recent example can be seen in the design of a water diversion project by the Sweetwater Reservoir. The diversion project was rerouted (from northside to southside) through an area of less abundant vireo habitat, changes guided again by the CSMP/HCP. As well, several communities within San Diego (e.g., East Elliot, Mission Valley, and Navajo communities), have modified, or are in the process of modifying, their plans to be consistent with the San Diego River HCP, including reclassifying certain lands as open space and incorporating the buffer standards contained in the plan.

The San Diego approach raises a number of concerns, however. Some environmental groups have been especially skeptical about the plan, especially members of the local Sierra Club. They have claimed, among other things, that the plan—at least as originally drafted—was "too vague," and contained too many potential "loopholes."[8] Indeed, there is much vagueness, even in the current Sweetwater/San Diego plan, despite the intent of the river basin plans to be much more detailed in focus. While the plans have been quite detailed in classification of habitat types and mapping, and in identifying areas that should remain as protected habitat, the plan is more uncertain about how such areas will be secured and protected (short of the case-by-case mitigation and habitat replacement). Moreover, movement away from the need for any additional acquisition will likely be of concern to some, raising questions about the ultimate ability to protect and control large contiguous blocks of riparian habitat. Furthermore, very heavy reliance is placed on local project review, and on the mitigation requirements stipulated in the plan. This, again, appears largely as an extension of the way habitat issues have always been handled, although now in the context of a comprehensive species management plan and process. While most agree that habitat creation and restoration is possible, at least in the case of vireo habitat, there remains some degree of uncertainty as to whether the cumulative impacts of projects in the future will leave the species in worse condition than would have been the case had the existing configuration of habitat been protected. Under the current Sweetwater/San Diego HCP, destruction of conserved habitat would be allowed only where unavoidable. It is precisely the interpretation of this type of standard that has caused uncertainty in the minds of Sierra Club representatives and others.

On a more philosophical level, then, the San Diego assumption of project-by-project review and conservation would seem to imply an acceptance of considerable habitat loss or degradation in the future. It seems to assume that habitat areas will continue to be besieged by highway expansions, flood-control projects, etc. Some question remains as to whether, despite aggressive mitigation requirements, the species will indeed be better off in the future under these circumstances. However, given the location of these habitat areas in southern California, it is extremely unrealistic to expect a cessation of these types of development-related projects.

During the preparation of the plan, questions have been raised by some observers about the cost and inconvenience of protecting what has been described as a visually unimpressive songbird. Advocates of the planning process have often argued that the vireo is like the "canary in the coal mine," and its status is indicative of the status and condition of the riparian habitat in general. Proponents of various public projects in the area are, on the other hand, quick to note the high cost of mitigation and the delays caused as a result of the species. The habitat restoration required in the case of the State Route 52 crossover (from Tierrasantita to State 67 in Santee) has been estimated to cost $12 million. This project is expected to reduce traffic on heavily congested Interstate 8 by some 20% and some proponents have argued that delay translates into accidents and loss of life on the interstate. Most observers agree, however, that the CSMP and HCPs have the potential of facilitating these project-by-project decisions.

The Least Bell's Vireo HCP process has also raised significant controversy among riparian farmers and property owners. Opposition to the planning process has been particularly vocal along the San Luis Rey River. This is a river which supports a predominance of agricultural activities. Farmers along the river perceive the vireo as a competitor for river water and have been suspicious from the start that an HCP would restrict their access to the water for irrigation purposes. In the words of one farmer along the San Luis Rey, the HCP process implies "that it's more important to grow willows than vegetables for people."[9] There is also the strong belief among these landowners that the vireo is really being used as a way of stopping all development. As an attorney for several of the San Luis Rey farmers stated: "These farmers are in competition for water [and] they question this almost religious need to take the country back, take this San Luis Rey Valley back to some historic point when there might have been more willows."[10] While a draft San Luis Rey HCP was prepared, the vociferous opposition led to dropping the river from the program, in turn raising questions about the effectiveness of the planning process. The loss of the San Luis Rey River from the process could be significant in terms of the relative importance of the river in providing future habitat for the vireo. Mike McLaughlin, who has spearheaded the planning effort at SANDAG, believes the San Luis Rey has the most potential of all the rivers to become a continuous, intact riparian habitat. It is currently the least urbanized and holds potential for restoring substantial vireo habitat.

Despite the biological background studies, there are clearly a number of uncertainties about the biology of the vireo. One of the more important of these with considerable implication for conservation and management is the potential impact of noise on vireos, especially construction noise. It is believed that construction noise can have a significant impact on vireos during the mating and fledging season (by displacing them). While the CSMP has identified the critical period of time as March to September, it also happens to be the non-rainy season and thus the optimal time for building construction. It is not clear what impact construction activities in adjacent locations in FPAs will have on the species.[11] The changing nature of vireo habitat also causes some concern. Because the extent and distribution of habitat within riparian areas changes from year to year, the information and mapping in the vireo HCPs may become quickly out-of-date. Indeed, the vireo plans reflect population and field survey data collected in 1988 and 1989 and may already be somewhat outdated.

As with a number of the other HCPs, concerns have been expressed along the way about the overemphasis of a single species. Recent versions of the Sweetwater/San Diego rivers HCP have sought to expand consideration of other species. It includes some provisions to conserve coastal sage scrub habitat, and the plan envisions eventually expanding the boundaries of the HMAs to encompass other species of concern. Still, the biological analysis and inventory, and development of the provisions of the plan, have focused heavily on the vireo and its habitat needs.

Conclusions

The Least Bell's Vireo HCP represents the considerable advantages of a range-wide approach, and an approach coordinated through a regional agency, in this case, SANDAG. Even though the plans have not yet been adopted they have already been influential in several project design decisions. The vireo planning process has clearly proven a useful overlay to the usual discrete, project-by-project review undertaken through Section 404/Section 7. Moreover, the SANDAG effort has explored some innovative implementation approaches, including the use of a habitat conservation assessment district. If successful, the process may generate funds for, and serve to more effectively coordinate, a variety of important management and species recovery activities (including, for instance, cowbird control programs).

The Least Bell's Vireo approach also exhibits a number of limitations. Without the strong need for a Section 10(a) permit (because most projects can go through Section 7 consultations) there is less incentive for jurisdictions and landowners to remain in the process. As a consequence, there was little support for the process by those along the San Luis Rey River—a river that may play an important role in the vireo's recovery. Moreover, while the plan provides a comprehensive perspective on highway crossing, flood controls, and a variety of other potential projects, it still appears largely driven by a reactive strategy—guiding mitigation on a project-by-project basis.

The vireo experience also further illustrates the time required and extensive process necessary to undertake a major HCP effort. If the latest version of the Sweetwater/San Diego rivers HCP is approved, the process may eventually end up having taken nearly seven years. To most involved in the local development process this seems like an excessively long time. Adding further frustration is the fact that biological and other conditions do not remain constant, and must be updated. By the time the first Sweetwater and San Diego rivers HCPs were completed and submitted, the biological and other information on which the plans were based were five or six years old, in turn making it difficult for USFWS to make an informed decision about the plans.

Endangered Rats and Endangered Homeowners: The Affordable Housing/Species Clash in Riverside County

In the late 1980s another major endangered species issue rose to the fore in Riverside County. While in the Coachella Valley conflict emerged over the endangered CV fringe-toed lizard, conflicts emerged in the eastern parts of the county, even closer to Los Angeles. The species of concern in this instance was the endangered Stephens' kangaroo rat.

Because of the proximity of rat habitat to the Los Angeles area, the conflict has been cast as one pitting a little-known endangered species against the need for affordable housing. Eastern Riverside County represents one of the last undeveloped segments of the Los Angeles metropolitan area, and the area has been receiving substantial growth pressures in recent years.

While the Stephens' kangaroo rat had been placed on the state's endangered list (as a threatened species) in 1971, it was not until its federal listing in 1988 that conflicts between the species and development became apparent.

Species of Concern

The Stephens' kangaroo rat (*Dipodomys stephensi*), like other kangaroo rats, has a large head, external cheek pouches, small front legs, and long rear legs. It is eleven to twelve inches in length, and more than half of the length is its tail. The SK rat is quite similar in size and appearance to the Pacific kangaroo rat although there are distinguishing features.

Stephens' kangaroo rats live in underground burrows; they either excavate these entirely on their own, or modify existing burrows of pocket gophers and ground squirrels (depending on how sandy or firm the soil

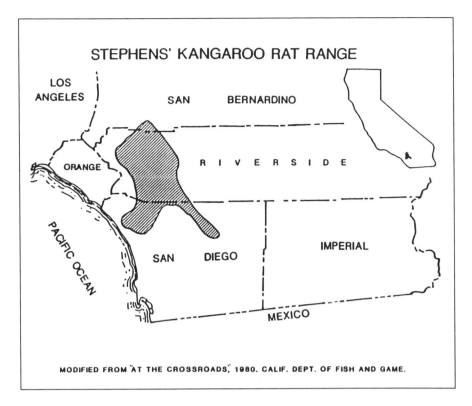

Figure 9.1. Historic Range of Stephens' Kangaroo Rat (Courtesy Regional Environmental Consultants)

is). SK rats are nocturnal and feed on vegetation, dry seeds, and insects. The rats forage and collect food in their cheek pouches, carrying the food back to the burrow.

Grasslands or herblands are the primary habitat for the SK rat. They prefer terrain of flat-to-gently-sloping topography with penetrable soils. The historic range of the rat is depicted in Figure 9.1, and includes portions of San Diego and San Bernardino counties, as well as Riverside County.

Habitat loss for the rat has been occurring for several decades. Disking and other agricultural activities have had substantial impacts. In recent years habitat loss has occurred as a result of grading for development and housing construction. It is estimated that only one-third of the species' original habitat remains, and this remaining land is highly fragmented. Because of this fragmentation into small habitat parcels, and the lack of movement corridors between them, population isolation and increasing extirpation are major concerns. Other threats include the use of rodenticides, invasion of non-native vegetation, and the potential increase in domestic pets associated with urban development. The USFWS declared the SK rat endangered on October 31, 1988.

The HCP process

Planning for the SK rat actually began before the species was officially listed. A Stephens' kangaroo rat Technical Advisory Committee was established in January of 1988, consisting of local planning staff, representatives of federal and state resource agencies, members of environmental groups—including the Sierra Club—and representatives of the Building Industry Association (BIA). This group met for approximately one year.

In December of 1987 Riverside County also responded to the Stephens' kangaroo rat issue by enacting an emergency mitigation fee ordinance. Similar ordinances were later adopted by each of the other localities in the area. These ordinances imposed a $1,950 per acre impact fee for all development occurring within the historic range of the rat. These funds have been used to hire consultants to undertake the necessary biological and land use studies. A formal HCP steering committee was formed in the spring of 1989, meeting for the first time in March of that year. The committee was chaired by Paul Selzer, the attorney who represented Sunrise Development Company in the Coachella Valley case, and consisted of a similar group of representatives of developers and builders, members of environmental groups, local government representatives, and representatives of state and federal resource agencies.

The HCP fee area includes approximately 565,000 acres of land. In addition to Riverside County, six incorporated cities are also located in the study area: Riverside, Moreno Valley, Perris, San Jacinto, Hemet, and Lake Elsinore. The vast majority of potential habitat, though, is located in the unincorporated areas of the county. Among the cities, Moreno Valley and Perris contain the most potential habitat. Current occupied habitat of the SK rat in Riverside County is estimated to be 19,849 acres.

The initial efforts of the steering committee were focused on the preparation and submittal to the U.S. Fish and Wildlife Service of an interim or short-term habitat conservation plan. The central idea was to devise a way to free large portions of the county where few, if any, rats were likely to be located, while protecting those areas where rat habitat and populations were concentrated, and where the studies and management activities of the long-term HCP would focus.

Under the interim plan, ten Stephens' kangaroo rat study areas have been identified and designated, including approximately 15,867 acres of occupied rat habitat, or what is estimated to be approximately 80 percent of the occupied habitat in the county. (See Figure 9.2; the individual study areas vary considerably in size from around two thousand to twenty thousand acres, with actual recognized habitat in these areas ranging from two hundred to 7,500 acres.)[1]

Under the provisions of the interim 10(a) permit, the U.S. Fish and Wildlife Service will allow incidental take of Stephens' kangaroo rats only in areas outside these designated study areas. This short-term permit will be in effect only for a period of two years. During this period the preparation of a comprehensive HCP will proceed for the study areas, including conducting extensive biological and field studies of the rat's habitat, land use compatibility studies, and the development of an appropriate long-term protection strategy.

Over the course of preparing the long-term HCP, the boundaries of rat habitat may be modified substantially as new and more detailed biological and land use information is generated (probably substantially reducing the boundaries). Proposed preserve boundaries may be quite different. In this refinement process, a number of factors are to be taken into account, including "the biological suitability of the land as part of conserved habitat (including buffers and movement corridors), the relative compatibility of land uses in the area, and the relative fair market value of the property."[2] Under the long-term HCP, a special subcommittee will be appointed to oversee the work for each of the ten study areas.

Several conservation measures—a combination of permit conditions and local actions—are proposed in the short-term HCP as a condition of the short-term 10(a) permit. These are briefly summarized below (largely following the short-term plan):

Limitations on take: Take will be permitted only in those areas outside of the designated study areas (except for essential utility projects) and only in local jurisdictions participating in the program.

Limitations on amount of take: Amount of take will be limited to a maximum of 20 percent of total occupied habitat for the study area. (This is based on the amount of occupied habitat believed to exist outside the reserve areas). This amounts to about four thousand acres, and determination of occupied habitat areas will be based on the map of habitat generated by CDFG (plus supplemental information provided by the consultants).

Mitigation of allowed take: Allowable take outside reserve sites will require several types of mitigation. First, for each acre of occupied habitat lost outside of reserve sites, an acre of habitat within reserves will be protected. The balance between acres to take and acres acquired as miti

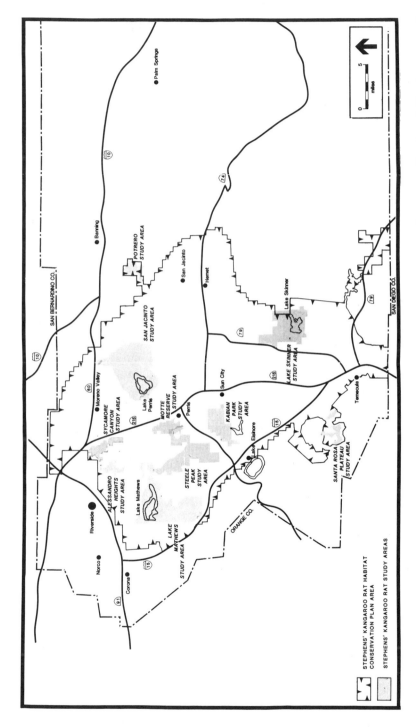

Figure 9.2. Area Proposed for Incidental Take for Stephens' Kangaroo Rat (Courtesy Regional Environmental Consultants)

gation will be reviewed quarterly. Developers will also be required to trap and relocate significant populations of SK rats.

Imposition of mitigation fees: Mitigation fees of $1,950 will be imposed by Riverside County and by the other localities participating in the 10(a) permit. This fee is applied to all projects proposed in the historic range of the SK rat. During the period of the short-term HCP, the funds collected will be used to pay for the costs of preparing the long-term HCP, any additional studies, and the acquisition of land within the reserve areas.

Reserve planning and funding: During the short-term HCP, efforts will be made to further identify the location and design of appropriate reserve sites and to develop a financing plan for paying for necessary acquisition. As well, an early acquisition program will be developed, which identifies early opportunities and priorities for acquisition.

Monitoring of potential reserve sites: During this period of the short-term HCP, the county and other participating localities will seek to ensure that the proposed development projects do not jeopardize the ability to protect necessary habitat for the species through the reserve system. In reviewing projects, attention will also focus on protecting potential habitat necessary for the species' recovery, movement corridors, and lands important as reserve buffers. The locality where a project is proposed must reach a finding that it will have "no significant adverse impact" on the ability to establish an SK rat reserve. "Significant adverse impact" is defined in the short-term plan as one of the following: "loss of occupied habitat, loss of potential habitat, loss of movement corridors, loss of buffer areas, and increased management difficulties."[3]

Quarterly review process: The localities will establish a quarterly review process through which any changes in study area boundaries will be considered, and through which early acquisition opportunities will be identified. The plan envisions the creation of a Quarterly Review Board (consisting of local representatives, USFWS, and CDFG). (When an interjurisdictional joint powers agency is found it will serve as the Quarterly Review Board.) Among other things, the quarterly review process will provide USFWS an opportunity to ensure that take of occupied habitat does not exceed allowable limits. USFWS, under their process, has the authority to require further acquisition before project approval, may veto any particular proposed habitat acquisition, and has the prerogative to revoke the 10(a) permit if it believes that reasonable progress is not being made.

Implementation agreements: The applicant governments, along with CDFG and USFWS, will enter into a series of implementation agreements which will specify responsibilities concerning collection of fees, acquisition of land, review of development projects, and management of reserve sites. This represents the first time such a short-term or interim mechanism has been approved by USFWS and may represent a major precedent for similar approaches elsewhere. Success with the SK rat short-term HCP encouraged the development of a similar short-term plan for the desert tortoise in Clark County (see Chapter 10).

An initial complication was the lack of involvement by the six cities which contain habitat within their jurisdiction and borders. All six have since adopted the interim mitigation fee, and are actively participating in the process.

Most of these study areas also contain other species of concern; at least seven of the study areas contain two or more of the following species:

— San Diego horned lizard
— Orange-throated whiptail
— Coopers Hawk
— Golden Eagle
— Black-tailed Gnat Catcher
— Coastal Cactus Wren
— Yellow-breasted Chat
— California orcutt grass
— Munz's onion
— Payson's jewel flower
— Many-stemmed dudleya
— Palmer's grappling hook
— Little mouse-tail

As can be seen in Table 9.1, several areas are known to contain as many as eight or nine additional species of concern.

Allowing take to occur outside the ten research areas is justified in part because of the fragmentation of occupied outside areas and the difficulty in sustaining their viability. As the short-term plan states, "The location and size of these small, isolated populations make it virtually infeasible to protect these sites as part of a viable preserve."

A final, revised HCP was prepared and submitted to USFWS in March 1990 and an interim Section 10(a) permit was issued later that year.

In 1990 the Riverside County Habitat Conservation Agency (RCHCA) was created. This agency was created through a joint powers agreement and has authority to identify and buy land, and to collect and disperse HCP funds, among other things. The agency is guided by a board of directors, with representatives of each of the cities, and a weighted vote

Table 9.1. *Areas Identified for Additional Study as Potential SKR Reserve Sites* **(in Alphabetical Order)**

Location	Size (Acres)	SKR Habitat[a] (Acres)	Local Jurisdiction	Species of Concern[b]
Canyon Lake/Kabian Park	9,324	2,165	Lake Elsinore Perris Riverside County	9
Lake Matthews/ Estelle Mtn.	16,510	7,520	Riverside County	6
Motte Reserve	2,200	>720	Riverside County Perris	8
Potrero/Beaumont	>2,200	NA	Riverside County	NA
San Jacinto Wildlife Area	19,600	2,335	Moreno Valley Perris Riverside County	3
Santa Rosa Plateau	3,221	NA	Riverside County	
Steele Peak	8,000	2,824	Riverside County	8
Sycamore Canyon &	3,742	2,160	Riverside City	4
Alessandro Heights[c]	2,970	1,950	Riverside County	
Winchester/Double Butte	6,900	241	Perris Riverside County	NA
Total	+74,667	+19,915		

[a] Estimate of occupied habitat based on CDFG report.
[b] Based on information provided by SKR TAC.
[c] Sycamore Canyon and Alessandro Heights are separate study areas.

provided to the county (representation allocated on the basis of the source of mitigation fees).

Even before the long-term HCP has been adopted, the RCHCA has been acquiring land. As of September 1992, the agency had acquired interests to approximately twenty-one hundred acres of occupied habitat within the study areas. Twelve hundred acres of this was acquired in the form of conservation easements on property owned by the Metropolitan Water District, as part of mitigation required for this project. The RCHCA put up $500,000 in management obligations for the property. The remaining acreage was purchased in fee simple. Land acquisition efforts have been focused on the study areas with the highest biological priority. In particular, acquisition has centered on three study areas: the Lake Skinner study area, the Lake Matthews study area, and the Motte Reserve study area. Several real estate brokers have been used to contact property owners who would be potential sellers in targeted areas. While the RCHCA has the power of eminent domain, it has not yet used it.

Approximately nine thousand acres of occupied habitat has already been protected through various forms of public ownership.

One of the more contentious provisions of the short-term HCP has been proposals to modify the boundaries of the study areas. Under the short-term HCP, proposals to modify the boundaries can be submitted to USFWS every six months. The first set of proposed boundary modifications was submitted in January of 1990, and has been recently acted upon by USFWS. Of the twenty-two proposed boundary changes, USFWS denied only three. One of these was for a very large project (involving about 900 acres of habitat in the Lake Matthews study area), and a parcel felt by USFWS to be important to the ultimate preserve design. The owner of the land has expressed frustration with the USFWS action and has threatened to initiate a legal action claiming an unconstitutional taking. A second set of proposed modifications has been prepared and has recently been submitted to USFWS. Under the short-term HCP, USFWS has 150 days to act on the proposed modifications, but has taken considerably longer than this. Environmentalists have been critical of these boundary changes and have characterized them as "deals," in which fairly large projects seek to become exempted from the study area restrictions. A case in point is the proposed Marina Highlands—a 2,500-acre project proposed within the San Jacinto study area (part of the second set of proposals). While the developer has offered to convey certain lands in exchange for boundary modifications, environmental groups have strongly opposed the proposal.

Disagreement over these proposed boundary changes stems in part from different perceptions of the original purposes of such an amendment process. Developers and landowners contend that they were led to believe that as subsequent biological analysis was conducted the study area boundaries would necessarily be reduced, and that this reduction process should occur quickly. On the other hand, others interpreted the provisions as intended to help the small landowner, and to cover circumstances where the impact of the boundary change was very small. In total, the permitted and proposed boundary modifications do not appear to have a major impact on the ability to craft an overall preserve system. The first and second round of boundary proposals would together reduce the total acreage in the study areas by 9%, and the amount of occupied habitat by only 2%.

Components of the Long-Term HCP

A preliminary draft of the long-term HCP was presented in November 1991, and has not been substantially modified since. A key strategy, as the interim actions have assumed, is the establishment of a system of habitat preserves. During the period of the short-term HCP, more detailed biological and land use analyses were conducted, and a computer model was developed to determine minimum acreage needed to preserve the rat, as well as to determine optimal preserve design and configuration. Results of the computer modeling concluded that a minimum of ten thousand acres of habitat will be necessary to preserve the SK rat. This has led some to believe that minimum levels of conservation may already have been reached when newly acquired acreage is combined with habitat already in public ownership. Precisely how much habitat should be protected remains an open question, however, and most observers believe that environmental representatives will find the 10,000-acre number to be too low. In purchasing lands, emphasis will continue to be on securing lands with the greatest concentrations of SK rats and with the greatest habitat value for the rat. Other factors will also be considered, including the cost of the land involved and the land use of the area. The consultants indicate that the 10,000-acre figure is meant as a starting point and that actual occupied habitat will likely be 10,000 to 15,000 acres.

The initial long-term strategy also analyzed the reserve opportunities for each of the study areas, identifying which areas are of greatest biological importance and are feasible for acquisition and long-term viability. Two study areas, Lake Matthews and Lake Skinner, are of highest priority, and will have little trouble meeting a 95 percent confidence standard (i.e., a 95 percent chance of population persistence over a 100-year period). On the other hand, Kabian Park would add little to the overall viability of the population and will have lowest priority. Decisions about whether, and the extent to which, the other study areas will be components of the reserve system will be decided in the months ahead.

Among the other design criteria discussed in the initial draft are the overall number of preserve units and the size of each unit. Several options were presented by consultants and discussed. One option is to protect three relatively large preserves, each meeting the 95 percent confidence standard. Another option discussed is the creation of five reserve units, with at least two that satisfy the 95 percent standard. It was recommended that each unit should be at least two thousand acres in size. Some concern has been expressed about attempting to link the different units together. The consultants have recommended that each preserve unit should be designed as a stand-alone unit, with efforts to be expended later to link them if possible.

The preserve system may also involve protection of potential habitat as well as occupied habitat. Exactly how much potential habitat would be included is uncertain at this point and hinges in part on analysis of area soils.

A major uncertainty in the preserve system is the amount of land needed for linkage and for buffers around occupied habitat areas. The question of buffers has been especially problematic, and there appears to be little scientific certainty or agreement on this (some have argued for 1,000 feet of buffer, others for 500 feet, etc.). Because there is little research or data on this, it's likely that a survey of scientific experts may be necessary to obtain the best scientific judgment.

The funding scheme also remains uncertain. Depending on decisions about minimum acreage and necessary buffers, total acquisition costs may range from $30 million to $50 million. Heavy reliance will continue to be placed on developer mitigation fees, but other funding sources are also being explored. The general belief is that the federal and state levels ought to share some of the costs, as should the broader local community. Additional local revenue sources are being explored, including tax increases and benefit assessment districts. The plan has already received $835,000 from the state, with revenue from its personal license plate program. The California Wildlife Conservation Board has purchased 200–300 acres of rat habitat as well, contributing to the plan.

The high cost of land acquisition will remain a critical consideration in assembling the habitat preserves. So far, the value of lands purchased ranges from $2,500 to $10,000 per acre. In certain areas, however, land prices are in the $40,000 to $50,000 range. Areas of high land value such as these will be avoided. A major concern has been the attempts by some developers and landowners within the study areas to take preliminary actions to raise the market value of their lands. While the recession has helped to keep land values low, there is the fear that as land values continue to rise, it may be difficult to secure important habitat land at reasonable prices.

In addition to high land values, extensive land parcelization is also a problem. The Sycamore Canyon Park study area has essentially been written off, for example, because it contains some 1,300 different private parcels. Trying to assemble a preserve there would be too time-consuming and costly, and possibly ineffective if there are property owner "hold-outs" (requiring a separate condemnation proceeding for each parcel).

The objectives of the HCP may also be advanced through the actions of the BLM. The BLM has recently issued its revised Resource Management Plan for the area which will protect those lands where prime SK rat habitat is located. It has proposed combining its holdings in certain locations through land trades, specifically in the Steele Peak study area (eventually to hold 9,600 acres here). The RCHCA has offered to assist BLM, to the extent that it can, in implementing its plan. For example RCHCA has offered to fund the salary of additional real estate staff it may need to undertake the land trades.

In 1991 the county also prepared a Multiple Species Habitat Conservation Plan (or Strategy) which sought to overcome the narrow species-by-species orientation that has occurred in the past. It identified different natural communities in the county, and high-diversity habitat locations, that should be protected in the future. While the plan holds potential for guiding future acquisition and management activities, it has apparently had little direct bearing on acquisitions made under the SK rat HCP. Acquisition decisions under the HCP have been made first and foremost on the basis of targeted high-importance SK rat habitat. The executive director of the RCHCA has indicated that to date the multi-species plan has not had much influence on their decisions as they feel constrained to direct their protection and acquisition efforts at SK rat areas. He indicated that they would indeed like to have the flexibility of buying related lands and getting credit for acquisitions of lands which may support other species of flora and fauna.

Acquisition efforts for the SK rat may also be aided through a newly created county open space district, created through a ballot measure in November of 1990. Unfortunately, an accompanying measure to fund the district through a yearly open space assessment did not pass.

The county is also in the process of updating the environmental element of its general plan. This update contains a variety of land management tools, including the use of transferable development credits, density limits in sensitive locations, riparian zones, and restrictions on developing on high slope areas. These measures may have more implication, however, for managing other non–SK rat sites delineated in the multiple species plan.

The RCHCA will likely remain in existence following completion of the plan and will coordinate management and plan implementation. A management committee will probably be appointed and will consist of representatives of USFWS, CDFG, and others. Multiple management entities also may be created in discrete units of the preserve system. There is speculation that as the SK rat acquisitions are completed, the RCHCA will then focus its energies on acquiring lands under the multi-species plan.

Under the original short-term HCP, the initial 10(a) permit for lands outside of the study was to expire in October of 1992 (two-year permit). In June 1992, the RCHCA applied for a twelve-month extension to the short-term permit. While pending, it is believed that USFWS will issue the extension. The RCHCA hopes that at that point sufficient acquisition of preserve sites would have occurred for USFWS to be willing to sign the long-term 10(a) permit. Uncertainty remains, however, about whether the preserve concept presented in the initial strategy report will be acceptable to USFWS, and the executive director of the RCHCA has expressed frustration at USFWS's noncommittal point of view.

New Initiatives: The Riverside County Multiple Species Habitat Conservation Plan

While the SK rat HCP has not been able to make acquisition decisions based on multi-species considerations, a Multiple Species Habitat Conservation Plan[4] was completed in 1991, and represents a major accomplishment, putting Riverside County in an excellent position to address future biodiversity issues. Funded entirely by local funds and costing approximately $290,000, the plan was prepared by consultants (Dangermond & Associates, and Regional Environmental Consultants), and took about eight months to complete. The plan involved a detailed analysis of significant habitat areas not currently under protection or management. The study methodology employed the technique of gap analysis which identified areas of important habitat for "sensitive, rare, threatened, endangered, or candidate species," not currently protected. The boundaries of these "resource areas" (also described as "potential reserve sites") were then refined, based on certain biological and management assumptions.

a. It is biologically important to provide connections among habitat areas to the maximum extent possible to enhance each areas' long-term viability.

b. It is desirable to build reserve areas around existing public lands whenever feasible to maximize the value of both those public lands and additional lands which may be acquired; this also promotes partnership opportunities.

c. Without compromising the integrity of the resource areas, it is desirable to avoid potential land use conflicts by coordinating resource area boundaries with existing and proposed land uses as identified in community plans, specific plans, the Open Space and Conservation Map of the general plan, and the draft Growth Management Element Map.[5]

The plan also identified and described a variety of conservation measures that could be used in implementing the plan, both regulatory and voluntary, and both public and private sectors. The plan stressed the need for partnerships and identified a variety of different public and private actors and the conservative roles they could play in bringing about the plan. Once approved, additional stages in the plan's development and implementation were envisioned, including more detailed vegetation mapping, inventory and sampling of wildlife and plant species in proposed preserve areas, a more detailed evaluation of threats to reserve areas, the development of biologically based management plans for each proposed reserve and corridor, and the preparation of a more formal multiple species HCP (i.e., consistent with the provisions of Section 10[a]).

Preparation of the plan was overseen by the county's Open Space Technical Advisory Committee. The MSHCS was presented to the County Board of Supervisors in July 1991, and went through extensive public hearings in the fall of that year. During these hearings the plan encountered certain opposition, particularly from developers and from the cities, who believed that their interests were not taken fully into account in the development of the plan. As a result of these objections, the plan was not adopted.

A number of specific implementation actions were identified in the MSHCP. Modifications were already underway to the Environmental Hazards and Resource Component (EHRC) of the county's general plan. Specific recommended changes to this element were contained in the MSHCP, including adding cluster requirements for development in sensitive lands (e.g., clustering development on the least sensitive 25 percent, with remaining 75 percent to be protected through dedication or easement); transferring density from sensitive area parcels to less sensitive lands; establishing a riparian protection policy requiring a minimum 100-foot setback from riparian areas and wetlands (setbacks to be greater within proposed wildlife corridors, to ensure minimum corridor width of 1,000 feet); and including future reserves and corridors on the county's Open Space and Conservation Map. Most of these proposals have been put on hold.

Even though the plan has not been formally adopted, some implementing actions are already underway. The SK rat reserve system, while not specifically looking at multiple species, may help to advance major components of this proposed countywide system. Private groups such as The Nature Conservancy have already utilized the strategy in its land acquisition decisions.

Consistent with the partnership approach, funding to implement this plan once it was completed, was to come from a number of different sources. A special open space property assessment as proposed recently by referendum, would be one possible mechanism for raising revenue. While voters passed the referendum creating the Parks and Open Space District they did not approve levying the open space assessment. Efforts may be made in the near future to again seek this authority. Full implementation of the plan would have been an expensive proposition. Crude estimates of the cost of buying all of the land identified as significant natural areas in the plan predict an exorbitant price. Paul Romero, executive director of the new Parks and Open Space District, estimated that the cost could exceed $500 million if these lands were purchased in the near future.

While the MSHCP was not officially adopted by the county, there is still considerable support for the concept behind the plan, and for the need to undertake multiple species approaches. Recently, the RCHCA entered into a memorandum of understanding with the Western Riverside Council of Governments and the Riverside Regional Open Space District to prepare a more detailed multiple species plan for the coastal sage scrub habitat in the county (habitat for the California Gnatcatcher). This effort would build upon the analysis and mapping of the MSHCP. The estimated cost of this plan is around $500,000 with a substantial amount of this already raised. A specific appropriation from Congress will provide $200,000, and another $75,000 has been donated by Southern California Edison.

Prospects for Success

The Riverside SK rat process involves two phases: an interim HCP, to cover a two-year period, and a long-term HCP, to come into existence on or before this two-year period expires. While to date the experience is mixed, the process has already had considerable success. USFWS approved the short-term plan and some 2,100 acres of occupied habitat within the study areas have already been acquired. Moreover, the amount of land protected has substantially exceeded official habitat take outside the study areas (now at about 1,700 acres). Substantial funds have been raised for acquisition and planning, mostly through developer mitigation fees. As of fall 1992, the Riverside County Habitat Conservation Agency had approximately $22 million in funds available for acquisition.

Despite these successes a number of questions can be raised about the Riverside SK rat program. Most distressing to observers is the large number of proposed boundary changes to the study areas, intended to exempt a number of large development projects. To many, these proposals amount to behind-the-scene "deals," and they question the integrity of the plan (some forty changes have been approved or proposed in the first and second boundary change packages). USFWS is understandably hesitant about approving such proposed changes.

Also, while habitat acquisition in the study areas has exceeded official take, there has been a considerable amount of illegal habitat alteration occurring through several means. In certain cases local jurisdictions (one city in particular) have simply permitted habitat destruction to occur. In other cases habitat destruction has occurred through agricultural grading, as have other activities for which no official permit is required. In response to the latter problem the county has been contemplating developing a certificate of compliance system for agricultural operations.

More fundamental will be the question of how much habitat protection is necessary. The minimum floor estimates of 10,000 acres would permit a substantial destruction of habitat and will likely result in vocal opposition, especially from representatives of the Sierra Club and Audubon Society. The development community, on the other hand, will accept this relatively low number and resist efforts to protect greater amounts of habitat. Most however, including the consultants, agree that actual acreage of occupied habitat will exceed 10,000, though there is uncertainty at this point about how much. Because there are currently an estimated 18,000 acres of occupied habitat within the study areas, even the minimum 10,000-acre figure would preserve more than 50 percent.

Another concern surrounds the county's multi-species habitat conservation plan. It represents an extremely promising tool and could be very useful in guiding a variety of public (and private) actions and decisions, but the SK rat HCP group appears to be operating with very little direct connection to it. Their mission is to protect and preserve important SK rat habitat. The failure to take a broader, multi-species approach is distressing, though other agencies, such as the open space district, may be able to adopt such a strategy. And, the failure on the part of the county to officially adopt the MSHCP raises serious questions about the county's commitment to seek a comprehensive, countywide solution to habitat conservation. The proposed coastal sage scrub habitat plan is a positive step, however, and will incorporate and implement major elements of the MSHCP.

One of the more interesting aspects of the SK rat HCP is the use of advanced conservation biology methodologies to predict the long-term effects on species of different sizes and configurations of preserves. This technique employs a GIS-based computer model, which is able to predict the probability of persistence of populations, into the future. A standard has been adopted of population persistance for one hundred years, at a 95 percent confidence level. Moreover, the computer model, developed by Michael Gilpin at University of California–San Diego, is being used by the consultants to determine ideal reserve configuration for the different study areas.

The Stephens' kangaroo rat HCP illustrates vividly the difficulty of protecting habitat in an area under extreme urban growth pressures. As a result, the fair market value of habitat is quite high, with land in certain study areas currently selling for $40,000 to $50,000 per acre. The RCHCA won't purchase habitat lands where the fair market value is so high. The downturn in the economy and in the real estate market represents a positive opportunity to acquire lands at lower prices. However, they have discovered that many property owners are speculating that values will go back up and will wait to sell under the improved market conditions. For these reasons, land acquisition has been been slower than some hoped.

To many, the SK rat issue represents what is wrong with the current ESA and the inflexibility of its application. It is one thing, the critics argue, for society to give legal protection to and spend large amounts of money to preserve the American Bald Eagle or the Florida panther, but another thing entirely to apply these to the protection of a rat. Indeed, this is a form of animal species, it is further argued, that many homeowners attempt to rid from their homes, and one otherwise not generally cared for. Many have difficulty understanding how public funds could be spent on such a conservation program during a period of layoffs and reduced funding for a variety of other social services and programs.

Moreover, the Stephens' kangaroo rat controversy has been treated in the media as a conflict between a rat—albeit a "cute" rat—and affordable housing. Western Riverside County has been characterized as one of the last remaining areas of affordable housing in the Los Angeles region, with the median price of homes at about $113,000. This compares to approximately $231,000 in Orange County, and $191,200 in Los Angeles. The Stephens' kangaroo rat HCP has been specifically mentioned and criticized in the recently issued report of the Advisory Commission on Regulatory Barriers to Affordable Housing. The high cost of establishing the rat preserves and the high development fees, the report concludes, will necessarily be passed along in the form of higher housing costs. In the words of the report: "Hence, for years to come, people buying new homes in Riverside County will be paying for the Stephens' kangaroo rat's preserves. While environmental protection efforts frequently raise the cost of land and housing, few instances provide as clear a picture of the process as this Riverside County situation."[6]

Interestingly, the development community in Riverside County continues to strongly support the HCP. According to the RCHCA director, the HCP is generally viewed as the most cost-effective and efficient approach to solving the endangered species problem.

Some could be critical of the Riverside plan for not attempting to address the entire range of the species, even including habitat in adjoining San Diego County, but consideration was given early on to an inter-county HCP, specifically including habitat located in northern San Diego County in addition to Riverside. This option was eliminated for several reasons, however, including a lack of interest on the part of San Diego County agencies, increased complications for coordination and funding, the fact that the majority of the existing population is located in Riverside County, and the fact that very little of the San Diego occupied habitat is on private lands (thus covered through Section 7 consultations).

Conclusions

This chapter has examined the ongoing efforts to conserve habitat for the endangered Stephens' kangaroo rat. While the long-term HCP has not yet been completed, the SK rat process has been innovative in crafting a short-term conservation program while the longer-term strategy is developed. The first short-term HCP in the country was approved by USFWS and a section 10(a) permit issued for limited take outside of designated SK rat study areas. During the interim period significant acquisition of occupied SK rat habitat has occurred, and in excess of take. Much of the process surrounding preparation of the long-term HCP has focused on determining the appropriate number, size, and configuration of SK rat preserve units. Preliminary analysis, based on computer modeling of different preserve configurations and utilizing a one hundred-year population persistance standard, suggests several different options. The resulting preserve system should include three to five reserve units, protecting between 10,000 and 15,000 acres of occupied habitat (and some potential habitat). Total cost should range between $50 million and $100 million.

Preserving the Desert Tortoise: The Clark County Habitat Conservation Plan

The Setting: Clark County and the Las Vegas Valley

Clark County is located in the southern tip of Nevada. It contains approximately 7,880 square miles of land, and a population of approximately 760,000 people (1990). It is the most populated county in the state and contains the city of Las Vegas and the concentration of urban development in the Las Vegas Valley (see Table 10.1). In addition to Las Vegas, the valley also includes the cities of North Las Vegas, Henderson, Boulder, and Mesquite.

Landownership patterns are unique compared with the other HCPs described in this book. Landowners in Las Vegas Valley are a mixture of federal and non-federal, with about half the land (some 277,000 acres) owned by the Bureau of Land Management. An even higher percentage of the land in the county as a whole is owned by BLM (about 60 percent).

The Plight of the Desert Tortoise

There are two distinct populations of the desert tortoise (*Gopherus agassizii*) native to desert regions of the southwestern United States—the Mojave and Sonoran populations. These populations are largely separated by the Colorado River.[1] The desert tortoise is a large reptile, with adults measuring up to fifteen inches in shell length. The tortoises have long lifespans (some adults live more than one hundred years) and are relatively slow to reproduce.

Once abundant in the desert regions of the western United States, the desert tortoise has experienced precipitous declines over the last few

Table 10.1. *Clark County Growth Trends and Forecast, 1980–2005*

	1980	1990	2000	2005
Clark County				
Population	461,000	761,300	997,200	1,074,200
Employment[a]	216,700	367,000	552,100	—
Las Vegas Valley				
Population	442,560	728,500	944,600	1,012,900

[a] Based on higher population forecast for 1990 and 2000.

Sources: Regional Environmental Consultants, *Short-Term Habitat Conservation Plan for the Desert Tortoise in Clark County, Nevada* (San Diego, Calif., 1990), p. 65.

years. Sharp declines in tortoise populations have been the result of a number of factors, such as direct loss of habitat as a result of land development, habitat degradation, tortoise deaths due to off-road vehicle use, deaths from shooting and other forms of vandalism, predation from ravens (a species whose numbers have risen dramatically in many desert areas as a result of the extension of telephone and power lines, the existence of dumps and landfills, and other results of increased human presence in the desert), and disease. The last, an upper respiratory virus, has had a particularly significant impact on desert tortoise populations in the wild, and was formerly thought only to exist in captive tortoises.

The emergency listing of the Mojave Desert tortoise was the direct result of a lawsuit filed by the Environmental Defense Fund, Natural Resources Defense Council, and Defenders of Wildlife. The decision to list the tortoise was based primarily on the impacts of the upper respiratory disease syndrome (URDS) but habitat loss and raven predation were also cited by USFWS as contributing factors. The USFWS gave the desert tortoise emergency listing as endangered on August 4, 1989.

The emergency listing of the desert tortoise was not taken lightly by the development community in Nevada, particularly those in the booming Las Vegas area who saw the tortoise as an obstacle that could bring development to a grinding halt. Immediately following the emergency listing a coalition of developers, development industry representatives, and government leaders (Summa Corporation, Southern Nevada Homebuilders Association, Nevada Development Authority, the city of Las Vegas, Building Industry Association of California, and the state of Nevada) petitioned the courts for an injunction, challenging the appropriateness of the emergency listing procedure. In particular, those groups argued that the listing should not apply in areas such as the Las Vegas Valley, where development was already taking place and where continual development would, in their eyes, have little influence on the overall desert tortoise population.

In response to the listing of the tortoise and the potential repercussions for development in the Las Vegas Valley the preparation of a tortoise HCP was quickly initiated. Clark County (which includes Las Vegas) took the lead, hiring Paul Selzer, the attorney who spearheaded the Coachella Valley HCP, to head the effort. A steering committee was formed, a mitigation fees ordinance enacted, and a consultant was hired to undertake the necessary background studies and mapping and to prepare the actual plan.

In late fall of 1989 an out-of-court settlement was reached on the emergency listing suit. Under the settlement USFWS would issue a scientific take permit to allow the limited take of tortoises on certain properties (e.g., Summa Corporation land) where development had already commenced. Tortoises would be relocated to the new Desert Tortoise Conservation Center, established under the agreement. Here they are to be used for research and education purposes.

Under the agreement, an extensive desert tortoise research program would be established to study among other things the upper respiratory disease syndrome, tortoise reproductive biology, tortoise nutritional needs, the interaction of tortoise and livestock, and the effectiveness of tortoise barriers and other tortoise management techniques. A Desert Tortoise Research Program Agreement was signed in February 1990, by the Nevada Department of Wildlife (NDOW), the Bureau of Land Management, and The Nature Conservancy. Under the agreement NDOW will supervise removal of tortoises from development parcels, BLM will own and operate the research center, and TNC will administer the funding.

USFWS did issue the scientific take permit, and it is expected that approximately 870 tortoises (between 312 and 1,060) will be collected from about seven thousand acres of habitat in the valley. Eleven separate land parcels are covered by the agreement, with the largest being the Summerlin/Del Webb development owned by the Summa Corporation (see Table 10.2), and consisting of forty-two hundred acres. The parcels included under this agreement were those deemed to have already commenced development on or before August 4, 1989 (the tortoise listing date). In addition, a team of biologists was assembled by USFWS and asked to evaluate each of the eleven parcels for their significance to the desert tortoise. Their assessment report concludes that: "There was unanimous agreement that the habitat on all the subject properties

Table 10.2. *Summary of Acreage and Population Estimates for the Eleven Parcels*[a]

Parcel Name	Acres	Estimated Numbers of Tortoises (Range)
Cosmo World	1,287	50 to 200
Summerlin/Del Webb	4,200	190 to 580
Vegas/Buffalo	30	1 to 5
Peccole Ranch	973	50 to 200
La Mancha	27	1 to 5
Candle Creek	23	1 to 5
Technology Park	310	15 to 40
Lewis Homes	80	1 to 10
Memorial Schools	40	1 to 5
Jacobson School	10	1 to 5
Navarre/Arroyo Grande	24	1 to 5
Total	7,004	312 to 1,060

[a] An additional 10 to 20 tortoises are expected to occur on the parcel of public land where the Conservation Center will be sited.

was unlikely to persist and that none was of special significance to the species."[2]

The commenced development settlement has not been uniformly accepted as a positive outcome. On the one hand it clearly helps to resolve some of the perceived inequities that resulted from the possibility that development projects already underway would be stopped or severely slowed as a result of the tortoise listing. Moreover, the compromise will clearly generate money and facilities to undertake basic, and most agree, badly needed research on the tortoise and its habitat requirements (and especially the upper respiratory disease syndrome). On the other hand, some in the environmental community have expressed concern that the compromise amounts to a circumvention of the protective provisions of the Endangered Species Act, and that the scientific take is largely a rationalization or justification for getting tortoises off the eleven properties covered by the agreement. To some observers the idea of establishing a Desert Tortoise Conservation Center, and the accompanying research agenda, were secondary considerations to solving the development problem on these parcels.

Another recently settled lawsuit involving the desert tortoise involved the Kerr-McGee Company. BLM had allocated fifteen thousand to twenty thousand acres of land to Clark County, which then sold it to Kerr-

McGee, an Oklahoma defense company relocating to Nevada. The tortoise listing could have halted construction on the site, and Sierra Club did sue in an attempt to stop the project. An out-of-court settlement was reached, however, in which Kerr-McGee agreed to donate $395,000 to the tortoise effort—of which $145,000 would go into research, and another $225,000 would be used exclusively for acquisition and enhancement of tortoise habitat (the latter amount was to be paid to The Nature Conservancy).

Preparing the Clark County HCP

Very shortly after the tortoise's listing, Clark County initiated a habitat conservation plan for the tortoise. Much of the county's undeveloped land was potential habitat and the desert tortoise was viewed as a major obstacle to future development and growth of the area. A steering committee was established to oversee the preparation of the HCP, consisting of, among other groups: representatives of Clark County and each of the five municipalities located in the county; development and real estate interests (the Summa Corporation, a major developer in the region, Southern Nevada Homebuilders Association, and the Board of Realtors); representatives from the environmental community, including the Desert Tortoise Council, Defenders of Wildlife, Environmental Defense Fund, and The Nature Conservancy; the Nevada Department of Wildlife; the Nevada Department of Transportation; the Nevada Department of Agriculture; USFWS; BLM; the Southern Nevada Zoological Park; the Nevada Cattlemans Association; the Southern Nevada Miners Association; representatives of off-road vehicle groups; and representatives of the state's congressional delegation. A full listing of active participants is presented in Table 10.3. This committee met on a weekly basis for the first two months or so of its existence and now holds monthly meetings. The Nature Conservancy was given the responsibility of directing the biological and other necessary technical studies and preparing the actual HCP (which was in turn subcontracted to an environmental consulting firm in San Diego). In addition to the steering committee, a technical advisory committee, consisting of biologists and scientific experts, was formed to oversee and advise the preparation of the plan (including experts from Nevada Department of Wildlife, BLM, USFWS, NPS, California Department of Fish and Game, TORT Group Nevada, and the University of Nevada, Las Vegas).

In October of 1989, the county and each of the five municipalities adopted a desert tortoise development ordinance which imposed a $250

Table 10.3. *The Desert Tortoise Steering Committee*

Clark County
City of Las Vegas
City of North Las Vegas
City of Henderson
Boulder City
City of Mesquite
Office of the Governor of the State of Nevada
Nevada Congressional Delegation
Nevada Department of Wildlife
Nevada Department of Agriculture
Nevada Farm Bureau
U.S. Fish and Wildlife Service (*ex officio*)
U.S. Bureau of Land Management
National Park Service
Summa Corporation
Southern Nevada Homebuilders Association
Joyce Advertising Inc.
Nevada Off-Highway Users Council
Nevada Cattleman's Association
Nevada Mining Association
Individual mining interests
Individual cattlemen interests
Desert Tortoise Council
TORT Group Nevada
Defenders of Wildlife
Natural Resources Defense Council
Environmental Defense Fund
The Nature Conservancy
University of Nevada, Las Vegas

per gross mitigation fee on all development in the county. These monies were placed in a special fund and were to be used to pay for the costs of preparing the HCP and for acquiring future habitat areas, among other things. The fee requirement applies to virtually all undeveloped land in the county. Payment of the mitigation fee, however, does not permit species take. Developers are also required to undertake biological assessments of their property to determine whether there are tortoises or evidence of tortoises present on the site (e.g., burrows, trails). If tortoises or evidence of tortoises are found, then development is considered to be prohibited without a 10(a) permit. The desert tortoise fund is administered by the Clark County Board of Supervisors, consistent with the recommendation and guidance of the steering committee.

The Short-term HCP

One of the key issues in the Clark County HCP process has been finding a way to allow some degree of development to proceed in tortoise habitat areas while the longer-term HCP was being prepared. The steering committee examined a number of different options and decided finally on preparing a short-term HCP that would allow take within Las Vegas Valley (which includes Las Vegas and most of the development pressures) for a three-year period, in exchange for certain short-term habitat conservation measures, primarily in the form of changing allowable land uses on BLM land and taking certain BLM habitat areas out of livestock, mining, ORV, and other damaging uses. This was to be accomplished through the designation of habitat as Tortoise Management Areas (TMA). The priority conservation areas were identified and short-term habitat protection has been focused here.[3]

Under the short-term HCP, allowable take is explicitly tied to protection and conservation of habitat areas. During the HCP process fourteen potential tortoise management areas (PTMAs) were identified, based mainly on earlier BLM analyses. Specifically, these are areas identified by the BLM as containing from 20 to more than 250 tortoises per square mile. Two priority areas were also identified (consisting of PTMAs 2, 6, 12, 13, and 14; see Figure 10.1). The short-term HCP established conservation thresholds that must be achieved over time in order for allowable take to continue. These thresholds specified not only the amount of habitat to be conserved but the location and type of these areas. Specifically, four thresholds were established:

1. At least 100,000 acres will be conserved within either of the two priority areas before any take is allowed in the permit area;
2. At least 200,000 acres will be conserved by the end of the fourth quarter after take is allowed;
3. At least 300,000 acres will be conserved before take exceeds 2000 tortoises or habitat loss exceeds 13,000 acres;
4. At least 400,000 acres will be conserved with at least 200,000 acres in either of the two priority areas before take exceeds 3500 tortoises or habitat loss exceeds 18,000 acres.[4]

Overall take during the three-year period will not exceed 3,700 tortoises.

The 10(a) permit covers approximately 300,000 acres in the Las Vegas Valley. The take area includes land in Las Vegas, North Las Vegas, Henderson, and Boulder City, the unincorporated towns of Sunrise Manor,

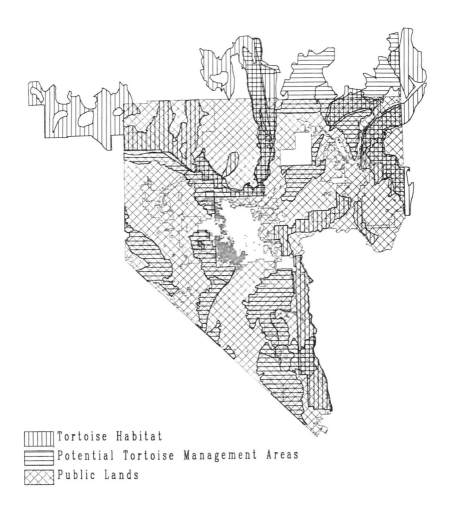

Tortoise Habitat
Potential Tortoise Management Areas
Public Lands

Figure 10.1. Potential Tortoise Management Area (Courtesy Regional Environmental Consultants)

East Las Vegas, Winchester, Paradise, and Spring Valley, and portions of the unincorporated areas of Love Mountain and Enterprise. The short-term HCP, and allowable take, will cover only a three-year period (or completion of the long-term HCP, whichever comes first). Habitat is to be conserved through several different types of land use controls, including the acquisition of grazing rights, additional restrictions on off-road vehicle use in habitat areas, and review of mining claims on BLM lands. Any proposed development would have to prepare a tortoise survey for the site and any tortoises found would be relocated (to be used for research, education, etc.). A $550 per acre mitigation fee would also be imposed (the $250 fee would still apply to areas outside of the permit zone). It is estimated that the costs of implementing the short-term HCP will be approximately $6 million over the three-year-plan period.

The placement of additional land use controls on conserved habitat areas is the heart of the mitigation effort under the short-term HCP. This has been somewhat controversial among members of the environmental community, who have critically questioned what these land use changes would actually be, how they would be brought about, and how tortoises and tortoise habitat would be protected by them.

The final short-term HCP envisions several types of land use controls in conserved habitat areas. In particular, grazing will be eliminated through the purchase of grazing rights from willing sellers, most commercial and competitive off-road vehicle events will be prohibited, intensive recreational uses will be restricted to existing designated areas, and mining claims will be reviewed for validity and Section 7 consultations conducted as needed (though existing claims will remain valid). An annual management plan will also be prepared for each conservation area, and it will address among other things physical maintenance, land use enforcement, and biological monitoring.

Management and Planning Issues

The Clark County HCP is different from other HCPs described in this book because of the pre-existing landownership patterns. With the exception of the Las Vegas Valley, the vast majority of habitat in the study area is under federal ownership, specifically the Bureau of Land Management. From the beginning there was an assumption that any significant amount of habitat protection or conservation would have to occur on BLM lands.

One of the initial tasks undertaken in the process was to identify prime tortoise habitat in the region. The BLM had already prepared a tortoise habitat map, identifying and categorizing different tortoise management areas. Based on this information and using additional criteria, such as the potential for land use conflicts, a subsequent habitat map was prepared by the Technical Advisory Committee and the planning consultant.

Because of the large amount of BLM land involved in the desert tortoise HCP, it was clear from the beginning of the process that conservation/mitigation would need to occur largely in these areas. The BLM must also go through its own planning process for these lands and a major complicating issue was the need to coordinate and dovetail the HCP with these BLM plans. Specifically, BLM must prepare, under the Federal Land Policy and Management Act (FLPMA) of 1976, a Resource Management Plan for the area. These plans are prepared and updated regularly. One of the early issues considered was whether the BLM planning process could somehow be speeded up to provide a timeframe closer to the HCP's. BLM began the process of preparing a Resource Management Plan in March of 1990, largely in response to the inadequacy of existing plans and the need to address the protection needs of the tortoise brought about by its federal listing as an endangered species. The plan will encompass about 4.2 million acres and will cover the entire Las Vegas District State Line Resource Area (parts of Clark and Nye counties) and will replace its current Framework Management Plan. The BLM maintained in the beginning of the process that it would be able to complete its RMP by approximately May of 1992. While a draft RMP has been prepared (and is out for public review) BLM has indicated that it does not intend to seek approval of the final plan until 1994. The draft RMP currently consists of several different land use alternatives (including a status quo alternative, a tortoise alternative, and a BLM-preferred alternative), and the BLM has been going through a process of soliciting public opinion on these different proposals. Both the tortoise and preferred alternatives would protect large amounts of habitat (approximately 800,000 to 1.5 million acres) and BLM officials believe that the alternative actually chosen will be a compromise between these two. Which alternative, or combination of alternatives, will be chosen by BLM will in turn depend on the USFWS Desert Tortoise Recovery Plan currently under preparation and the long-term tortoise HCP. It also remains to be seen what sort of political clout mining interests, ORV users, and other public land users will bring to bear. The BLM has received harsh and vocal criticism from these groups during the RMP review process, and it is clear that they strongly object to any additional restrictions on public lands.

Legislative constraints also clearly prevent BLM from making land use changes very rapidly. Current users of BLM land have rights of appeal, and proposed land use changes of a certain magnitude (e.g., removing 5,000 acres of mining) require congressional approval.

As with most of the other HCPs, funding for habitat protection has been a major uncertainty. Estimates vary, but the cost of setting aside tortoise conservation areas and buying out current user rights should be less than $20 million. The development mitigation fees have already generated substantial funds, but additional monies will probably be needed. The HCP process has initiated discussion about alternative funding sources and a number of ideas have been discussed. From the beginning of the discussions the development community made it clear that while it did not mind contributing its fair share, it was not willing to be the sole source of funding for tortoise conservation.

The state has also been identified as a potential funding source. Some funds have already been made available for HCP through a state-wide bond referendum, passed in November of 1990. Referred to as "Question 5" the resource provided funds for a variety of parks and wildlife projects. Approximately $1 million of this $47.2 million has been tentatively earmarked for the desert tortoise.

One idea which has been discussed is the possibility of tapping into monies generated through federal land sales. BLM sells land in the region under several different legislative provisions. Most of these monies, however, go to funds for use outside of Clark County. Much of the land BLM sells is sold under the Burton-Santini Act, with proceeds designated for replenishment of the federal Land and Water Conservation Fund to cover the costs associated with land purchases around Lake Tahoe. In other cases, land sold to local governments sends monies to the Bureau of Reclamation. In addition there are a variety of land uses on BLM land which generate revenue (e.g., an estimated $1 million per year for gravel pits) with the resulting funds going to Washington. The feeling locally is that some of these revenues ought to be returned to the area for use in implementing the HCP.

The need to generate other local revenues has also been discussed. It has been argued by some in personal interviews with the author that the casino community should be required to contribute in some way. It is this sector, it is claimed, that's generating much of the growth pushing into habitat areas in the first place. Some have suggested that the HCP ought to be allocated a share or percentage of gambling receipts.

Section 7 consultations have remained an option for many projects in the valley, and tend to illustrate the limitations of project-by-project approaches. One Section 7 consultation involved a proposal to construct a new elementary school. Several tortoises were discovered on the site and at least one was kept for educational purposes as part of the required mitigation. Another Section 7 consultation involved a runway extension at McCarran Airport, specifically because of the potential effects on habitat of gravel excavation. Required mitigation included a $250 mitigation fee, and an agreement to develop and present an education display at the airport. (No-jeopardy opinions were reached in both of these cases). The mitigation provided in these and similar Section 7 consultations, as in many of the other cases in this book are of questionable merit. Nevertheless, it appears that many landowners have been searching for a federal connection in order to utilize the Section 7 mechanism, and there is currently a backlog of consultation requests.

Potential success

While it is still early in the desert tortoise habitat conservation process, much has already been accomplished. Under the conditions of the short-term 10(a) permit, conservation of tortoise habitat on BLM land has in fact occurred, and has actually exceeded the required thresholds. As of the fall of 1992, some 400,000 acres of tortoise habitat had been protected (primarily through the securing of private grazing rights)—the total acreage required to be conserved at the end of the short-term permit. Thus, the final short-term conservation levels have already been achieved, some two years ahead of schedule. Moreover, these lands have been protected within one of the two priority management areas (specifically in the southern preserve), as specified in the short-term permit. Even though the short-term thresholds have been reached, conservation efforts are continuing, focusing on acquiring grazing rights in the other priority habitat area, the northern preserve site. While acquisition of grazing rights there has been slower, it is probable that by the expiration of the short-term permit, protected land will well exceed existing protected acreage.

The long-term HCP has also progressed during the interim. A draft long-term plan has been released for comment and review. It mainly continues the philosophy behind conservation efforts under the short-term permit, supporting the protection and maintenance of two large preserves (the northern and southern sites), and an ultimate conservation acreage of 800,000 to 1 million.

While the acreage conserved so far is impressive, some concerns have been expressed about the level of protection afforded these lands. The primary conservation strategy has been to purchase grazing rights in these prime habitat areas. Other threats remain, however, including off-road vehicle use and mining, and some (especially in the environmental community) have questioned the stringency of the controls over these lands. There is a general concern that the BLM's Resource Management Plan will not assure enough long-term protection and management of preserve sites.

Also, while the southern preserve has been mostly secured, efforts at purchasing grazing rights in the northern preserve area have been slow. Grazing rights are acquired on a willing-seller basis, and few of the ranchers in the northern site apparently want to sell these rights. These individuals are apparently much more skeptical of the objectives of tortoise protection efforts. A more creative approach is being considered there, including the possibility of TNC purchasing grazing rights elsewhere (in non-tortoise habitat locations) as an added inducement for recalcitrant ranchers in the northern preserve area. These ranchers would be offered replacement grazing rights in these other locations, in addition to having their own existing rights purchased.

Take of tortoise and tortoise habitat in the valley has been small, largely as a result of a slow economy. As of September 1992, only 4,200 acres of habitat had been converted, and only 10 tortoises had been collected within the permit area (there were also approximately 300 tortoises collected from the exclusionary zone, and as a result of Section 7 consultations). Levels of take are quite low compared to the 3,500 tortoises and 18,000 acres of habitat allowed to be taken under the short-term permit. Low level of development is a result of the economic slowdown, as well as limitations on domestic water supply (until recently). The small numbers of tortoises found in the permit area have surprised some, but may reflect that many of these development sites had already been heavily graded.

Funding for the HCP effort has been steady, largely through the generation of mitigation fees. As of September 1992, $5.8 million had been collected through mitigation fees. Approximately $1.5 million of these funds have been expended, with $700,000 paying for the initial acquisition of grazing rights. The remainder has paid for consultant fees and other costs associated with the planning process.

An interesting question from the beginning is why it requires the efforts of the Clark County HCP to protect and conserve habitat on federal land. BLM must also satisfy the provisions of the Endangered Species Act. Yet, many of the activities allowed on BLM land are damaging to the tortoise's habitat and threaten tortoise take, including ranching and cattle grazing, recreational uses such as ORV activities, and mining. Several answers have been given to this question. First, the mission of BLM has not been historically one of conservation and protection, but rather one of making resource lands available to a variety of potential users. Even with the passage of mandates like ESA, the BLM mission remains one of providing for multiple uses. And, while BLM must adjust its management plans to protect listed species, there are certain obstacles, including financial, involved. Many current land users, such as ranchers, have vested rights which would require compensation if taken away. The HCP is seen as a viable way to generate the funds to allow this kind of compensation.

Much more fundamentally, there are basic political difficulties faced by BLM in effecting major new restrictions on the use of their lands. Such proposals, not surprisingly, bring tremendous opposition by ORV users, mining companies, and other traditional BLM constituents. It is not at all clear that BLM is either willing or able to act against the interests of its traditional constituents.

A related question is why, if in theory the BLM must protect tortoises on BLM land, it should be permissible for take to occur in the Las Vegas Valley in exchange for this additional BLM protection, i.e., in exchange for something that should, and legally must, occur anyway. It has struck some observers that what is being offered in exchange for take is a level of protection on BLM lands that should be expected anyway. BLM has in the past, for many of the reasons already mentioned, had little interest in wildlife management.

Conclusions

The Mojave Desert tortoise has experienced dramatic population reductions in recent years as a result of a number of pressures. These include an upper respiratory virus, raven predation, death from vandalism, and increasing loss of habitat due to urban development. Las Vegas Valley has been one of the fastest growing metropolitan regions in the country, and this urban expansion has translated directly into loss of habitat for the tortoise.

The Clark County HCP is different from other HCPs because the mitigation and habitat protection areas are primarily federally owned—specifically, by the BLM. This has added further complexity to the HCP process, and has sought to connect what is allowed to occur on private lands, i.e., land development, to mitigation and conservation on public lands. This has raised questions about the merits and integrity of the federal land planning process.

The Clark County experience is also the only one to craft a temporary or interim HCP to cover a three-year period during which the full-fledged HCP is prepared. Under this short-term HCP, allowable take of tortoise was explicitly tied to the establishment and protection of tortoise conservation areas. Conservation of tortoise habitat under the short-term permit has been impressive—with some 400,000 acres of priority habitat protected through the purchase of grazing rights. While concerns have been expressed that other land use threats, such as off-road vehicle use and mining, have not been as adequately addressed, this level of short-term conservation is commendable.

CHAPTER

ELEVEN

Preserving the Kit Fox
and Other Flora and Fauna
of the San Joaquin Valley:
The Bakersfield and Kern County
Habitat Conservation Plans

The Bakersfield, California area lies in the southern end of the San Joaquin Valley. Much of the original grassland habitat has been replaced by agriculture, oil and gas development, and increasing urban development. The San Joaquin Valley is habitat to a variety of plant and animal life, including the endearing San Joaquin kit fox. This chapter examines an HCP prepared for the metropolitan Bakersfield area and an HCP process currently under way by Kern County, where Bakersfield is located.

The Metro-Bakersfield HCP: Species of Concern

While the Metro-Bakersfield plan addresses a number of species, primary attention is given to the plight of the San Joaquin kit fox. The foxes are quite small, measuring about fifteen to twenty inches long and weighing about five pounds. They have large ears, long legs, and a black-tipped tail. The population of the fox was estimated at seven thousand in 1975, but its numbers are much lower today. While it is found in fourteen counties in central California more than 40% of the existing population is estimated to be in Kern County.[1]

Other species of concern in addition to the kit fox are also addressed in the plan and include: the blunt-nosed leopard lizard, the Tipton kangaroo rat, the giant kangaroo rat, the San Joaquin (Nelson's) antelope squirrel, the short-nosed kangaroo rat, and the San Joaquin pocket mouse (although the last two species are no longer found in the

Table 11.1. *Species of Concern in Metro-Bakersfield HCP*

Animals	Plants
State and federally listed endangered or threatened	State and federally listed endangered
• San Joaquin kit fox	• Bakersfield cactus (*Opuntia treleasei*)
• Blunt-nosed leopard lizard	• California jewelflower (*Caulanthus californicus*)[a]
• Tipton kangaroo rat	
• Giant kangaroo rat	Federally listed endangered or threatened
	• San Joaquin woolly-threads (*Lembertia congdonii*)
State listed threatened; federal candidate for listing	• Hoover's woolly-star (*Eriastrum hooveri*)
• San Joaquin (Nelson's) antelope squirrel	Federal candidate for listing
	• Cottony buckwheat (*Eriogonum gossypinum*)
State and/or federal candidate for listing	
• Short-nosed kangaroo rat[a]	
• San Joaquin pocket mouse[a]	

[a] Recent studies indicate that these species may no longer be found in or near the 2010 General Plan area.

Source: Thomas Reid Associates, 1990. *Metropolitan Bakersfield Habitat Conservation Plan and Environmental Impact Report,* 1990.

study area). Plant species addressed by the plan include: Bakersfield cactus (*Opuntia treleasei*), San Joaquin woolly-threads (*Lembertia congdonii*), Hoover's woolly-star (*Eriastrum hooveri*), cottony buckwheat (*Eriogonum gossypinum*), and the California jewelflower (*Caulanthus californicus*). (The last plant species is no longer found in the study area). Table 11.1 lists these species of concern. In the Metro-Bakersfield HCP, while all these species are addressed, the kit fox has received primary attention. From the beginning of the process it was assumed that by preserving and restoring habitat for the kit fox, many of these other species would also benefit.

The Emergence of Conflict and the HCP Response

The endangered species issue emerged in Bakersfield in 1986 when environmentalists charged that the proposed Sand Creek Golf Course along the Kern River would result in take of the federally listed San Joaquin kit fox. Local environmentalists were instrumental in bringing these potential threats to the attention of USFWS, which began to scrutinize development projects in the area more carefully.[2] As a result, plans for the Sand Creek Golf Course (on city-owned land) were scrapped and several development projects were placed on hold. The need to find a solution to the local species problem led to the city's initiating an HCP.

It was decided early on that the focus of analysis would be the area conforming with the city's 2010 general plan. This includes an area of 405 square miles. A steering committee was appointed to oversee the plan preparation, and a biological consultant was hired (Thomas Reid Associates). The steering committee consisted of developers, environmentalists, and city officials, and met from 1986 to 1990. The city and county both adopted an interim mitigation fee requirement for all development occurring in the metro area while the HCP was prepared (with the exception of urban infill areas which are clearly not habitat).

Like the Coachella Valley case, USFWS has tacitly approved this temporary arrangement even though it leads to some take of endangered species. The temporary mitigation fee is $680 per gross acre. Fees are assessed currently for any new development anywhere in the metro area except for:

1. Additions, remodels, or reconstructions totaling not more than 50 percent of the square footage of the pre-existing development.
2. Commercial farming or related farm accessory structures, oil field development, or development within the Downtown Redevelopment Agency project boundary.
3. Development of any parcel of less than one-half gross acre where at least half of the adjacent parcels have been developed prior to September 23, 1987.

A temporary moratorium in prime habitat areas was considered but discarded because these are the fastest growing areas in the county (the southwest and northeast quadrants). The USFWS has issued a strongly worded special notice to developers requiring that potential kit fox dens found on site be hand-excavated prior to development (allowing any kit foxes present to "escape unhindered"). Most developers in habitat areas appear to be adhering to this requirement.

The steering committee met for approximately three years, completing the final HCP in 1990. The city and county adopted the plan in 1991, but as yet, the plan has not been submitted to USFWS for approval. The delay is primarily the result of certain concerns expressed by the California Department of Fish and Game over several specific provisions in the proposed implementation agreement. (The city and county want to submit the plan for a state 2081 permit under the California Endangered Species Act, at the same time that they request a 10[a] permit.)

Provisions of Metro-Bakersfield HCP

A draft HCP was issued in September 1990. Its main strategy is a combination of habitat acquisition and restoration. More specifically, the plan calls for the acquisition and management of 500 to 1,000 acres in the northeast portion of the study area, primarily to preserve the Bakersfield cactus, the acquisition and management of 5,000 to 10,000 acres of land adjacent to the Kern County Water Bank project, and cooperative agreements for restoring and enhancing 3,000 to 12,000 acres of land within the Kern County Water Bank project. These proposed acquisition and restoration areas are presented in Figure 11.1.

Dovetailing the HCP's habitat acquisition-enhancement efforts with

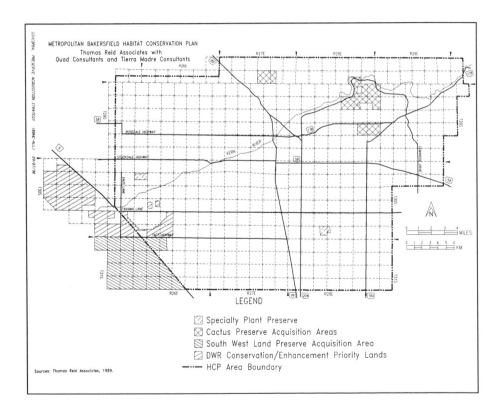

Figure 11.1. Local Preserve Acquisition Strategy, Bakersfield (Courtesy Thomas Reid Associates)

the water bank project is a major component of the Metro-Bakersfield strategy. Under this project, the State Department of Water Resources has recently purchased some twenty thousand acres of farmland southwest of the city to become the Kern County Water Bank. (These are areas to be used by the state to replenish regional groundwater supplies.) Past experience suggests that it is relatively easy to convert agricultural land back to grassland habitat suitable for the fox and other species of concern.

The proposed plan calls for the issuance of a 10(a) permit for a twenty-year period, which would allow take in areas outside of the primary floodplain of the Kern River (which is an important kit fox movement corridor connecting populations in the northeast foothills and valley to the southwest), and lands within the Kern Water Bank. The Section 10(a) permit will cover development activities, but will not cover oil extraction or agricultural activities in natural habitat lands.

The Bakersfield plan takes a "pay-as-you-go" approach, with yearly mitigation intended to stay ahead of take. The amount of mitigation called for in the draft plan is to be directly proportional to the amount of habitat destroyed. A distinction is made in the plan between open lands (agricultural lands) and natural lands (which provide superior habitat). Natural land is defined in the plan as "land generally in grazing and with original soil and topography in tact," while open land includes "natural land as well as agriculture and all other non-urban lands in the area."[3] Under the plan, each acre of natural land lost to development will be mitigated by the enhancement of three acres elsewhere. (For open lands the mitigation ratio is one-for-one.)

A contingency plan is also included in the HCP which would provide for acquisition of lands outside the study area should acquisition of local land not be possible (see Figure 11.2).

Funding to implement the plan will come primarily from development mitigation fees (proposed in the plan to be increased to $1,200–$1,250 per gross acre in 1990 dollars), and be supplemented as necessary with federal and state funds. The plan projects that at current metropolitan growth rates approximately $537,000 in fee monies will be generated each year. This will allow the purchase of 300 to 800 acres of land each year. The plan also proposes to secure additional federal and state monies to supplement this local funding. Responsibility for administration of the plan will be given to a specially created Implementation Trust. Representatives of the city and county will serve as the trustees, with USFWS and CDFG as "mandatory advisors." Each year, the Implementation Trust will monitor and report the cumulative status of take and enhancement to USFWS. This annual accounting will serve as the basis

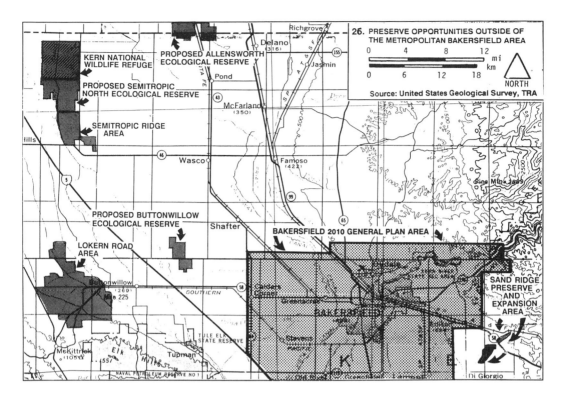

Figure 11.2. Preserve Opportunities outside the Metro-Bakersfield Area (Courtesy Thomas Reid Associates)

for determining HCP compliance. If the amount of acquisition and/or enhancement does not occur according to the mitigation ratios established (i.e., one acre of enhancement for each acre of open land lost, three acres for each acre of natural land lost, whichever is greater), USFWS will deem the jurisdictions not to be in compliance with the 10(a) permit.

The plan also allows for periodic amendments, including such things as adjustments to the fee assessment area, or charges to preserve boundaries. A proposed amendment must be agreed to by all parties to the implementing agreement.

Development has continued while the plan has been under preparation. The city and county have received tacit agreement from USFWS that as long as the $680 mitigation fee is collected, and progress is being made on the HCP, development may proceed. Actual take of species is still forbidden, however, and USFWS has required the city and county to distribute a special notice to developers that they may be held civilly and criminally liable if kit foxes are killed during construction.

Success of the Metro-Bakersfield Plan

Because the Metro-Bakersfield HCP has not yet been approved by USFWS, and not yet implemented, it is premature to reach conclusions about its success or effectiveness. The plan does reflect, however, a number of very positive approaches. First, while the plan focuses on the kit fox, it explicitly incorporates the needs of other species, including plant species. Moreover, the level of habitat conservation, including a combination of acquisition and habitat restoration, is fairly high and in the case of natural habitat must be replaced on a three-to-one basis. The plan is admirable in its intention of returning large blocks of agricultural land back to grassland habitat. There are also positive features of the preserve system, including attempts to protect the Kern River flood-plain, so that a movement corridor is ensured for kit foxes.

A number of important issues were raised during the process of preparing the Metro-Bakersfield plan, however. One contentious issue is whether it is appropriate to promote or allow the mitigation of local take through habitat acquisition/restoration in other areas, i.e., outside the Metro-Bakersfield study area. Provisions for this are included in the HCP on a contingency basis. Proponents of this view have argued that habitat can be more easily secured, and purchased at a much lower cost in areas outside the Bakersfield metropolitan area. Land within Bakersfield may go for as much as $15,000 per acre, as compared to $500 or $600 per acre in rural areas. On the other hand, groups such as the Sierra Club have argued that a large portion of the land protected/restored in exchange for local take ought to be within the study. The sentiment seems to be that the problem is here, so the solution should be here as well. Along with this seems to be the attitude that local monies are being used, therefore preserved habitat ought to be in or near the city where residents can see the results, and enjoy the open space and perhaps even the species. There has also been concern about what effect going outside the study area would have on the ability of the county to find appropriate mitigation sites of its own under its valley HCP.

On the other hand, some have expressed concern that in the long run, closer areas would be surrounded by development, thus weakening their long-term ecological viability. Moreover, it was observed that many members of the public view conserved habitat areas as recreational facilities—clearly, heavy public use of such areas, even for passive recreation, would be detrimental to the species.

The fact that the Metro-Bakersfield HCP process did not include agricultural and oil interests is also seen by some as a deficiency. There were attempts early on to involve these groups, but oil companies in particular felt that they could continue dealing with USFWS on a project-by-project basis. The relationship between agricultural operations and endangered species has always been uncertain and because most of these activities do not require a local permit, the city and county did not press to have agricultural representation in the process. Agricultural operations do have potential impacts on species of concern, especially the kit fox. Evidence suggests that if lands are left fallow for even a short period of time, kit foxes will move in and reestablish themselves. Thus, the reestablishment of agricultural operations could involve take. Moreover, even where agricultural operations are continuous, kit foxes are often able to live in peripheral areas, such as along canal banks. Certain types of agricultural operations could threaten these populations.

Another source of concern has been the development activity that has been occurring during preparation of the plan. As noted, developers are permitted to build in kit fox habitat as long as they hand-excavate potential kit fox dens. If foxes are actually found, they are in essence shooed away. While this may prevent the actual death of the species, such actions would seem to constitute harassment and fall within the definition of take. Impacts on kit fox populations from such gradual loss of habitat cannot be positive.

Other concerns about the process have been cited by participants. One difficulty cited by the chief city planner in charge of the HCP process in Bakersfield has been the unwillingness to purchase habitat areas in the interim while the plan was under preparation. Both the city and county had opportunities to secure lands—opportunities that may not be available after the plan is adopted—but chose not to. The steering committee had no authority or mechanism for acquiring such lands, and the local governments were generally hesitant to buy lands before the plan was completed. Participants have also expressed frustration over uncertainty about the minimum threshold of habitat conservation or mitigation to be included in the plan. USFWS staff, while participating throughout the process, was unable to provide much specific guidance on this.

The Metro-Bakersfield HCP has clearly benefited from having as its key species of concern a cute species, the kit fox. Most agree that this species has a high "cuddleability quotient" and people find it easier to understand the expenditure of large amounts of time and money to preserve it compared to a fringe-toed lizard or kangaroo rat. However, it has been observed that another factor has tended to work at cross purposes. As habitat for the kit fox has shrunk over time, the species has been increasingly forced to scavage and to move into areas where inter-action/conflict with humans is more frequent. As a consequence, kit foxes have become quite visible in certain areas of the city. This visibility has conveyed to some the impression that foxes are plentiful in number and therefore not endangered.

The Metro-Bakersfield HCP has received widespread political support in the community, especially from the development sector. According to the chief city planner, developers generally view the plan as an efficient and cost-effective approach to dealing with endangered species. They believe that participating in the HCP, and solving the problem by paying a modest fee, is far preferable to negotiating individual mitigation plans. There is a widespread belief that the HCP will serve to keep down the cost of new housing in the region, as a result of the lower costs associated with a community or regional HCP effort. Moreover, developers do not object to payment of mitigation fees because they are able to see where the funds actually go, and to recognize clear and tangible results from the plan. The environmental community strongly supports the plan because they see it to be capable of protecting larger blocks of habitat, and therefore much preferable to the more scattered and fragmented approach that would result from project-by-project mitigation.

Kern County HCP and Endangered Species Element

Kern County has initiated its own habitat conservation planning process, as part of its land use plan update. The HCP will specifically encompass the approximately thirty-one hundred–square–mile valley floor portion of Kern County. Federally listed species to be addressed in the HCP include the San Joaquin kit fox, the Buena Vista lake shrew, the giant kangaroo rat, and the blunt-nosed leopard lizard. In addition to the HCP, the county is also preparing an endangered species element of its general plan. The endangered species element will include other species that have not yet been federally listed, and will serve as the umbrella policy document for the more specific HCPs. In addition to the San Joaquin kit fox and the blunt-nosed leopard lizard, other species of concern in the county include the San Joaquin antelope squirrel, the short-nosed kangaroo rat, the Tipton kangaroo rat, and the American badger, and some endangered plant species.

For approximately four years, the county has convened a threatened and endangered species work group, consisting of representatives from state and federal resource agencies, private conservation groups, private land developers, the oil and gas industry, and agriculture. This group oversees the preparation of the valley floor HCP and the endangered species element, and generally advises the county on endangered species issues. The objectives of the Kern County program are "(1) to develop a cooperative program among public agencies with permit authority over threatened and endangered species of concern which will ensure that activities or private parties comply with applicable laws and regulations concerning species of concern in Kern County and; (2) assure the long-term protection of species of concern while allowing for the continued economic growth of Kern County."[4] A memorandum of understanding has been entered into between USFWS, the Bureau of Land Management, California Department of Fish and Game, California Energy Commission, California Department of Conservation (Division of Oil and Gas), and Kern County. A consulting firm has been hired to prepare the HCP, the endangered species element, implementing agreements, and related environmental documentation (e.g., the necessary environmental impact reports). A large portion of the money to fund the HCP and endangered species element ($350,000) has been obtained from a grant from the State Division of Oil and Gas.

A draft of the Endangered Species Element of the Kern County General Plan has been prepared. The element establishes goals and policies concerning endangered species and identifies general strategies for mitigating impacts on these species. It presents a comprehensive inventory of species of concern found in the county and the locations of their primary habitat areas. Consistent with the county general plan, the endangered species element recognizes three distinct planning regions, each representing different ecological conditions: the valley floor, the foothill and mountain region, and the desert region. Species of concern in the valley floor region include the San Joaquin kit fox, the blunt-nosed leopard lizard, the giant kangaroo rat, the Tipton kangaroo rat, and the San Joaquin antelope squirrel. Species of concern in the foothill and mountain region include the Kern Canyon slender salamander, the Tehachapi slender salamander, the Willow Flycatcher, and the Yellow-billed Cuckoo. Species of concern in the desert region include the desert tortoise and the Mohave ground squirrel.

The endangered species element provides goals, policies, and discussions of implementation measures. The element states that the county will use, wherever possible, multi-species, habitat-based conservation programs, and will seek the cooperative efforts of local, state, and federal agencies, along with private organizations. Several of the more detailed policies address planning and environmental review. The element establishes policies that the county will, among other things, establish "thresholds of significance" to be used in CEQA review, provide guidelines on the need, timing, and scope of biota reports, assist project proponents with early identification of endangered species conflicts, develop mitigation guidelines for discretionary projects, and encourage acquisition of mitigation habitat near existing preserves. The endangered species element, once adopted, will provide guidance for all future county actions and activities regarding endangered species. Once adopted, it will carry the weight of the law, and other provisions of the plan will be modified for consistency. The general plan land use element, for example, will be reviewed and modified to be consistent with protection of species.

The element will be largely implemented through more detailed habitat conservation plans. Eventually the county intends to prepare an HCP for each of these regions, or appropriate subregions. It has already embarked on preparation of the valley floor HCP (as well as participating in the Metro-Bakersfield HCP). To date, the consultant has undertaken a series of background studies and has prepared detailed maps indicating habitat areas, and areas where future protection and acquisition efforts ought to be focused. All lands in the study area have been categorized according to their overall habitat quality. Land in the study area has been divided into three classes: 1) highly sensitive, natural habitat areas; 2) moderate habitat areas; and 3) areas used intensively for agriculture. Analysis of the various threats to species of concern has been undertaken, and the extent of future incompatibility between species and various land uses.

The planning process and endangered species work group have focused much of their energy on considering a number of alternative mitigation strategies for activities occurring in the study area. Although a number of possible strategies have been identified, there has yet been no consensus on which should be adopted. These alternative strategies have generally assumed that required mitigation should vary according to the habitat class with the most stringent mitigation required in the sensitive/natural habitat areas. The use of mitigation ratios has received considerable attention and it is likely that whatever mitigation alternative is adopted will apply them in some form, again depending on the habitat class involved. In considering alternative mitigation strategies much of the debate has focused on how to treat the sensitive/natural habitat areas, with resource agencies, on the one hand, arguing for high mitigation ratios and very stringent mitigation standards, and oil industry representatives, on the other hand, supporting much weaker mitigation requirements. In these natural habitat areas the USFWS has been arguing for a two-pronged mitigation ratio which would require both permanent acquisition or replacement at the rate of three acres for every acre destroyed, as well as temporarily protecting habitat (i.e., securing options to buy) at a ratio of sixteen to one. Representatives of the oil industry see this combined mitigation ratio of nineteen to one as excessive and unacceptable.

Potential success

Substantial progress has already been made in habitat conservation planning in Kern County. An endangered species element of the general plan, though not yet officially adopted, has been completed and holds the potential for guiding a variety of future county decisions in ways which protect biodiversity. Incorporating endangered species and biodiversity into general comprehensive planning represents an extremely promising strategy and a model for other local governments. It is too early, of course, to tell whether the plan element will have any real effect on habitat conservation.

The endangered species element also provides an important framework in Kern County for the more detailed HCPs to follow. Substantial progress has already been made on the Valley Floor HCP including habitat mapping and classification, and extensive discussions of a number of alternative mitigation approaches. According to county officials, oil and gas companies, agricultural interests, and other key actors continue to support the process and see the advantages of staying at the bargaining table. County officials continue to believe that these different factions will reach agreement on key aspects of the plan, including the mitigation standards for different habitat types. While completion of the plan has taken longer than expected, county staff believe agreement on the mitigation provisions can be reached by March 1993, with plan completion (including all necessary environmental documentation) occurring by the end of 1993.

Conclusions

The Metro-Bakersfield HCP is commendable for its attempt to address the habitat needs of multiple species. It is also impressive in its use of a mitigation ratio that should, in the long term, result in a net increase in habitat. The Bakersfield effort, however, effectively illustrates the dilemma of whether to use limited financial resources to protect local habitat, or whether it is more logical to protect species habitat at some distance away from urbanizing areas (e.g., at lower costs, adding onto existing protected areas). While this issue has not been completely resolved in Bakersfield, the HCP does represent a practical compromise between these two perspectives.

The efforts at habitat conservation planning by Kern County are equally impressive. The preparation of an endangered species element of its general plan, and the notion of incorporating species conservation into the overall county planning function, make a great deal of sense and should be emulated elsewhere.

TWELVE

The Promise of Regional, Multi-species Approaches: The Balcones Canyonlands Conservation Plan

Many HCPs have a relatively narrow biological or geographical focus on a single species or a limited range of one or more species. More recent HCPs appear to acknowledge the great long-term biological and economic benefits of a multi-species approach and regional geographical focus. One of the more ambitious of the multi-species plans is the Balcones Canyonlands Conservation Plan (BCCP) prepared for the Austin, Texas region.

The Balcones Canyonlands Conservation Plan: Background and Context

The Balcones Canyonlands is a region located in the hill country and Edwards Plateau to the west and northwest of Austin, Texas. Its steep canyons, ridgetops, and plateaus are home to two species of endangered migratory songbirds—the Black-capped Vireo, and the Golden-cheeked Warbler. The limestone geology of the area has resulted in a series of subterranean caves, sinkholes, and fissures which are home to a diversity of unique and rare invertebrates. Six cave-adapted invertebrates have been federally listed. Two federally listed species of plants are also found in the area and are also addressed by the plan. The BCCP addresses the habitat needs of ten federally listed species.

The Black-capped Vireo (*Vireo antricapillus*) is a small migratory songbird which nests in Texas, Oklahoma, and northern Mexico during the summer months and winters in the highlands of southwestern Mexico. It was listed as an endangered species under the federal Endangered Species Act in November of 1987. The vireo relies on an "edge" form of habitat, consisting of mid-successional clumps of shrubs and trees, including juniper, shin oaks, and sumacs, in otherwise grassy open areas. Threats to the vireo include the loss of this habitat to development, the impacts of overbrowsing by sheep and goats (making vireo nests more vulnerable to predators), the proliferation of domestic cats, and nest parasitism by the Brown-headed Cowbird. The cowbirds lay their eggs in vireo nests and the cowbird chicks, which are larger and grow faster, displace vireo chicks. Together these factors have taken a toll on the vireo population, and nesting pairs seen in the Austin area have declined substantially. Only twenty-eight nesting pairs were counted in the Austin area in the 1990 breeding season.

Although also a migratory songbird, the habitat needs of the Golden-cheeked Warbler (*Dendroica chrysoparia*) are quite different. Emergency listed as an endangered species in May 1990 (and permanently listed in December), the warbler relies on mature dense canopy forest, consisting of juniper and mixed oak woodlands on steep canyons. The warbler's nesting range is in Texas, and it winters in Mexico, Guatemala, and Honduras. It has been estimated that the number of breeding pairs of warbler in the area is eleven hundred to twenty-three hundred—much higher than the vireo, but also on the decline. The threats to the warbler are similar to those for the vireo and include cowbird parasitism and habitat loss. It has been estimated that the area has been losing warbler habitat at a rate of 6% per year. Considerable amounts of land clearance for development projects and the loss of closed canopy forests prompted the USFWS to undertake emergency listing of the species.

Perhaps the most interesting biological aspect of the Balcones Canyonlands is its subterranean habitats. The Edwards Plateau, consisting primarily of limestone, is underlaid with an intricate system of caves, fissures, and sinkholes. The gradual erosion caused by streams and rivers has caused isolation and evolution of unique forms of fauna. Six cave-adapted invertebrates have been federally listed as endangered (in September of 1988) and are considered in the plan. Those include the Tooth Cave pseudoscorpion (*Microcreagis texana*), the Tooth Cave spider (*Neoleptoneta myopica*), the Tooth Cave ground beetle (*Rhadine persephone*), the Kretschmarr Cave mold beetle (*Texamaurops reddelli*), the Bee Creek Cave harvestman (*Texalla reddelli*), and the Bone Cave harvestman (*Texella* n. sp.). In addition, recent studies have identified some thirty such invertebrates which have yet to receive scientific names and to be fully characterized. The diversity and uniqueness of this habitat has led some to describe the area as a subterranean archipelago. The ecology of these underground environments is not well understood, but threats in recent years have included the paving over of cave openings, the introduction of fireants, and the generation of non-point run-off from development and other land use changes.

The BCCP also addresses several species of plants, including the canyon mock-orange (*Philadelphus ernestii*) and the bracted twistflower (*streptanthus bracteatus*).

Several species of rare salamanders are also found in the BCCP study area, and are also addressed to some degree in the plan. Specifically, the central Texas *Eurycea* salamanders inhabit springs along the Balcones Escampment, including areas in the BCCP study area. Three species have been identified, including the Barton Spring salamander, the Jollyville Plateau salamander, and the Texas salamander. Primary threats to these species are changes to quality and quantity of groundwater that may result from development (e.g., in recharge zones). Non-point source run-off from construction sites and urban development may also damage the sensitive spring environments.

The Conflicts Emerge

As noted, this biologically rich habitat of the Balcones Canyonlands has come under tremendous development pressure in recent years. Things came to a head in 1988 when a number of public and private projects threatening Black-capped Vireo habitat were halted (the other species had not yet been listed). In particular, several public road projects, and a large forty-five hundred–unit housing project, known as the Steiner Ranch, were stopped because they would have affected vireo habitat. Public awareness about the problem of habitat loss in the Austin area was facilitated by the actions of the environmental group Earth First! which staged a variety of public protests receiving national as well as local attention. Among other things, members of the group chained themselves to bulldozers in vireo habitat and occupied a series of karst caves threatened by a proposed shopping mall. Almost all observers in Austin agree that Earth First! has played a remarkable role in monitoring habitat loss and in alerting USFWS to these activities, as well as heightening overall public concern about the issues.

Concerns about the endangered species problem led to the appointment by the city of Austin of an Endangered Species Task Force and the preparation of an endangered species ordinance. Among other things, the ordinance would have prohibited development in occupied habitat areas without a conservation plan, mandated a three hundred-foot buffer around occupied habitat areas, and provided density bonuses for setting aside land in occupied habitat or buffer areas. These restrictions would apply to land within the city's extra-territorial jurisdiction, in a way similar to its comprehensive watersheds ordinance. The land and development community in Austin, unhappy with the prospect of yet another impediment to development, protested the ordinance to state legislators. The result was Senate Bill 1461, which essentially prevented the city from the application of these types of restrictions outside its corporate boundaries, thus largely gutting its new ordinance.

The development of a regional habitat conservation plan for the Austin area was formally initiated in 1988 through a joint proposal of the Texas Nature Conservancy and Austin's Department of Environmental Protection (now called the Environmental and Conservation Services Department). An executive committee was formed to oversee the preparation of the plan and was chaired by the director of the Texas Nature Conservancy. The committee includes representatives of the development community (attorneys for local developers) and representatives of the environmental community (the Audubon Society and Sierra Club). Several local governments are also represented on the committee, as are relevant state agencies (e.g., Texas Parks and Wildlife Department, the Texas General Land Office). In addition to the executive committee, a Biological Advisory Team (BAT) was also appointed and consists of some twenty leading scientists and biologists from the area (e.g., from the University of Texas, and the city of Austin). Consultants were hired to collect land use and other necessary data, and to prepare the plan itself.

The process of biological assessment began with the BAT reviewing a list of endangered and threatened species identified by one or more public and private conservation groups (USFWS, Texas Parks and Wildlife Department, and the Texas Natural Heritage Program) as a species of concern. Species were targeted for inclusion in the plan based on whether there was a significant population in the area, the extent of the threat to the species, and the extent to which the HCP would be effective at protecting or conserving the species.[1] A series of biological background studies were conducted, including specific studies of the biology and habitat requirements of the migratory songbirds, botanical studies, and studies of the underground cave ecosystems. The overall findings of the BAT are contained in a comprehensive biological assessment issued in January 1990. The assessment contains specific recommendations about the necessary size and characteristics of habitat preserves. Specifically, the BAT recommended that protection of large blocks of contiguous habitat be undertaken. Minimum necessary preserve acreage is also estimated for each species of concern. For the Golden-cheeked Warbler the BAT recommends establishing two separate preserves, each at least 12,000 acres in size (to support 500 to 1,000 breeding pairs). For the Black-capped Vireo the BAT recommends that a minimum of 123,500 acres of contiguous habitat be protected (again to support 500 to 1,000 breeding pairs). For the karst habitat the BAT recommends protection of all known caves, but stresses that smaller, interconnected cavities may also prove important. A series of habitat maps has been generated by the planning consultant and BAT, based in part on remote sensing (for example, see Figures 12.1 and 12.2). Especially useful has been the ability of the consultant to overlay the different habitat areas and to identify areas and locations where the needs of multiple species can be satisfied. The ability to overlay these types of data was further assisted by the development of a regional geographical information system (GIS). The development of this system was coordinated by the Texas Natural Resources Information System (TNRIS), a unit of the Texas Water Development Board.

Substantial cost has been incurred in preparing the plan and necessary background biological work. Approximately $200,000 was needed to conduct the background biological studies, and approximately $400,000 to pay for the preparation of the plan. An additional $160,000 was necessary to prepare the environmental impact statement and associated environmental documentation. Funding for the planning process and necessary background studies has come from a number of sources. Funding was initiated by TNC in the form of a $20,000 pledge. Other participants in the process have offered similar contributions. Grants of $100,000 have been made by both the city of Austin and Travis County, while the Texas Parks and Wildlife Department, the lower Colorado River Authority, and The University of Texas have each contributed $20,000 to the process. Developers have also contributed funds, with the largest contribution at $25,000.

Main Components of the Plan

Much of the work of the consultants, in collaboration with the executive committee, has been directed towards developing a viable preserve design. The development of the preserve concepts began with an analysis of different macro-sites in the study area. Early on the study area was divided into a series of macro-sites, with an analysis of the relative abundance and quality of species habitat located in each. From the beginning there was an assumption that land to be acquired or set aside should also add to or build upon land already protected in a public park or under the city's Comprehensive Watersheds Ordinance. Thus, in determining a preserve design for the region a process of overlaying these different layers of information was used. There were already large blocks

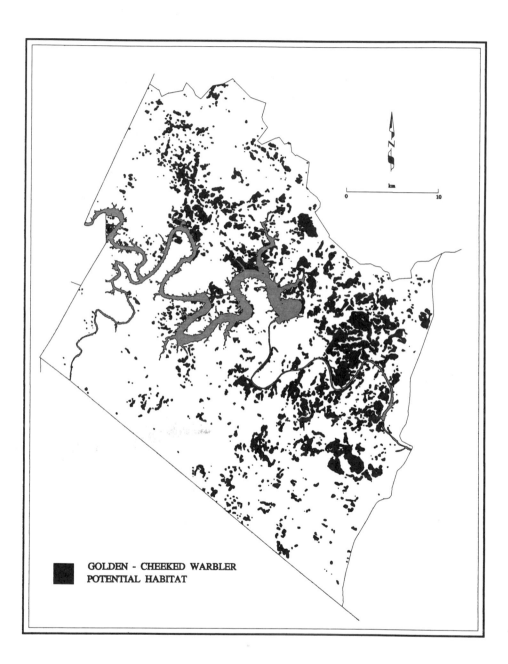

Figure 12.1. Potential Habitat for the Golden-cheeked Warbler in the Balcones Canyonlands Conservation Area (Courtesy Butler/EH & A Team, City of Austin Environmental and Conservation Services, *Balcones Canyonlands Conservation Plan*, Preapplication Draft, Austin, 1992)

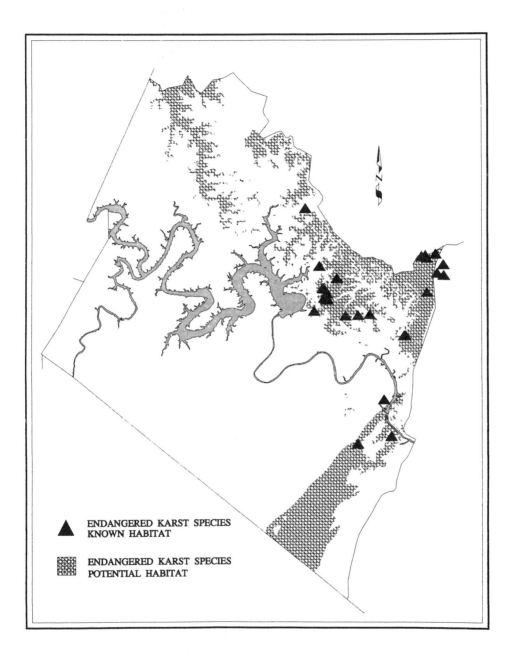

Figure 12.2. Known and Potential Habitat for Endangered Karst Species in the Balcones Canyonlands Conservation Area (Courtesy Butler/EH & A Team, City of Austin Environmental and Conservation Services, *Balcones Canyonlands Conservation Plan*, Preapplication Draft, Austin, 1992)

of public land protected; for instance, the city's Emma Long Park contains a large amount of potential warbler habitat. As well, under the city's Comprehensive Watersheds Ordinance, certain areas are classified as off-limits, also containing substantial habitat. Again, this process was greatly facilitated through the development of the regional GIS.

From this analysis and the recommendations of BAT, the plan identifies priority protection areas. The plan proposes to establish a preserve system containing a minimum of 29,160 acres of 35,338 acres identified as suitable for acquisition.[2] The preserve system proposed would include six primary preserve units, ranging in size from 400 acres to more than 9,000 acres (see Figure 12.3.) The proposed system generally comprises "a broad interrupted band which extends from west Austin northwestward towards the proposed National Wildlife Refuge" (p. 8-1). As Figure 12.3 illustrates, the system seeks to build upon existing patterns of public ownership, and accepts certain gaps because of existing development centers and the economic impracticability of securing certain lands. The preserve system also identifies certain core preserve units which are deemed essential to the preserve design (those in the Cypress Creek, Bull Creek, and North Lake Austin macro-sites especially).

Approximately 7,526 acres of this is already in public ownership or otherwise protected (in city and county parks and preserves, private preserves, and Lower Colorado River Authority [LCRA] property). In addition, as a result of the BCCP process, some 9,633 acres of habitat has already been secured (through a below-market value sale). This leaves, then, an additional 12,000 acres of habitat that would need to be acquired to complete the proposed preserve system.

Another important component of the regional preserve system is the newly created Balcones Canyonlands National Wildlife Refuge (the Post Oak Ridge site). Containing extensive warbler habitat, this eventual 41,000-acre site refuge was largely an outgrowth of early BCCP efforts. The Post Oak Ridge site was contained in early versions of the plan. Congress has already appropriated extensive funding for the refuge (from the Federal Land and Water Conservation Fund) and the BCCP process served as an important catalyst in establishing this refuge. Much of the acquisition for the refuge has already occurred (through the early assistance of the Texas Nature Conservancy). When the refuge habitat acreage is taken into account the Austin initiative is even more impressive, ultimately protecting more than 70,000 acres of habitat.

The plan envisions that private preserve lands will be acquired primarily through voluntary sale. This is the major reason why a larger preserve area is delineated than is planned for protection. Planned acquisition is to be achieved within three years of the issuance of a 10(a)

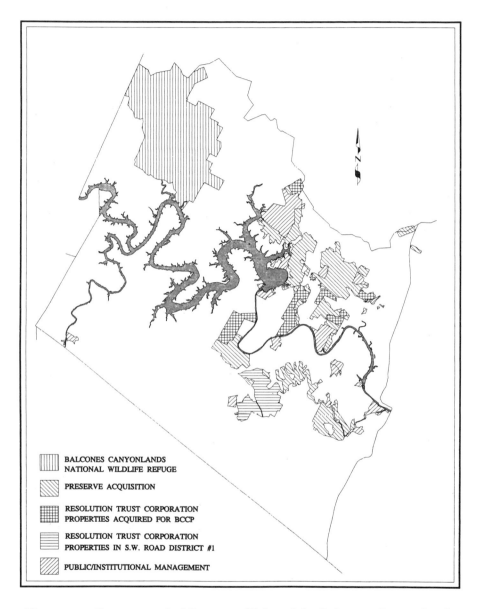

BALCONES CANYONLANDS
NATIONAL WILDLIFE REFUGE

PRESERVE ACQUISITION

RESOLUTION TRUST CORPORATION
PROPERTIES ACQUIRED FOR BCCP

RESOLUTION TRUST CORPORATION
PROPERTIES IN S.W. ROAD DISTRICT #1

PUBLIC/INSTITUTIONAL MANAGEMENT

Figure 12.3. Recommended Preserve Units of the Balcones Canyonlands Conservation Plan (Courtesy Butler/EH & A Team, City of Austin Environmental and Conservation Services, *Balcones Canyonlands Conservation Plan*, Preapplication Draft, Austin, 1992)

permit. The plan envisions the use of both fee-simple and less-than-fee simple acquisition. It states that at a minimum, 2,000 of the 12,000 acres to be acquired will be through conservation easements or other less-than-fee simple mechanisms. The plan designates the Texas Nature Conservancy as the land acquisition agent for the plan. To protect area designated for preserve acquisition from development or habitat destruction, the plan imposes certain restrictions within these areas. Specifically, development could occur in these areas only under one of three conditions: (1) through a development agreement (with the BCCP management committee and relevant local government); (2) through a finding by USFWS that the action is not a take and that the development does not impair the ability to acquire habitat in size and configuration necessary to meet design requirements for that particular macro-site; or (3) through an individual Section 10(a) permit.

The plan also suggests that incentives should be provided to private landowners to protect as much habitat as possible on lands in or adjacent to preserve sites. Incentives suggested include deductions or waivers from mitigation fees and the use of development intensity transfers.

The plan operator and permit holder for the 10(a) permit will be a specially created BCCP Management Committee. The committee will oversee implementation of the plan, and will consist of representatives of local government (Travis County, city of Austin, LCRA), as well as the Texas Parks and Wildlife Commission. A USFWS representative will also serve in an *ex officio* capacity. The creation and duties of the management committee, and the duties and responsibilities of the other plan participants, are delineated in a more detailed interlocal agreement.

A major and important element of the HCP is its funding program. The plan estimates that land acquisition will cost approximately $56 million. A number of funding options have been considered during this process. Much of the initial funding for the plan would be generated through a public bond referendum. The cost of issuing bonds (debt interest, transaction costs) is estimated at around $35 million (depending on financing assumptions). Preserve management and administrative costs have been estimated at about $82 million.

While the funding program is still evolving, ultimately it envisions a mixture of local revenues, including developer impact fees, a building fee surcharge, local property tax revenues, a percentage fee applied to public capital improvements projects started in the conservation area, a utility surcharge, user charges (visitation, hunting), and grants and donations, among others. The plan explicitly states its philosophy of ensuring an equitable distribution of the costs of habitat protection. Various entities will have responsibilities for collecting these funds, and they will be pooled in a Habitat Mitigation Trust Fund.

Much of the discussion in the final months of the plan has centered on the use of a $1,500-per-acre mitigation fee, and a surcharge on city and county building fees, from which much of the plan's funding would be derived. The building fee surcharge would apply to development activities (e.g., building, remodeling . . .) in most areas of the city and county, not simply for projects in the habitat planning area. This has caused some critics to charge that these recent funding schemes shift too much of the burden of the plan away from those developers who will benefit the most from a 10(a) permit.

As mentioned, one way in which the BCCP team has sought to acquire habitat is through below-market sales from the Resolution Trust Corporation (the agency created in response to failed savings and loans). The RTC, as well as the FDIC, owns a considerable amount of acreage in the Austin area, much of it involving species habitat. Members of the BCCP team have for some time sought to secure the donation or below-market sale of these lands, arguing that RTC, as a federal agency, has clear responsibilities to protect listed species under ESA. Furthermore, they have been arguing that RTC's land holdings in the region will generally be more valuable and saleable if a Section 10(a) permit is obtained and that for these reasons RTC should be willing to take a "loss-leader." Recently, a deal with RTC has been struck, in which RTC will be selling nearly 10,000 acres at relatively low prices.

The plan includes provisions to ensure that habitat protection occurs rapidly and exceeds take. Specifically, the plan requires a mitigation-take ratio of five-to-one, in the first few years (for warbler and vireo habitat). Special additional restrictions are placed on conversion of vireo habitat, because so little of it exists in the BCCP conservation area. Specifically no loss of occupied vireo habitat will be permitted until certain minimum protection and management measures have been implemented (e.g., until 50 percent of the minimum preserve area in certain macro-sites is secured).

Land in the habitat preserve system will be owned and managed by a number of different entities. The BCCP originally envisioned the creation of a Balcones Canyonlands Conservation Authority with overall responsibility for implementing the plan.[3] The authority would own and manage any new habitat preserve areas acquired through local funds, and would coordinate management of all the preserve units in the BCCP preserve system. Other landowners will include: USFWS, U.S. Army Corps of Engineers (Lake Georgetown and surrounding riparian areas),

Texas Parks and Wildlife Department, Lower Colorado River Authority, The University of Texas, city and county governments, and several non-profit organizations (e.g., Travis Audubon, Wild Basin Wilderness Board of Trustees). Recent thinking is that the Texas Parks and Wildlife Department will act as the primary preserve manager (through a management services agreement with the management committee).

The plan also provides for long-term preserve management and habitat restoration (e.g., oak wilt control, habitat revegetation, fire ant control, cowbird control, fire ant management, etc.). It is expected, however, that a detailed management plan will be prepared for each preserve unit (originally to be submitted for review and approval to the Balcones Canyonlands Conservation Authority). The BCCP also incorporates an extensive research and monitoring program. Both short-term and long-term research needs are identified.

Short-term research needs identified in the plan include:
- Black-capped Vireo modeling to investigate a more efficient means of evaluating reproductive success rather than pair success, and to help direct preserve acquisition and management.
- Continuation of the western Travis County Black-capped Vireo monitoring and banding.
- Continuation of Brown-headed Cowbird trapping.
- Golden-cheeked Warbler census in the Bull Creek area.
- Evaluation and synthesis of available Golden-cheeked Warbler data.
- Fire ant control study in karst features and first stage of management.
- Study of nutrient input to karst features.
- Rangewide mapping of Golden-cheeked Warbler habitat using recent satellite imagery.
- Research to identify threats to the *Eurycea* salamander and to develop protection strategies.

Long-term research needs identified in the plan include:
- Analysis of Black-capped Vireo habitat characteristics and development of vireo habitat management strategies.
- Continued Black-capped Vireo nest monitoring and banding in conjunction with observations to acquire dispersal data.
- Theoretical modeling of vireo disposal data to better determine vireo dispersal patterns and refine existing population models.
- Vireo habitat inventory and sampling on the Lampasas Cut Plain (i.e., Post Oak Ridge to Fort Hood) and the eastern edge of the Balcones Fault (i.e., Austin to San Antonio).

- Golden-cheeked Warbler study on the characteristics of pair bonding in fragmented versus unfragmented habitat areas.
- Golden-cheeked Warbler censusing/inventory, including density estimates for varying patch sizes.
- Investigation of effects of urbanization on Golden-cheeked Warbler densities and reproductive success.
- Study of Golden-cheeked Warbler fecundity, survival, and dispersal.
- Investigation and implementation methods to reduce impact of cowbird parasitism on the Golden-cheeked Warbler and the Black-capped Vireo throughout the conservation area.
- Research of extent of fire ant infestation of karst habitat and development and implementation control strategies.
- Continued biogeographic survey of BCCP karst areas.
- Continued taxanomic evaluation of karst invertebrates.
- Geologic and hydrogeologic studies of karst areas identified for protection.
- Continued baseline karst ecology studies to describe the microclimate, organic input, and biotic components of, and seasonal variation in, cave systems supporting endangered cave invertebrates.
- *Streptanthus bracteatus* demographic and bank study.
- Study of pollinator biology of *Streptanthus bracteatus* and *Philadelphus emestii.*
- Continued surveys of potential plant habitat in or near proposed preserves and conservation easements.
- Study of negative factors affecting Black-capped Vireo and Golden-cheeked Warbler populations in wintering habitat.

Once approved by USFWS the 10(a) incidental take permit would be in effect for a thirty-year period, and plan progress would be evaluated at least every five years. The plan remains politically contentious and has not yet made it through all steps in the local approval process. Environmental impact documentation must also be prepared and the plan submitted and approved by USFWS. Implementation of the plan, moreover, will require certain enabling legislation from the state legislature (several bills are currently before them, for example authorizing the building fee surcharge).

Potential for Success

Preparation of the BCCP represents a tenuous balancing of development and environmental interests, and a coalition that may or may not hold up in the months ahead. Those in the development community, while recognizing the need for an HCP, have consistently expressed concerns about the amount of habitat to be protected and the cost involved. In interviews with representatives of the development community, frustration was frequently expressed about the overly ambitious and unrealistic proposals being made. On the other hand, some members of the environmental community have expressed concerns about the adequacy of the plan and its ability to ensure the preservation of the species. Earth First! in particular, while more open-minded about the BCCP than it typically has been in other parts of the country, has maintained a level of skepticism from the beginning. In the words of one leader, "We'll see what they come up with before we decide." They have threatened to undertake legal action under ESA if the plan does not protect enough habitat. Interestingly, the Austin environmental community appears somewhat split on the issue of adequacy—while groups like Earth First! are questioning the current plan, other groups like the Austin chapter of the Sierra Club appear to view the proposal more favorably and support it as a practical compromise.

More serious concerns expressed by some in the environmental community relate to the perceived fragmented nature of the preserve system. This is especially a concern with respect to the warbler. Recent evidence suggests that Blue Jay proliferation has a negative effect on warblers, and that fragmented preserves which allow interspersed development patterns may allow the expansion of Blue Jay populations, in turn leading to severe impacts on warbler populations. A second major concern expressed relates to the percentage of the costs of the plan that are paid for by the development community. Some environmentalists claim an agreement was made that developers would pay for at least 50 percent of the cost of acquisition and management (for areas outside of the Post Oak Ridge site). It was believed that the plan succumbed to the interests of the development community and that the actual percentage of the costs that will be covered by this group will be much smaller.

The development community has expressed a number of concerns, in addition to the size of the habitat preserves and the costs of protection. One source of concern expressed by several developers is the failure of the BCCP to consider habitat conservation needs on a rangewide basis. They find it unfair to require the Austin community to carry the burden of saving species, such as the vireo, that also inhabit other jurisdictions in the hill county.

Others have expressed concern about the potential side effects of the plan, especially its potential impacts on future growth and tax base. As

Gordon Gorychka, president of the Austin Board of Realtors, maintains, "It is our concern that any solution, with or without an approved plan, protect endangered species, permit economic and tax base development, and be affordable to local taxpayers."[4] There is special concern by the real estate and development communities that new development will be forced to unfairly shoulder the lion's share of the costs of the plan, in the form of new development fees. In the words of Gorychka, "If local financial participation is required, it should be fairly shared with as broad a base as possible, such as every resident of the county or a multi-county, regional tax base."[5] The plan seems to strike a fair balance in spreading these costs.

In an effort to estimate the potential economic costs and impacts of the BCCP, the Bureau of Business Research at The University of Texas was commissioned to prepare an Economic Impact Study. The purpose of this study was to "evaluate the comparative effects on Austin's and Travis County's future economic development, property values, and government tax revenue of two approaches to complying with the habitat provisions of the ESA."[6] One option considered was simply leaving ESA compliance to individual property owners, while the other option evaluated was the BCCP. The study looked at impacts over a twenty-year period and concluded that the average cost of individual compliance (without the BCCP) by landowners and public agencies is $9,000 per acre. If the BCCP is not adopted, it is estimated that 8,763 to 39,050 jobs will be lost (depending on the extent of developable habitat), and the BCCP is found to generate additional property tax revenue of $244 million to $439 million (in 1992 dollars). Overall, total compliance expenditures without the BCCP are found to be much greater than the total cost of the BCCP. The study concludes that the total net benefit of the BCCP will range from $291 million to $756 million, and is " . . . from an economic perspective . . . the preferred compliance approach when compared to the alternative of individual compliance."[7]

From the very beginning some in the Austin community have threatened to seek changes in ESA. The Texas Farm Bureau has been particularly vocal in its criticism of ESA and its belief that the law must be softened. Members of the Farm Bureau have a larger agenda, focused on substantially modifying ESA when it comes before Congress for reauthorization. Dan Byfield, the Farm Bureau's associate director for state affairs in Austin, describes their position towards the BCCP:

The local plan is onerous. Too many acres are involved and the city needs to realize that the property will be taken out of the tax base . . . . It's a no-development, no-growth, land use plan . . . . The law was never meant to preserve every species in the world or to stop development . . . .[8]

Some private landowners have sought to go through their own individual Section 10(a) or Section 7 reviews. The USFWS has been demanding stringent mitigation requirements and has, as a result, tended to discourage individual development projects. Perhaps the most notable case of an individual project review is the recent Section 7 consultation undertaken for the proposed expansion of the 3M complex on RR 2222. Under their proposed plan, 3M intends to destroy approximately 11 acres of Golden-cheeked Warbler habitat. What has allowed them to utilize the Section 7 consultation provisions is the fact that they are seeking an amendment to their air pollution permit, required under the federal Clean Air Act (3M operates its own cogeneration plant on-site). The mitigation package offered by 3M is fairly impressive and to many has set a high standard for other projects and developments considering private solutions. Among other things, 3M has agreed to acquire 215 acres of warbler habitat (located in a desired preserved site), establish a $50,000 trust fund to manage the site, offer a cash donation of $15,000 to the BCCP, conduct a three-year Golden-cheeked Warbler census, undertake a three-year cowbird trapping program, and agree to develop the 3M expansion site in such a way as to minimize impacts on warblers (including controlling the timing of land alteration and revegetation of altered areas). All told, 3M estimates that the cost of these mitigation actions is around $2 million. Previous Section 7 mitigation requirements have not been as impressive, however. When the Steiner Ranch, a forty-five hundred acre housing development, went through a Section 7 consultation (because it required a Section 404 wetlands permit from the Corps of Engineers) the mitigation provided was quite limited, resulting in setting aside 115 acres of warbler habitat. These types of parcel-by-parcel review, have often resulted in the protection of small, unconnected slivers of habitat, and strongly highlight the importance of a more comprehensive, regional approach such as the BCCP.

Funding for the BCCP was one of the biggest uncertainties in the minds of many. In particular, would voters be willing to pass bond referenda to protect endangered species? Whether they would or not was seen to depend largely on how such referenda were actually presented to the public. Opinion research in the past has shown that the general public is less likely to support conservation of less aesthetically appealing species, many of which in the Austin case would fall into this category. Would the general public be willing to pay for habitat preservation when much of it is karst habitat intended to preserve cave-adapted invertebrates? On the other hand, if attention were focused on the water quality, recreation, and open space benefits of habitat acquisition, voters and the general public might have an easier time supporting such initiatives. The local chapter of the Sierra Club stressed these types of benefits in a recent newsletter:

> The biggest benefits of the plan will be creation of permanent open spaces for public recreation, water quality enhancement, and wildlife protection, regardless of whether or not the species survive.[9]

A recent public opinion survey by RPC Market Research shed some light on this. Of four hundred Travis County residents surveyed, 80 percent said they would be willing to support a land acquisition plan aimed at protecting the environment, and more than 50 percent indicated they would support a bond referendum to pay for it. Indeed, during the summer of 1992, a series of referenda in support of habitat preservation was passed by the public (including more extensive watershed regulations and a measure authorizing $22 million in bonds for BCCP land acquisition), which suggests that in Austin at least, the general electorate is able to see the merits of such programs.

The state legislature in Texas seems to have presented some obstacles early on to the plan's funding. While local governments in Texas currently have the power to impose development impact fees, these fees are restricted to certain specified areas, including the provisions of public facilities. Most believe that to impose a fee to preserve habitat will require state-enabling legislation. A bill to provide this authorization was beaten back in the 1991 session, largely as a result of political pressure from realtor groups and the Farm Bureau. Similar opposition may arise in response to the current bills before the legislature and there is, consequently, no assurance that the localities will have the authority to impose the mitigation fee and building fee surcharges so important to the funding of the plan.

The Balcones Canyonlands Conservation Plan is impressive in a number of respects when compared to many other HCPs described in this book. Its focus on multiple species—including ten federally listed species—and its regional geographical scale make much sense in terms of the overall efficiency of protecting biodiversity. There is considerable economic value to such a multi-species approach. Moreover, its focus on protecting larger ecological processes is likely to better ensure the survival of all species. The emphasis on preserving large blocks of contiguous habitat areas may also result in more ecologically defensible and viable population and habitat areas.

The BCCP preserve system will also achieve other important local objectives. Much of the acreage to be protected is land providing drain-off into Austin's major water supply, thus protecting the diminishing water source. The recreational and open space benefits will also be substantial.

The BCCP is also extremely impressive in the amount of habitat land it proposes to acquire and protect, and considerable habitat is already being protected under the plan. It has already been a major catalyst for the Balcones Canyonland National Wildlife Refuge, with 41,000 acres of habitat eventually to be protected there. Much of this land has already been secured (at least in the short term) through the work of Texas TNC. The city of Austin also designated about $20 million in its 1991–1992 fiscal year budget to secure land around Barton Springs, an acquisition commitment which will do much to advance the goals of the plan. And, as already noted, an agreement was recently reached with RTC which provides for below-market acquisition of some 10,000 acres of habitat lands held by them. On balance, considerable progress has already been made in Austin.

The BCCP has clearly been a major catalyst behind the establishment of the Balcones Canyonlands National Wildlife Refuge. There remains the possibility, however, that the refuge will not be completed if the BCCP falls through. Representative Pickle has strongly supported the refuge and pushed for congressional funding. He has indicated, however, that he will withdraw his support for the refuge if it is not part of a regional solution to the protection of species. Thus, while the refuge is moving ahead, it is still in political jeopardy if the larger BCCP should become stalled.

Like most HCPs, the BCCP is necessarily founded on limited biological understanding of the species of concern. Indeed the plan itself acknowledges these limitations. Biological understanding is particularly limited, for example, with respect to the underground karst ecosystems. And, again, concerns have been expressed about the effectiveness of the preserve design for the Golden-cheeked Warbler. An extensive biological study of warbler habitat and behavior and impacts of various land uses has been underway by several University of Texas researchers. By the fall of 1991, when the final preserve design was being hammered out, the study had not yet been completed, raising serious questions about the design.

The BCCP preserve concept might also be criticized for a failure to adequately fulfill the BAT's recommendation concerning minimum

Black-capped Vireo habitat. The plan, however, explicitly acknowledges that full achievement of the ideal preserve system proposed by the BAT must be balanced against issues of economic feasibility. The 1991 draft version of the plan was particularly direct:

It should be emphasized that the proposed preserve system does not fully meet either the biological or socioeconomic criteria established early in the process . . . . The process of designing a preserve system that is both biologically viable and economically feasible necessarily involves compromises. The recommended preserve system is a product of such compromises and is intended to provide the maximum protection of the species of concern within the recognizable financial limitations.[10]

It should also be kept in mind that for two of the species addressed in the BCCP—the Black-capped Vireo and Golden-cheeked Warbler—severe habitat degradation can occur in its wintering areas, and this is largely beyond the control of the plan. It is critical that the vireo's highland habitat in southwestern Mexico be protected, as well as the tropical highlands of Guatemala, Honduras, and Nicaragua in the case of the warbler. Deforestation in the Central American wintering areas is on the rise and should be the cause of considerable concern. This highlights the unfortunate fact that for many migratory species great effort and expense can result in habitat protection in one portion of its migratory range, but may be unsuccessful because habitat is not protected in other areas of its migratory range. The BCCP highlights the need for international agreements to go hand-in-hand with local and regional habitat conservation efforts.

While the BCCP clearly takes a multi-species approach, and as comprehensive an approach as any HCP to date, it still does not seek to protect all biodiversity, broadly defined, in the region. As with most HCPs, the BCCP focuses heavily on *species,* and the habitat needs of these species. There are certain endangered *communities* in the region that, because they do not contain endangered species, have been left out of the conservation strategy. Notably, native blackland prairie is becoming quite rare in Texas, yet no attempt is made in the BCCP to protect these communities to the east of the city. Thus, while the BCCP is extremely ambitious, it does not protect (but perhaps should be expected to) all biological diversity in the region.

The plan has not turned out to be quite as regional as originally conceived. Specifically, Williamson County to the north of Austin has recently dropped out of the plan. The reason appears to be unwillingness to be involved in a process and plan orchestrated (or perceived to be orchestrated) by Austinites. Most believe that as a result Williamson County will be forced to prepare its own plan at some later date.

The Austin experience also effectively highlights in many ways the failure of local land use planning and growth management efforts to reduce these types of species/development conflicts. Austin has a long history of attempting to plan for and manage its growth in ways which minimize impact on the natural environment. A major initiative in the 1970s—called *Austin Tomorrow*—carefully analyzed and identified environmentally sensitive areas and proposed a north-south growth corridor in which to funnel the bulk of growth so as to avoid these areas. Had this plan been effectively implemented, fewer development and growth pressures would have resulted in sensitive habitat areas.[11] However, this plan was never realized for a number of reasons. The city was unable to put into place the infrastructure to accommodate growth in desired locations (largely a result of failed bond measures) and housing demand proved great for the sensitive hill country areas to the west and northwest. Austin has also had difficulty controlling growth beyond its corporate boundaries. Under Texas law, land developers can essentially provide city services through the creation of municipal utility districts or MUDs.[12] Had the city and the other jurisdictions in the region had an effective, coordinated growth management program, a great deal of development pressure might have been deflected away from sensitive habitat areas. Moreover, reducing and deflecting such growth pressures would also have had the benefits of reducing the acquisition costs of habitat and making it easier to secure and protect large blocks of habitat.

It has also been observed that had the Golden-cheeked Warbler been federally listed earlier, this would have prevented much of the land speculation which occurred in the area, and would have saved substantial public facility investments. Scientific papers had been written as early as 1975, raising concerns about the plight of the warbler.

Conclusions

The Balcones Canyonlands Conservation Plan is impressive in its efforts to take a regional multi-species approach and may well represent the best model for habitat conservation in the future. It is further commendable in its ecosystem orientation and in its ability to achieve other important local objectives, such as water quality protection and open space conservation. The methodology used in preparing the plan, including an overlay or gap analysis approach, in which efforts are made to build onto existing protected lands, is also notable. Achievements of the

BCCP process have already been substantial, including serving as an important catalyst for creation of the Balcones Canyonlands National Wildlife Refuge, and securing nearly ten thousand acres of habitat from the Resolution Trust Corporation.

While the Balcones Canyonlands plan is impressive in a number of respects, it has not yet been fully adopted or implemented, and a number of potential political and financial obstacles loom ahead. Especially problematic will be raising the large amounts of money needed to implement the plan. It is also not entirely clear that the plan will be able to hold together the tenuous coalition of developers, environmentalists, and others involved. Overall, though, Austin represents an impressive model for future habitat conservation efforts in the United States.

Evaluating the Success of Habitat Conservation Efforts: Lessons Learned and Recommendations for the Future

Introduction: Evaluating a Moving Target

Because the HCP mechanism is being used increasingly to resolve species protection/development conflicts, and because the conflicts will likely increase in the future, it is important to evaluate the success and desirability of the device and perhaps to offer suggestions for improving habitat conservation efforts. Several factors make it difficult to definitively evaluate the success of the 10(a) provisions. First, the program is clearly a moving target, in that a large number of HCPs are in progress but few are completed or fully settled in their implementation. Second, to judge certain important criteria—especially the extent to which such plans result in the protection and recovery of listed species, without loss of community prosperity—will require a number of years and extensive monitoring and study. At this point in time an evaluation must be speculative and tentative. This lack of definitiveness, however, is in my mind far outweighed by the need and opportunity to influence habitat conservation policy at a critical point in its development in this country.

This chapter summarizes the key findings concerning this study and evaluates the experience to date with HCPs based on the following criteria: the extent of habitat protected and restored, the ability to promote constructive political compromise on species development conflicts, the ability to implement resulting compromises, the biological adequacy of conservation measures and the long-term viability of habitat areas, the cost of habitat conservation efforts, and the time required to prepare and obtain approval of an HCP.

Successes to Date

HCPs have been responsible for setting aside considerable amounts of natural habitat. In the Coachella Valley HCP, for instance, more than 16,000 acres of desert habitat have been protected, in three different preserves.[1] Within these preserves, some 8,000 acres of lizard habitat (blowsand) have been protected in perpetuity. The San Bruno Mountain HCP has resulted in setting aside a vast amount—nearly 90% of the proposed acreage—of butterfly habitat (some 2,700 acres). Even in places like North Key Largo, where the HCP has never been officially adopted or approved by the USFWS, it clearly served as a catalyst for public acquisition of substantial amounts of habitat (under the state's Conservation and Recreation Lands program). Even though it has not yet been formally approved, the San Diego River HCP, prepared for the Least Bell's Vireo, has been influential in the design and review of several highway and bridge projects (required to undergo Section 7 consultation—e.g., the extension of State Highway 52 across the San Diego River).

Furthermore, HCP processes, even where plans have yet to be completed or approved, are generating revenue and funds necessary to undertake management activities and biological research that would not be undertaken otherwise. For instance, in the Coachella Valley HCP, revenues generated from developer mitigation fees are being used to undertake a variety of management and research activities, including fencing certain areas to keep off-road vehicles away from lizard habitat, dismantling certain windbreaks that interrupt natural blows and movement, and conducting an annual lizard count, as well as other research activities which will ultimately enhance understanding of the ecology and population dynamics of the species. As already mentioned, funds generated from the San Bruno Mountain HCP (annual mitigation fees) are being used to restore native grasslands essential for butterfly survival.[2] These native grasslands had been declining for many years as the result of the invasion of non-native vegetation. In both of these cases, it appears that the species of concern would have been in considerable jeopardy even if the habitat had been left undeveloped.

Furthermore, it appears that the HCP device has served as a pressure valve and has added some needed flexibility to ESA, promoting compromise and negotiated settlements between the development and environmental communities in particular, where confrontation and litigation would have been the likely alternatives. The HCP concept acknowledges that some degree of development and human use of species habitat may not be inconsistent with the conservation and survival of threatened or endangered species. And, to the contrary, some degree of development may have a positive impact, if it serves to generate funds to be used for habitat restoration and conservation.

It is also remarkable how well the HCP process is functioning in many places, given the potential volatility of the different community factions and stakeholders involved. While there has been considerable acrimony in many of the HCP processes, warring factions often have come together to strike a balance between development and conservation. As a result, developers have recognized the need to set aside habitat, while members of the environmental community have acknowledged that much can be accomplished through collaboration and pursuit of common interests.

To be sure, environmental and development communities have remained as good faith participants in these processes, because they have seen it in their best interests to do so. From the development community's perspective, HCPs represent an efficient solution to a major development obstacle. The alternatives would be either to expend considerable time and expense in legal fights or to attempt to deal with the endangered species problem on an inefficient site-by-site, project-by-project basis. The development community has also clearly seen the HCP process as a way to spread the costs of habitat conservation to the broader public. Members of the environmental community frequently view the HCP mechanism (although there is clearly not unanimity among environmentalists) as a way to marshall financial and political support for the establishment of habitat preserves—resources that would otherwise not be available. Many in the environmental community also recognize the political difficulties the USFWS has in shutting down development in habitat areas and the likely political fallout that would result if such actions were taken.

Areas of Concern, and Future Directions

A number of factors in habitat conservation planning give cause for concern. Because the HCP process is a relatively recent one, and because it will be many years before we will be able to adequately evaluate the effectiveness of these efforts, what is presented here must necessarily be tentative and inconclusive. At the very least, however, my evaluative observations raise some serious concerns about HCPs, which the USFWS (and others) should address. In each of these areas of concern, there are strategies appropriate for overcoming or at least minimizing them. From this study it is possible to identify lessons learned and future directions that should be taken in habitat conservation planning.

The adequacy of habitat conservation measures

Perhaps the most serious issue is whether the extent and nature of the conservation measures contained in the plans adequately protect the endangered or threatened species involved and ensure the protection of overall biodiversity. Yet to be fully answered are a number of key questions regarding the level of habitat conservation required, the level of species protection actually demanded under section 10(a), and the amount of habitat loss that is acceptable. Recall that ESA states that a section 10(a) permit can be issued and incidental take allowed only where the taking "will not appreciably reduce the likelihood of the survival and recovery of the species in the wild."

The issue regarding the amount of habitat conservation required has yet to be resolved; there is considerable variation between the HCPs. Different HCPs have adopted different philosophies concerning the amount of habitat conservation necessary or desirable. At least three different approaches can be identified. One approach might be described as the "minimal survival" position, where the minimum amount of habitat needed to protect a species is set aside. The amount of loss of existing habitat is not as important. The key question often asked is what is the minimum number and size of preserves? The answer is often determined through consultation with leading biological experts and the USFWS.

The Coachella Valley HCP is perhaps the best example of this approach; while many biological experts (including the USFWS recovery team) found the preserves large enough to sustain the species, only about 10 percent of the occupiable habitat that existed at the time the plan was prepared is protected. And, although much of the habitat was already undergoing degradation due to sand shielding, it is still questioned whether this much habitat destruction should be allowed. It is hard to imagine how an 85 to 90 percent reduction in the existing habitat of a listed species could satisfy the section 10(a) criteria contained in ESA. Moreover, many of the scientific authorities involved in the HCP who endorsed the plan have expressed concern about the long-term prospects for the lizard. Many of the participants interviewed described the plan as a gamble and claimed that there was no assurance that the lizard would survive in the long term. However, many participants also stated that what was accomplished in terms of habitat conservation was certainly better than nothing and probably constituted the best deal that could have been struck. Concerns about the extent of habitat loss are further reinforced by the dramatic population swings exhibited by the lizard population in the three Coachella preserves. Several years of data indicate that lizard populations are prone to extreme yearly fluctuations, closely tied, it appears, to precipitation patterns, though this is not understood very well.[3] Some members of the Coachella Valley HCP steering committee have been critical of the plan because it sacrifices large areas of potentially occupiable habitat. And, again, while much of this land has been undergoing degradation due to sand shielding, no serious consideration was given to such options as removing existing sand shields (such as the Southern Pacific Railroad windbreaks which are estimated to be a major cause of sand shielding and habitat degradation). For many of these reasons the Coachella Valley plan has been the most heavily criticized of the HCP efforts to date. Richard E. Webster, for instance, concludes that the HCP

> . . . can only be described as doing, under the guise of an "incidental take," great violence to the concepts of recovery and survival. Taking a "threatened" species, with a range already reduced by one-half, and permitting it to be reduced to less than one-quarter of its remaining range, makes its reclassification as "endangered" certain. Even if the biological evaluation is correct and adequate preserves will remain to prevent extinction, the fringe-toed lizard probably will warrant reclassification as an endangered species in the near future.[4]

A second approach exhibited in several of the HCPs might be characterized as the "mitigation ratio" position, where the amount of habitat protected, restored, or created is in some sense directly related to the amount of habitat destroyed or lost. In a variety of environmental laws, such mitigation ratios are applied. Developers who are allowed to fill an acre of wetland, are then often required to create, restore, or protect an acre somewhere else—this is the "no net loss" concept and has a fairly convincing equity appeal to it. Those who are responsible for destroying or degrading habitat ought to be required to "make it right" or to compensate for these impacts in some way. The mitigation ratio concept has been used extensively in wildlife habitat issues. The California Department of Fish and Game, for instance, has in some recent cases been requiring mitigation for habitat loss on as much as a five-to-one ratio (under the California Endangered Species Act). Mitigation ratios greater than one to one are generally intended to compensate for the inherent riskiness of allowing natural habitat to be replaced with newly created or rehabilitated habitat. Several HCPs appear to have the concept of a mitigation ration as their underlying philosophy. The Metro-Bakersfield HCP is a notable example of this kind of approach, in that a goal of the plan is to restore/protect three acres of kit fox habitat for each acre destroyed. The Least Bell's Vireo HCP is assuming a similar philosophy with its heavy emphasis on project-by-project mitigation. Obviously this approach will be more difficult to apply where restoration or re-creation of habitat is difficult or impossible (e.g., it may be impossible to re-create desert blowsand habitat). In maintaining or even expanding the existing habitat of threatened or endangered species, the results of this type of strategy seem more consistent with the section 10(a) standards contained in ESA.

A third approach might be described as the "minimal footprint" position, where the absolute extent of habitat loss is reduced and the consumption of habitat areas used for development or other destructive uses is minimized. The San Bruno Mountain plan is an example of this, for instance, because it resulted in a minimal consumption of habitat for development, and it set aside some 90% of the butterfly habitat. This strategy is the most attractive from a biological and conservation standpoint, but is obviously going to be less desirable to developers and others who wish to maximize their use of habitat lands. And, because of constitutional restrictions on the extent to which land can be restricted or regulated before such actions constitute government takings (requiring compensation), determining the minimum footprint becomes closely related to what is needed to ensure some reasonable economic return for the landowner or developer. What level of use or development is necessary to ensure such a reasonable economic use is of course controversial and admittedly difficult to dictate by regulatory and resource management agencies such as USFWS.

In a number of the HCP cases described in this study, participants have expressed frustration in not being given guidance from USFWS as to what the minimum threshold of conservation in fact is. While this may be difficult to do biologically, USFWS may need to provide some degree of minimum conservation/protection standards that should be achieved. Moreover, USFWS must ensure that the benefit of doubt goes to the species of concern. USFWS should demand more adequate levels of habitat conservation, providing greater assurance that species survival *and* recovery will be achieved. Moreover, many in the scientific and biological communities argue that the long-term success of habitat conservation will require much larger regional conservation strategies (e.g., larger contiguous and interconnected blocks of habitat), and USFWS must in the future ensure that local HCPs contribute to such strategies.

Long-term viability

A related concern is whether the conserved habitat areas that are being set aside are going to be viable over the long term. In many cases HCPs will serve to create habitat islands which are surrounded by development, but are not connected to and do not relate very well to the broader natural landscape. One has to wonder about the long-term viability of areas like the east dunes in Sand City—a small habitat island which will inevitably be surrounded by intensive human uses. In Coachella Valley the long-term viability of the lizard preserve system, particularly the two satellite preserves, is not assured. There have already been serious adjacent land use conflicts, for instance, the recent proposals to construct a racetrack adjacent to the Whitewater floodplain preserve. Incompatible adjacent land uses threaten even the large Coachella Valley preserve (e.g., by sand shielding, flood control, and other activities).

These concerns suggest that greater efforts should be made to design defensible habitat areas, which join, wherever possible, existing contiguous protected areas, and to incorporate landscape linkages. The Metro-Bakersfield HCP is encouraging in this regard in its efforts to join conserved habitat areas, and to protect a contiguous corridor along the Kern River. Greater attention should be given to placing stringent controls on adjacent uses and activities. Conservation buffers around habitat areas may do much to protect them from adjacent activities. Here again is the question of what level of habitat protection is needed before 10(a) approval should be given.

Conservation decisions based on limited biological knowledge

It is problematic that conservation decisions must be made without full and complete biological knowledge, and it is particularly troubling given the magnitude of the policy decisions based on this limited knowledge (e.g., approval of plans which may seal the fate of endangered species), and the speed with which these decisions are to be made. A basic contradiction exists between the timeframes of developers, who want relatively quick conservation answers, and the timeframes of scientists and wildlife biologists who may require many years of study to adequately understand the biology of even a single species.

Examples of the biological uncertainties present in HCPs are numerous. Key questions include the extent of habitat which must be set aside to protect a species, and the appropriate number, size, and configuration of preserves. Scientists still do not understand why lizard populations fluctuate dramatically at Coachella Valley. The Coachella Valley HCP itself is quite honest about this rudimentary biological understanding, outlining in its long-term biological program a variety of basic research and monitoring activities, including: establishing a population baseline; tracking fluctuations in populations; developing reliable and cost-effective methods for monitoring; conducting basic research to identify important factors affecting habitat quality, essential elements of lizard diet, and a better understanding of reproduction and lifespan; and identification of important predators and competitors of the lizard.[5]

The Coachella Valley situation is not unique. Each HCP contains serious deficiencies in biological knowledge and examples are numerous. In the San Diego Least Bell's Vireo HCP, for instance, there are considerable uncertainties about the extent to which noise from automobile traffic or farm equipment is disruptive to the bird's life functions (e.g., mating and establishment of territory).[6] In the Balcones Canyonlands Conservation Plan, little is known about the biota of the underground karst habitat (areas of porous limestone), where the six federally listed cave invertebrates live. Because these underground cave areas are relatively inaccessible to humans (with cave openings and fractures too small for humans to fit through) and have not received much study in the past, it is believed that numerous other rare species may live in the caves. Some thirty new species of cave-adapted invertebrates have been discovered. These species have yet to undergo taxonomic study, or an analysis of relevant biological or ecological characteristics.[7] Moreover, understanding of the impacts of human activities on these karst habitats is crude at best (e.g., effects of water contaminants, modifications to surface vegetation, introduction of fire ants).

Unfortunately, little can be done to adequately address these biological limitations, given the time and monetary constraints of the HCP schedules. Policy decisions must be made quickly. Obviously, the best biological studies possible in the short term should be prepared as part of the HCP process. More fundamentally, however, these basic biological uncertainties should be clearly acknowledged in the HCP process and conservation measures should err on the side of caution and conservatism, for example by requiring habitat mitigation on a five-to-one ratio. In the Balcones Canyonlands Conservation Plan, uncertainties about karst biota suggest the conservative strategy of protecting representative pieces of karst habitat, centered on areas of endemism in each of five biogeographic zones that have been identified in the HCP study area.

The potential benefits of comprehensive, multi-species approaches

In evaluating the merits of the HCP mechanism, one is initially struck by the failure of many HCPs to take a broader, comprehensive, multi-species approach. Several HCPs have identified other important species of concern, and have given lip service to the concept of a multi-species approach, but have remained focused on one key species. The single-species nature of most plans is perhaps not surprising given the structure and orientation of the federal Endangered Species Act, and given the perceived need to arrive at a solution to the problem quickly, but it does not make much sense when considering the time and tremendous expense involved in preparing HCPs. More comprehensive approaches would provide a greater payoff for limited conservation dollars, could serve to prevent conflicts in the future, and could more effectively save important biological resources. Moreover, such comprehensive, multi-species approaches are more likely to result in setting aside ecologically viable and defensible habitat areas.

Taking a more comprehensive approach would mean considering not just federally listed endangered or threatened species, but also candidate species, state-listed species, other species of concern, and overall patterns of biodiversity in a locality or region. Such a strategy would allow the consideration of habitat needs of species that are not yet legally covered by ESA, but are likely to be listed at some time in the future and would allow the identification and protection of critical areas of overlapping habitat. Several of the more recent HCPs—the Balcones Canyon-lands Conservation Plan and the Kern County HCP in particular—are taking such an approach and seem sensible.[8] Despite the possibility of restricting more land to preserves, the development community often supports such a strategy as a way of taking care of the species conservation needs in the region through a single plan and process (i.e., they will not have to confront myriad HCPs in the future).

In some circumstances, of course, there may be relatively few opportunities to set aside overlapping habitat. To take a comprehensive species approach, however, would not only mean studying how species' habitats overlap, but also studying preservation of other species of concern within the jurisdiction. It would have been logical for jurisdictions such as Riverside County, California to protect the Stephens' kangaroo rat at the same time it protected the Coachella Valley fringe-toed lizard. Similarly, it would make sense for Monroe County, Florida to protect the habitat of the endangered key deer at the same time it helps the Key Largo woodrat, Key Largo cottonmouse, etc.

On the other hand, comprehensive multi-species approaches are expensive and time-consuming and may be inconsistent with the views of many participants in the HCP process, particularly those in the development community. State and federal agencies could help by laying the biological groundwork, where possible, for such comprehensive multi-species plans.

Methodologies such as gap analysis hold particular promise in their ability to identify areas which are rich in biological diversity and which are not currently protected through acquisition. Gap analysis, developed by USFWS scientists, identifies areas of high species' diversity through a process of overlaying information on vegetation types and species ranges and densities (for endangered and non-endangered species), and comparing the location of high diversity habitat with existing protected lands to identify gaps in habitat protection (i.e., important areas of species diversity not currently protected by parks or preserves).[9] The USFWS is successfully applying the analysis at a state level in Idaho and Oregon, and such studies could be extremely useful in facilitating local and regional multi-species HCPs. The Riverside County Multiple Species HCP is the best example of such an approach and represents a positive model that ought to be emulated elsewhere (even though it has run into some political problems).

Utilizing approaches such as gap analysis also highlights the importance and power of Geographic Information System (GIS) technology. Through this computer technology it is possible to overlay many different layers of data, and to simultaneously consider the habitat needs of different species, existing patterns of land use and development, and other important spatial information. GIS technology can also be useful in modeling habitat and land use changes over time and for testing the ecological viability of different preserve configurations. Movement toward comprehensive, multi-species approaches will require the increasing use of GIS technology at state, regional, and local levels.

Federal and state resource agencies also need to expend considerably greater funds on basic biological research, at least for those species of concern whose habitat is or is likely to be threatened by urban development and other human activities. Early strategic planning might reduce the need later to undertake eleventh-hour biological assessments for individual HCPs.

As noted earlier, habitat fragmentation can be overcome to some extent by providing corridors and landscape linkages. Several of the HCPs profiled in this study have used or plan to use such corridors, and future habitat conservation designs should, where possible, take advantage of this strategy. In the Metro-Bakersfield HCP, for instance, the Kern River floodplain is critical as a movement corridor connecting several populations of San Joaquin kit fox. Considerable controversy still remains in the scientific and conservation communities about the merits of wildlife corridors, however.[10] First, such corridors can also allow for transmission of disease and pests, putting entire populations at risk. Second, it is not clear that such corridors are always of much practical benefit for endangered species. Habitat planners must safeguard against the use of wildlife corridors as a way of justifying habitat fragmentation and loss.

It is clear, as well, that in the long run, protecting biodiversity and viable habitat areas will require maintenance of basic physical and ecological processes. The increasing attention of conservation efforts such as the Balcones Canyonlands Conservation Plan to protecting watersheds and other ecological processes is encouraging. Even very large blocks of protected lands are subject to a variety of threats to ecological processes, including acid deposition, groundwater contamination, etc. In the long run, protecting large areas of habitat will be ineffective if these cross-boundary ecological threats are not addressed.

Larger, multi-species approaches will have considerable advantages, both from biological and economic perspectives. Such approaches again argue for attempting to protect and conserve habitat at a much larger geographical scale. Increasing attention has been given to bio-regions or bio-reserves.[11] Future HCPs must avoid saving isolated habitat pieces, and instead promote protection of lands that fit into a larger geographical conservation strategy (see Figure 13.1). Such a strategy should promote protection of multi-species, link existing parks and protected areas, and work to insulate habitat areas from future major development and growth pressures. Such a bio-reserve strategy is currently being pursued by The Nature Conservancy, in recognition of the pitfalls of preserving detached and isolated parcels of land. This approach may question the view that HCPs should necessarily seek to protect *local* habitat, and may argue that certain lands directly in the path of development should not be preserved.

Integration with land use planning

It is unfortunate that HCPs and species conservation efforts have not been more closely tied to local land use planning. Local land use plans ideally should incorporate the kind of comprehensive biodiversity analysis and planning discussed above; these efforts could prevent the species/development conflicts that frequently give rise to HCPs in the first place. For example, local plans could direct growth away from areas rich in biodiversity and could serve as the basis for comprehensive, long-term land protection and acquisition programs.

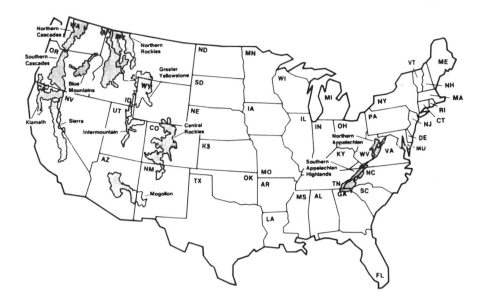

Figure 13.1. Potential Bioregions within the National Forest System (adapted from Hal Salwasser et al., "The Role of Interagency Coopera-tion in Managing for Viable Populations in M. E. Soule, ed., *Viable Pop-ulations for Conservation, 1987,* by permission of Cambridge University Press, publishers)

More emphasis should be given to prevention—effective land use planning and growth management—than quick cures. In many ways the HCP process is analogous to bailing water from a sinking ship; the integrity of the ship should first be ensured. Kern County's current ef-forts to prepare an endangered species element of its general plan are encouraging in this respect. In the long term this may be one of the most cost-effective ways of dealing with species conservation issues. The USFWS or state governments should consider providing small amounts of seed money to facilitate this kind of local planning (e.g., perhaps in the form of small planning grants). Many states mandate the prepara-tion of local land use or general plans, often stipulating in considerable detail the types of issues and policy areas which must be addressed.[12] The importance of such a tool in preventing or minimizing species/de-velopment conflicts suggests the need for states to specifically require endangered species components such as that being prepared for Kern County.[13]

In order to avoid future conflicts between species conservation and development, communities need to re-examine their current development and growth patterns. The assumption prevalent in most HCPs is that current patterns and types of growth are appropriate and that the HCP is primarily intended to find a way to overcome the legal obstacles presented by ESA, and thus to facilitate this existing growth. By modifying growth types or patterns—for instance by encouraging denser, more compact and contiguous growth patterns, and by encouraging in-fill, development pressure on open space and natural areas can be substantially reduced.[14] In many localities and regions with substantial numbers of endangered wildlife and important biological resources, it may no longer be possible to just accept existing inefficient and wasteful patterns of development.

Problem of Funding HCPs

Perhaps the most striking aspect of many of the more recent HCPs is the amount of money required to undertake the habitat acquisition and other activities needed to protect an endangered species. For example, the Stephens' kangaroo rat HCP of habitat acquisition may ultimately cost $50 million to $100 million. The Balcones Canyonlands Conservation Plan may cost more than $170 million. Acquisition costs may be the greatest implementation obstacle influencing the potential effectiveness of the HCP mechanisms. Where will the funds come from to finance HCPs?

It is paradoxical, in a sense, that species are not usually endangered until the occurrence of significant human development. However, by the time such species are in jeopardy and society recognizes the need to protect remaining habitat, the market value of these lands is extremely high. A recent survey of land prices for Stephens' kangaroo rat habitat in eastern Riverside County, for example, found some land selling for as much as $400,000 per acre.[15] Acquisition of habitat in a highly urbanized context, sufficient to ensure the long-term survival of endangered species, may require tremendous funds.

It is apparent in discussing funding sources with participants in a number of ongoing HCPs that many people expect the federal government to provide most of the habitat acquisition money. At Coachella Valley, the federal government covered approximately 60 percent of land acquisition costs (through a combination of appropriations from the federal Land and Water Conservation Fund and BLM land swaps). To many this is an equitable solution, in that it is a federal law—the Endangered Species Act—that creates the need for HCPs in the first place, and thus it is fair to expect the federal government to assume a major portion of the cost of conservation. Species conservation, the argument continues, is a public good, and thus its costs ought to be borne by the broader public.[16] Recent indications from Washington, however, are that Uncle Sam cannot be counted upon to bail out HCPs in the future; this heightens the need to explore other long-term funding sources. This is perhaps the greatest single challenge facing the HCP process in the future.

One component of this solution is to increase the contributions made by the development community, specifically in the form of mitigation fees. It can be argued that in many cases the extent of development contributions is low, particularly since these very activities (e.g., development in habitat areas) threaten loss of species. The Coachella Valley HCP is a case in point. Under this funding scheme the $600 per acre mitigation fees will ultimately generate approximately $7 million or 28 percent of the total $25 million cost of the preserve system. Given the tremendous profits to be made in opening up development in the valley, such a per-acre assessment seems modest. Furthermore, early in the fringe-toed lizard controversy, some argued that development fees should be assessed at least on the basis of an acre-for-acre replacement—that is, a per-acre fee should be assessed which would be sufficient to purchase and protect an acre of lizard habitat somewhere else. Given that in the early 1980s habitat land in Coachella Valley was selling for $3,500 to $8,000 per acre, a $600 per acre mitigation fee falls greatly short of a one-for-one replacement ratio. Indeed, landowners and developers consequently are being asked to protect habitat at about a one/fifth-to-one ratio at best (i.e., $600 providing enough to purchase only about 0.2 acres of habitat).

A straight per-acre mitigation fee, used in most HCPs, may however not be the most equitable way in which to assess new development. In Clark County, Nevada, a developer of a four-acre parcel would pay the same $250 per acre (or $1,000 fee total) regardless of whether this was going to the site of a new detached single family home or a multi-million dollar hotel and casino. Equity would suggest the need to explore other ways of imposing such fees, to take such differences into account.

There is some validity to the arguments of developers, of course, that the costs of HCPs should be shared to some extent by the broader public. Often, of course, it is the previous growth and development in the community, from which everyone benefits to some extent, that causes a species to become endangered or threatened. Would it not be equitable, then, for the broader public to contribute to these conservation costs?

This is an especially compelling argument when the resulting habitat set aside serves important open space, aesthetic, or recreational functions for the community or region. Local governments faced with HCP costs in the future should consider utilizing other sources of revenue in addition to exactions and development fees on new development. Local funding for land acquisition is not a novel idea, and numerous examples exist of successful, locally funded acquisition programs around the country (e.g., Boulder, Colorado uses a sales tax; the Mid-peninsula Open Space District in the San Francisco Bay area uses an annual property assessment; Nantucket, Massachusetts uses a land transfer tax).[17] The size of the funds needed for habitat acquisition also suggests the need to continue to move towards greater state funding, such as the bond referenda considered in several states (e.g., Question 5 in Nevada which may provide funds for the desert tortoise; the California Wildlife Protection Initiative, Proposition 117, which was recently passed).

These costs of habitat conservation and preservation could be reduced by utilizing alternatives to fee-simple acquisition (e.g., some combination of regulation/transfer of development rights; easements and other forms of less-than-fee-simple acquisition), adopting a much longer time-frame, and acquiring land well in advance of when it is needed (this ties in closely with the advantages of a comprehensive/multi-species approach). It might also help to utilize mitigation funds generated in one jurisdiction by buying habitat areas in other jurisdictions, perhaps where land is less expensive and where larger, more ecologically viable lands can be obtained. And, again, comprehensive regional HCPs, which simultaneously consider the habitat needs of many species, will serve to facilitate these types of cost efficiencies.

Gaining support for habitat conservation, and the large expenditure of public funds that may be necessary, will require careful thought and planning. The case studies illustrate well that some arguments will carry greater political and popular support than others. Protecting large habitat areas will receive more support for providing public open space and recreational benefits than for protecting a rare or endangered species. For example, public officials in Coachella Valley were convinced of the benefits of supporting habitat conservation largely because they saw the need to preserve a desert park, and not because the fringe-toed lizard was especially worthy of such expenditures. Furthermore, it may often be wise to emphasize protection of species that are more aesthetically appealing to the public, such as the San Joaquin kit fox, while downplaying species such as cave-invertebrates that may actually be repugnant to many people. These types of strategies may be essential for winning public support for bond referenda, special taxing districts, or various other means for funding habitat conservation programs.

Managing the HCP Process and the Need for Interim Conservation

In reviewing past and ongoing HCP programs a number of concerns about the process have been expressed by individuals the author interviewed. One concern is that the decisionmaking structures of HCPs are oriented and biased in certain directions. In many ways these types of concerns reflect a general uncertainty about the actual status of HCP steering committees and other decisionmaking structures. Are they to be informal working groups, allowing anyone and any group interested to participate? Or are they to be considered formal groups, with membership defined to reflect a genuine balance of community interests and perspectives? Concomitantly, should decisionmaking procedures reflect this objective of more formal representation, as perhaps through voting, rules of order, etc.? There are HCPs which fall into these two camps, and various points in between.

While most HCPs are balanced in terms of interest groups and perspectives, some interests are underrepresented in a few. For instance, some people stated that environmental interests are currently underrepresented on the Clark County desert tortoise steering committee. While each meeting is typically attended by a host of representatives of resource users and developers, often only one environmental group is consistently represented. The tenor of discussion and the substance of the policy decisions are influenced by this membership composition. In the North Key Largo HCP many observers believe that the process was biased in favor of the interests of large landholders. Smaller landowners do appear to have been underrepresented in the process. While it is difficult to generalize about biases in representation, there is sufficient merit to these concerns that additional thought and attention should be given to best ensuring representation and public accountability.

Perhaps the most troubling aspect for participants involved in HCPs is the sheer length of time typically required. While the Coachella Valley HCP was started in the early summer of 1983, for example, a section 10(a) permit was not officially issued by USFWS until April of 1986. Moreover, some plans like the North Key Largo HCP, initiated in 1984, have for a variety of political and technical reasons become derailed. These lengthy plan preparation and adoption periods are, of course, particularly troubling to those in the real estate and development community where even brief delays can be costly. Such delays are of concern also from a standpoint of species conservation because in many cases (e.g., the gradual replacement of natural grasslands on San Bruno Mountain) failure to complete the HCP quickly may place endangered species in greater jeopardy. While earlier recommendations concerning the need for comprehensive multi-species approaches may seem to work against such concerns, in the long run such efforts may prevent the constant and continual preparation of more limited species HCPs. The temporal demands of any carefully prepared HCP, however, do suggest the need to explore possible interim conservation measures.

HCPs take time to prepare. This raises the question: what happens while the plan is being prepared? It would often be economically disastrous and politically infeasible to expect to completely shut down development in a community, particularly in high growth areas, while an HCP is being prepared. On the other hand, to permit take to occur prior to any protective actions is certainly risky. In the Coachella Valley HCP, the USFWS tacitly agreed to allow "take" of lizards prior to the adoption and approval of the HCP as long as developers and landowners paid the necessary mitigation fee. Despite a warning about the need to hand-excavate kit fox dens, it could be argued that "take" is being permitted in the case of the Metro-Bakersfield HCP as well, again as long as a $680 mitigation fee is paid by the developer (excavating a species' den and chasing it off should be considered harassment and thus covered in the definition of take). On the other hand, the general feeling in Clark County was (prior to the issuance of the short-term permit) that only developers or property owners who do not have tortoises on their land are able to build, and thus only they were paying the $250 mitigation fee.

Recent approvals by USFWS, of interim or short-term HCPs for the Stephens' kangaroo rat, and the desert tortoise are perhaps one appropriate way to deal with this interim question. Large areas in Riverside County have been identified where few rats are likely to be found, and development is allowed to proceed while the full HCP is being prepared (a section 10[a] permit has been issued for these areas). Development will not be allowed to proceed, on the other hand, in ten designated study areas, encompassing some 20,000 acres of habitat where the vast majority (some 80 percent) of kangaroo rat habitat is found (that is, unless developers obtain 10[a] permits on their own). Under this arrangement the USFWS has issued a 10(a) permit only for a period of two years, during which time the long-term HCP will be under preparation. Separating major habitat study areas from minor, mostly non-habitat areas may prevent the county from coming to a development standstill. While some very small amount of habitat may be lost outside of the study areas (perhaps on the order of 5%) this approach seems a reasonable compromise.

A three-year, short-term HCP was prepared in Clark County for the desert tortoise. Approved by USFWS, the plan begins to establish a system of desert tortoise management areas, where new limitations would be placed on incompatible land uses such as grazing, mining, and ORV use.[18] By the end of the three-year period at least 400,000 acres (mostly BLM land) will be included in these management areas. In exchange for these protective actions, a section 10(a) permit has been issued for the Las Vegas Valley, where most of the development pressures in the county are centered. This incidental take area encompasses approximately 300,000 acres of potential tortoise habitat, generally felt to be low-quality habitat already heavily degraded from development, and where few tortoises remain (actual loss of habitat over the three-year period is estimated at around 22,000 acres). Take is permitted in the valley under certain conditions, including removal of any tortoises found on-site and payment of a higher ($550-per-acre) mitigation fee. In addition, allowable take is pegged to achieving certain conservation thresholds over the three-year period. These and other options represent practical solutions to the problem of interim conservation. However, short of a clear and logical plan for protecting the bulk of species habitat and regional biodiversity during the preparation of the long-term HCP, prohibitions against interim takes should be strongly enforced by USFWS.

Developer Satisfaction and Support

A major issue in the HCP process, as the case studies effectively illustrate, is how and the extent to which certain stakeholder groups see this mechanism as positive and of direct benefit to them. In particular, developers are frequently skeptical about environmental and other programs which impose extra costs and additional bureaucratic requirements on their projects. Can it be argued, however, that HCPs do directly benefit this constituency? Can developers be convinced of the positive benefits of participating?

The case studies presented in this book effectively illustrate that HCPs can and do positively benefit developers. These benefits take several forms, and the cases presented here generally provide evidence of strong support on the part of developers. While sometimes initially resistant to the HCP idea, the majority of the developers do in fact recognize the advantages and benefits of HCPs. There is the general feeling, as expressed directly in a number of personal interviews, that the HCP process represents a far less costly approach than attempting to satisfy federal and state endangered species requirements on a case-by-case or project-by-project basis (by obtaining individual project 10(a) permits). Developers have seen the HCP process as one which efficiently and effectively deals with the habitat protection problem, and one which simplifies compliance for them. Usually developers are able to pay a per-acre mitigation fee, a cost substantially lower than for a private solution. Developers in some places have supported HCPs as a way to keep down the cost of housing (in the Metro-Bakersfield case, for instance). And, while there have been few attempts to quantify the economic and financial benefits of regional HCPs, this has been attempted in Austin, Texas. The results are impressive and show quantitatively that the per-acre costs of compliance with ESA are *much* higher if attempted individually.[19]

Furthermore, developers appear not to object to payment of mitigation fees partly because they are able to see the resulting uses of these funds in ways which benefit them directly. Just as most developers have come to view sewer and water hookup fees, schools, parks, and other kinds of impact fees as legitimate and a normal part of the development process, habitat mitigation fees are being viewed in the same way.

Also, depending on the specific HCP and the nature and location of the habitat protected or set aside as a result, development projects may directly benefit from the open space and other amenities provided in close proximity. In HCPs such as San Bruno Mountain, the development that is permitted to occur—while less in density or size than would be allowed if habitat protection were not needed—is situated in close proximity to protected preserves.

Protected lands serve not only as important habitat for endangered species, but also as parklands and open space adjacent to residential areas—and, land that will remain such in perpetuity. One San Bruno developer described to me the resulting islands of development as providing a "pretty unique and spectacular ambiance," which would make the units much more attractive to prospective buyers. He believed that the protected habitat and open space would make his project much more attractive and marketable and would allow him to receive higher prices.

In some HCPs, such as those along the San Diego and Sweetwater rivers, surrounding or adjacent development will be set back a certain distance from habitat to protect certain buffer zones. While developers may have less buildable space, there are frequently provisions which allow the landowner or developer to use this density on the buildable portion of the site (i.e., to use the entire area of the parcel, even the land in unbuildable habitat or floodplain areas, in calculating allowable density). In this way, habitat setbacks and buffer zones do not impose economic hardship, but again help to enhance the attractiveness of a development. Community planners in San Diego observed that owning homes along and adjacent to the protected open space and habitat corridor on the San Diego River (Least Bell's Vireo habitat) was viewed as very desirable. Homes in these areas tend to be larger and more valuable (outside of the floodplain) in large part because of the assurance of having a protected and undevelopable corridor on one side of their property.

For HCPs such as Marina Dunes, where eventual development will be hotel-resort in nature, there is a strong likelihood that the extensive beachfront habitat protected under the plan will further enhance the attractiveness of visiting and staying in these developments. While no direct empirical research on these economic side-benefits was undertaken as part of this study, anecdotal evidence suggests that these market effects may be substantial. A representative of one of the major landholders there (one of the sand mining companies) expressed strong support for protecting shorefront open space, and believed that it would enhance the attractiveness and desirability of any development project they initiate (they are considering a combination motel and RV park for the site). There appears to be a clear trend in the direction of development projects which incorporate and emphasize the natural environment, and housing consumers appear increasingly to want and demand such amenities.

In HCPs where the habitat acquired or protected is a great distance from existing development, or current development pressures, these economic benefits may be less apparent. Even in these cases, however, the market value of private lands surrounding preserve sites will probably rise. Another potentially important factor is the extent to which the habitat set aside under an HCP will be open to direct public use or access. Often the sensitivity of the species or habitat conditions requires that public access be prohibited or severely restricted. Such restrictions may in turn reduce the practical benefit of having adjacent protected habitat.

While these economic and marketing benefits will vary depending on the nature of the HCP and local development patterns, they may be substantial enough that developers and private landowners are more supportive of the HCP concept than they otherwise would be.

Community Prosperity and Support for HCPs

The political feasibility of HCPs, especially regional HCPs, will also depend on the extent to which local communities, and the local officials in these communities, view the results as positive. The case studies do illustrate that, at least initially, local officials often view habitat planning requirements in a negative light, considering them additional requirements that may be costly to the community and serve to thwart local growth. The case studies suggest, however, that local officials do eventually view HCPs as a very positive tool. As with developers, community-wide or regional HCPs are seen as cost-effective strategies for dealing with the issue of endangered species protection—strategies which have the potential for addressing the issue through a single process, and at a single point in time. This is seen, again, as far preferable to the higher cost and inconvenience of leaving mitigation to be handled on a project-by-project basis.

While some local officials have certainly been critical of the time involved in preparing HCPs, and gaining approval, those having finished or completed the process appear to view the mechanism favorably. The HCP outcome has generally not impeded or slowed local growth, has not appreciably reduced the local tax base, and has not negatively affected local economic activity. Indeed, it is frequently perceived that the habitat protection has provided clear and direct community benefits. There is a certain local pride in Coachella Valley, for instance, now that a major portion of the desert ecosystem has been set aside and protected in perpetuity. This is seen as an extremely important public benefit—and one which probably would not have been possible without the catalyst of the HCP. There is a perception in Coachella Valley and other HCP sites that the resulting land protection can substantially enhance local quality of life.

There has, moreover, been a growing concern in recent years in communities around the country to protect and preserve open space and natural areas. There has been much discussion of the virtues of establishing greenbelts, wildlife and open space corridors, riverfront parks, and so on, in recent years. The local initiatives and activities in this area are impressive with a number of communities establishing and expanding greenbelt and open space systems (e.g., Portland, Oregon; Raleigh, North Carolina; Boulder, Colorado; Montgomery County, Maryland; and many others).[20] These are priorities which are likely to grow in the future and which again will dovetail effectively with the preparation of HCPs.

Few studies have been undertaken on the community-level economic benefits that could result from extensive habitat protection. Concerns are sometimes expressed about the loss of tax base, and the stifling of economic activity, but these concerns so far appear to be unwarranted. In all the HCPs studied here, sufficient land for development has remained and there was little tax base loss. Furthermore, as noted earlier, approval of an HCP may serve to substantially enhance the economic attractiveness of land covered under a 10(a) permit. Also habitat protection does not itself eliminate or reduce development demand, but instead displaces this demand onto other developable properties (perhaps leading to increased densities in these areas). Furthermore, the community tax base also benefits from rising land values adjacent to and surrounding protected lands.

A Final Checklist

The case studies presented here suggest that despite the limitations cited, successful HCPs can be crafted and implemented. While there are no easy ways to overcome certain fundamental issues in the HCP process, the experiences to date do suggest that those about to embark on an HCP should keep in mind the following checklist:

The HCP process should include representatives of all affected stakeholder groups. All individuals and groups who have a potential stake in the outcome should be included. Those not included in the process may create legal or other obstacles to the plan after it has been prepared.

The HCP should incorporate as complete and as thorough a biological and scientific information base as possible. The defensibility of the plan—politically, legally, administratively—will depend largely on its biological and scientific integrity. Major data deficiencies, and failure to consult key biological experts, may jeopardize approval and support of the plan.

Integrate the HCP into local and regional long-range planning. In preparing the HCP and in identifying proposed conservation areas, all efforts should be made to ensure consistency with local and regional land use and growth management plans. Long-term viability of protected areas will be enhanced if they can be located and configured in ways which insulate them from future development pressures.

Develop an equitable long-term funding program. Successful HCPs will require steady long-term funding sources for acquisition, management, and research. Equity and political considerations suggest the desirability of seeking a mixed and balanced funding package, spreading the financial burden over a number of benefiting groups (e.g., developers, general public, property owners).

Protect simultaneously habitat for multiple species; seek to protect broader patterns of diversity. Consideration of the habitat needs of many species will in the long run reduce conservation costs, reduce uncertainty to the development community, and enhance political and community support for the plan.

Look for ways of dovetailing habitat conservation with other community goals.
HCPs will be much more politically feasible if these efforts can be combined with other local and regional goals, such as the need for public
recreational lands, open space, and water quality protection.

Conclusions

This book has attempted to summarize the main experiences of the use
of regional habitat conservation plans. Because the HCP provisions are
a relatively recent addition to the Endangered Species Act, and because
few HCPs have been completed, it is premature to definitively critique
or assess the success of these plans. There has been sufficient experience, however, to suggest tentative observations about how successful
and useful a tool the HCP mechanism is in terms of protecting and preserving biodiversity. Without doubt the next decade will witness even
greater conflicts between urban development and endangered species
protection. HCPs will be even more extensively utilized, and it is important to reflect on their limitations and the potential for improvement of
this conservation tool.

Generally, HCPs do appear to provide a necessary pressure release
valve under ESA and do seem to be resulting in the protection and preservation of substantial amounts of species habitat. Furthermore, the
HCP process has generated substantial funding for conservation and
management activities which would otherwise not have been available.
However, despite these positive outcomes a number of concerns have
been expressed about the amount of habitat loss permitted through
HCPs, the defensibility and long-term viability of conserved habitat
areas, the failure to take broader comprehensive and multi-species approaches, the necessity of making habitat and management decisions
with limited biological understanding, the common failure to integrate
species conservation with local land use planning and growth management, the failure to adequately address the long-term funding needs of
HCPs, and the failure to adequately consider the question of interim
protection. While it is relatively easy to accuse the USFWS of failing to
provide leadership on these issues, responsibility also lies with local and
state governments. State governments, for instance, will tend to have
the financial and other resources to facilitate the preparation of efficient
comprehensive habitat protection plans.

One role which the USFWS must continue to play, and play perhaps
more aggressively than it has in the past, is in the area of enforcement.
Clearly, if developers and land users do not perceive the liabilities of
undertaking activities in habitat areas to be significant they will be less

inclined to participate in HCPs. For instance, there is apparently only one USFWS enforcement officer for the entire state of Nevada. The USFWS must also make it clear that the failure to prepare a strong HCP, which protects a large proportion of species habitat, will result in a local development moratorium, as politically unpopular as this may be. It is also clear that there are many situations where private development has deleterious effects on listed species but where no HCP is required by USFWS under a narrow interpretation of take. For example, on Big Pine Key, Florida, development in the northern end of the island is substantially increasing traffic along the major north-south road (Big Pine Boulevard), in turn leading to increased road kills of the endangered key deer. The USFWS should make development in these circumstances conditional upon the submittal and implementation of an acceptable HCP.

The increasingly frequent use of the HCP mechanism also suggests an important research role in documenting and disseminating information about successful strategies and approaches. Until recently, participants involved in preparing HCPs have had relatively little information about the experiences and issues confronted by HCPs prepared in other areas. While each HCP will have its own unique circumstances, much can be learned from the others.

Notes

1. Land Development and Endangered Species: Emerging Conflicts

1. For instance, see Edward O. Wilson and Francis M. Peter, eds., *Biodiversity* (Washington, D.C.: National Academy Press, 1988); Paul Ehrlich and Anne Ehrlich, *Extinction: The Causes and Consequences of the Disappearance of Species* (New York: Ballantine Books, 1981).

2. For a discussion of global population trends, see Paul Ehrlich et al., *The Population Explosion* (New York: Simon and Schuster, 1990).

3. "The Current State of Biological Diversity." In Wilson and Peter, eds., *Biodiversity*.

4. See Walter V. Reid and Kenton R. Miller, *Keeping Options Alive: The Scientific Basis for Conserving Biodiversity* (Washington, D.C.: World Resource Institute, 1989).

5. This discussion draws heavily from Timothy Beatley, "Planning for Endangered Species: On the Possibilities of Sharing A Small Planet," *Carolina Planning*, vol. 15 (1989).

6. See, for example, Norman Myers, *The Sinking Ark: A New Look at the Problem of Disappearing Species* (New York: Pergamon Press, 1979).

7. John A. Murray, *Wildlife in Peril: The Endangered Mammals of Colorado* (Boulder, Col.: Roberts Rinehart, Inc., 1987), p. 5.

8. See Jane E. Brody, "Scientists Eye Ancient Plant as Better Source of Pulp for Paper," *New York Times*, December 10, 1988.

9. Ehrlich and Ehrlich, *Extinction*, pp. xi–xiv.

10. Aldo Leopold, *Sand County Almanac* (New York: Oxford University Press, 1949).

11. Ibid. p. 204.

12. Ibid. pp. 224–225.

13. David Ehrenfeld, *The Arrogance of Humanism* (New York: Oxford University Press, 1978), pp. 207–208.

14. E.g., Paul Taylor, *Respect for Nature: A Theory of Environmental Ethics* (Princeton: Princeton University Press, 1986).

2. The Federal Endangered Species Act: Key Provisions and Implications for Land Development

1. For an overview of this history see Kathryn A. Kohm, "The Act's History and Framework," in K. A. Kohm, ed., *Balancing on the Brink of Extinction* (Washington, D.C.: Island Press, 1991).

2. Endangered Species Act, Section 2(b).

3. Ibid., Section 3.

4. For a discussion of the limitations of the listing process, including the injection of politics, see U.S. General Accounting Office (GAO), "Spotted Owl Petition Evaluation Beset by Problems," February 1989.

5. Endangered Species Act, Section 3(5)(A).

6. For a recent analysis of the efforts of the Section 7 consultation requirement, see GAO, "Limited Effect of Consultation Requirements on Western Water Projects," March 1987.

7. As Yagermann notes, USFWS regulations have essentially collapsed the no-jeopardy and no-adverse-effect-on-habitat requests into a single standard. Destruction or adverse modification of critical habitat is not generally deemed to occur unless it threatens the existence of the listed species. See Katherine Simmons Yagermann, "Protecting Critical Habitat under the Federal Endangered Species Act," *Environmental Law* 20 (1990): 811–856.

8. For a more detailed review of this case see Edwin Smith, "The Endangered Species Act and Biological Conservation," *Southern California Law Review*, vol. 57 (1984).

9. 437 U.S. 153 (1978).

10. E.g., Ruth Marcus, "Endangered Species Act Must Change, Bush Says," *Washington Post*, Tuesday, September 15, 1992.

11. Endangered Species Act, Section 3-19.

12. See Robert D. Thornton, "Search for Consensus and Predictability: Habitat Conservation Planning under the Endangered Species Act of 1973," *Environmental Law* 21 (1992): 588–604.

13. 471 F. Supp. 985 (D. Harv. 1979) affirmed, 639 F. 2d 495 (9th Cir. 1981).

14. 50 C.F.R. Section 17-2.

15. 631 F. Supp. 787 (D. Harv. 1985). The court concluded the following: "A finding of 'harm' does not require death to individual members of the species; nor does it require a finding that habitat degradation is presently driving the species further toward extinction. Habitat destruction that prevents the recovery of the species by affecting essential behavioral patterns causes actual injury to the species and effects a taking under Section 9 . . ." (649 F. Supp. 1071). For a discussion of the implications of the so-called "Palila-II" decision see Frederico Cheever, "An Introduction to the Prohibition against Takings in Section 9 of the Endangered Species Act of 1973: Learning to Live with a Powerful Species Preservation Law," *University of Colorado Law Review*, vol. 62 (1991).

16. General Accounting Office, "Endangered Species: Management Improvements Could Enhance Recovery Program," GAO/RCED-89-5, December 1988.

17. See Lindell Marsh and Robert Thornton, "San Bruno Mountain Habitat Conservation Plan," in *Managing Land Use Conflicts* (Durham, N.C.: Duke University Press, 1987).

18. Endangered Species Act, Section 10(a)(2)(A).

19. Ibid.; see U.S. Fish and Wildlife Service, Conservation Planning Guidelines, 1990.

20. For a review of state endangered-species laws and programs see Steven T. King and J. R. Schrock, *Controlled Wildlife*, vol. 3 (State Wildlife Regulations, Association of Systematics Collections, Lawrence, Kansas, 1985).

3. Overview of Past and Ongoing Habitat Conservation Plans and Processes

1. An earlier and shorter version of this table appeared in Timothy Beatley, "Regional Wildlife Conservation Programs," in *Urban Land* (Washington, D.C.: Urban Land Institute, August 1991).

2. For a more in-depth discussion of this issue see Beatley, "Land Development and Endangered Species: The Coachella Valley Fringe-toed Lizard Habitat Conservation Plan," technical report prepared for the National Fish and Wildlife Foundation, Washington, D.C., 1990.

4. The Politics of Habitat Conservation Planning: Key Actors and Perspectives

1. For a good discussion of the Wise Use Movement see Kate O'Callaghan, "Whose Agenda for America," *Audubon*, September–October 1992.

2. Susan Sward, "Secretary Lujan and the Squirrels," *San Francisco Chronicle*, May 12, 1990, p. A-1.

3. See for instance U.S. General Accounting Office, "Spotted Owl Petition Beset by Problems," February 1989.

4. Walter E. Williams, "Liberty in Retreat," *Richmond Times-Dispatch*, August 16, 1991, p. A-19.

5. E.g., John Lancaster, "Public Land, Private Profit: U.S. Ranchers Face Off over Grazing Limits," *Washington Post*, February 17, 1991.

6. See Stephen Kellert, *Public Attitudes toward Critical Wildlife and Natural Habitat Issues* (Washington, D.C.: U.S. Fish and Wildlife Service, 1979).

7. Steve Moore, "Fringe-toed Lizard Flares Anew in Desert Area," *Press-Enterprise*, November 19, 1983.

8. "County Planners Tentatively Favor Condos Although Lizards Are Issue," *Press-Enterprise*, June 24, 1984.

9. Ibid.

5. Habitat Conservation Plans to Protect Butterflies and Invertebrate Species

1. Lindell L. Marsh and Robert D. Thornton, "San Bruno Mountain Habitat Conservation Plan," in David J. Brower and Daniel S. Carol, eds., *Managing Land Use Conflicts: Case Studies in Special Area Management* (Durham, N.C.: Duke University Press, 1987), p. 116.

2. Ibid., p. 120.

3. County of San Mateo, *San Bruno Mountain Area Habitat Conservation Plan*, vol. 1 (San Bruno Mountain Habitat Conservation Plan Steering Committee, November 1982).

4. Marsh and Thornton, "San Bruno Mountain," p. 121.

5. County of San Mateo, *San Bruno Mountain*, pp. 5–8.

6. For a full discussion of this see Michael J. Bean, Sarah G. Fitzgerald, and Michael A. O'Connell, *Reconciling Conflicts under the Endangered Species Act: The Habitat Conservation Planning Experience* (Washington, D.C.: World Wildlife Fund, 1991).

7. 596 F. Suppl. 518 (N. Cal. 1984) aff'd 760 F. 2d 976 (9th Circuit 1985).

8. For a review, see Frederico Cheever, "An Introduction to the Prohibition against Takings in Section 9 of the Endangered Species Act of 1973: Learning to Live with a Powerful Species Preservation Law," *University of Colorado Law Review* 62 (1991): 109–199.

9. For a full review of amendment proposals see Bean, Fitzgerald, and O'Connell, *Reconciling Conflicts,* pp. 57–59.

10. Marsh and Thornton, "San Bruno Mountain," p. 137.

6. Conserving Habitat for a Threatened Desert Lizard: The Coachella Valley Habitat Conservation Plan

1. Portions of this chapter have been published in "Balancing Urban Development and Endangered Species: The Coachella Valley Habitat Conservation Plan," *Environmental Management,* 16, no. 1 January (1992): 7–19.

2. Coachella Valley Association of Governments, "Coachella Valley Area Growth Monitor," 1988; Coachella Valley Association of Governments, Regional Housing Needs Assessment," 1989.

3. See Coachella Valley HCP Steering Committee, *Coachella Valley Habitat Conservation Plan,* 1985, Section II; J. Cornett, "Uma, the Fringe-toed Lizard," *Pacific Discovery,* vol. 36 (April–June, 1983); C. C. Carpenter, "Patterns of Behavior in the Form of Fringe-toed Lizards," *Copeia,* vol. 2 (1963).

4. "Occupiable habitat" is defined in the HCP as "all undisturbed lands within CVFTL historic range which now provide or have the potential to provide habitat for CVFTL when considered over geologic time. The limits of occupiable habitat are determined by historic and present CVFTL distributions and by considerations of topography, geology, and meteorology. The area designated as occupiable habitat is a subset of the historic range: historic CVFTL populations in areas south of the Whitewater River and between Indio and the Salton Sea are considered to be extirpated with virtually no possibility of recolonization and these areas are excluded from the designation of occupiable habitat. Unless noted as 'scattered,' most areas within occupiable habitat can be expected to be actually occupied by CVFTL now or at various times in the future, as lizard microhabitats and populations themselves change distribution over time." *Coachella Valley HCP,* p. II-19.

5. Professor Mayhew stated in an interview: "The lizard was selected intentionally, but on the other hand, there were other species that could have been selected to try to get listed as endangered or threatened. We had more information on the fringe-toed lizard. I had done a good deal of work on the reproductive activities and temperature regulation of these animals. Other people had worked a lot in other aspects of their biology. They are restricted to windblown sand deposits, and this species occurs only in the Coachella Valley. This seemed like the prime target to use as our lever for acquiring habitat. We felt that if we could not get the people in the valley to support an organism for which they had the entire world's population, we had little chance of getting them to sup-

port anything to be listed . . . This seemed like the best organism to use in our attempts to get state and federal money for the acquisition of an ecological reserve." Gloria Schaepfer, "A Model for Land Conservation: An Oral History Analysis of Habitat Preservation for the Coachella Valley Fringe-toed Lizard, an Endangered Species," M.A. thesis, California State University–Fullerton, 1985, pp. 143–144.

6. U.S. Fish and Wildlife Service, *Recovery Plan for the Coachella Valley Fringe-toed Lizard* (Portland, Ore., 1984).

7. A. S. England and S. G. Nelson, "Status of Coachella Valley Fringe-toed Lizard," Inland Fisheries Administrative Report No. 77-1, California Department of Fish and Game, 1976.

8. England and Nelson conclude that the current range of the lizard (in 1975) was 236 square miles, compared to its historical range of 324 square miles, or a 27 percent reduction of the range existing in 1975. They estimated that only 51 percent of it, or about 120 square miles, was suitable habitat (i.e., blowsand habitat). See England and Nelson, *Status*, p. 10.

9. Riverside County Planning Department, "Desert Habitat Preserve: A Preliminary Study," December 1973.

10. Dave Michaels, "Lizard Termed 'Grave Threat,'" *Desert Sun*, November 9, 1978.

11. There was considerable confusion about what had actually been withdrawn by USFWS. Some news reports wrongly indicated that the proposal to list the lizard as threatened had been withdrawn. See for example Martin Saldith, "Fringe-toed Lizard Withdrawn from Proposed Endangered List," *Desert Sun*, March 28, 1979.

12. Martin Hill, "Lizard Reserve Is Endorsed: Five-Square-Mile Area Gets C-VAG Backing," *Desert Sun*, March 28, 1978.

13. The letter states in its second paragraph: "The opinion of the Foundation is that the Specific Plan projects a cavalier attitude and remarkable insensitivity to the biological consequences of the proposed project. The Biological Resources Investigation is superficial and of questionable value for determining the biological resources that are actually present on site." Allan Muth, "Letter to John Crista, Riverside County Planning Department," June 5, 1982.

14. Sunrise also agreed to contribute the $25,000 mitigation fee if the process failed. The California Department of Fish and Game called this figure inadequate. Holly Kurtz, "Supervisors tentatively OK 433-Acre Tract in Fringe-toed Lizard Area," *Press-Enterprise*, September 21, 1983.

15. Schlaepfer, "A Model for Land Conservation."

16. Specifically, the county adopted a modified version of its "N-A" or "Natural Assets" zone. Under this zone, intensive urban development is prohibited. A minimum lot size of twenty acres is required and potentially incompatible uses such as golf courses require a conditional use permit. This zoning was adopted on an interim basis originally but was essentially kept in place after the HCP was adopted and the preserve established.

17. U.S. Fish and Wildlife Service, *Recovery Plan*, 1984.

18. Kathleen Franzreb, "Economic Impact of Designation Critical Habitat for the Coachella Valley Fringe-toed Lizard" (Sacramento: U.S. Fish and Wildlife Service, 1980).

19. These include: Riverside County, Coachella, Indio, Cathedral City, Ran-

cho Mirage, Palm Desert, Indian Wells, LaQuinta, Desert Hot Springs, and Palm Springs.

20. Rita Lewis, "Grower Criticizes Preserve," *Desert Sun,* November 15, 1984.

21. As a result of turning over these twelve hundred acres for the preserve, the Coachella Valley Water District was given permission by USFWS to construct additional dikes and groundwater settling ponds near Windy Point. Under an agreement with the Desert Water Agency and the Metropolitan Water District CVWD receives water diverted from the Colorado River. Water is channeled into ponds and used to recharge local groundwater. See "CVWD to Add 1200 Acres to Preserve," *Press-Enterprise,* May 25, 1984.

22. The ACEC designation provides a special level of management and protection by BLM. BLM prepares a special management plan for each designation, and in times of financial and personnel shortages, ACECs receive priority. Incompatible uses such as oil and gas development and ORV recreation are usually prohibited in these areas.

23. The steering committee realized that acquisition for the Coachella Valley Preserve might actually be between $20 million and $22 million, and between $1 million and 2 million for the Willow Hole–Edom Hill preserve. For planning purposes the $20 million and $2 million estimates were assumed.

24. Coachella Valley HCP Steering Committee, *Coachella Valley Habitat Conservation Plan,* 1985, p. V-6.

25. To date The Nature Conservancy has purchased 12,087 acres. A total of $18,201,365 was paid by TNC for land with a fair market value of $25,136,350. This reflects the fact that some lands were acquired through gifts or "bargain sales." Correspondence from Jennifer Johnson, The California Nature Conservancy, August 31, 1989.

26. The Nature Conservancy estimates that USFWS has spent a total of $8,973,058 to purchase land in the preserve from TNC. Correspondence from Jennifer Johnson, California Project Coordinator, TNC, August 31, 1989.

27. The actual total value of BLM exchange lands received by TNC was $6,066,255. Correspondence from Jennifer Johnson, The California Nature Conservancy, August 31, 1989.

28. The Press-Enterprise, "Bill Seeks Land Trade for Lizard Preserve," *Press-Enterprise,* June 26, 1987.

29. Johnson, correspondence, August 31, 1989.

30. Cameron Barrows, "1989 Monitoring Report: Coachella Valley Fringe-toed Lizard," Southern Area Manager, California Nature Conservancy, 1989.

31. Phone interview with Cameron Barrows, California Nature Conservancy, October 21, 1992.

32. Richard W. Webster, "Habitat Conservation Plans under the Endangered Species Act," *San Diego Law Review* 24 (1987): 255.

7. Habitat Conservation in the Florida Keys: The North Key Largo Habitat Conservation Plan

1. See Rick Boling. "Reef Madness," *Amicus Journal,* Fall 1987, pp. 3–7.

2. "Preliminary Discussion Outline: North Key Largo Habitat Conservation Plan," August 14, 1984.

3. North Key Largo HCP Study Committee, *North Key Largo Habitat Conservation Plan*, 1986, pp. 59–60.

4. Rosemary Harold, "County Stalls Plan for Habitat Location," *Miami Herald*, July 22, 1987.

5. "HCP: The Final Day: Conservationists Decry Outcome," *Miami Herald*, August 7, 1986.

6. Ibid.

7. "Agencies Criticize Habitat Plan," *Miami Herald*, July 31, 1986.

8. As quoted in Boling, "Reef Madness," p. 7.

9. Rosemary Harold, "North Key Largo Growth Plan Tabled," *Miami Herald*, March 4, 1987.

10. Ibid.

8. Protecting Migratory Songbirds: The San Diego Least Bell's Vireo Habitat Conservation Plan

1. Regional Environmental Consultants, *Comprehensive Species Management Plan for the Least Bell's Vireo*, July 1988, pp. ix–x.

2. San Diego Association of Governments, "Vireo Project Update: Planning Process Overview," 1989.

3. See Regional Environmental Consultants, *Sweetwater River Habitat Conservation Plan*, July 1990.

4. See Regional Environmental Consultants, *Sweetwater River Habitat Conservation Plan*, 1990, p. 16.

5. San Diego Association of Governments, *Conservation Plan for the Least Bell's Vireo and Riparian Habitat on the Sweetwater and San Diego Rivers in San Diego County, California*, August 13, 1992, p. 9.

6. Ibid., pp. 11–12.

7. Lou Cannon, "Opportunities, Obstacles in Songbird's Fate," *Washington Post*, September 22, 1991.

8. Steve LaRue, "Detours Are Found around a Little Bird," *San Diego Union*, July 31, 1989.

9. Tim Mayer, "Needs of Endangered Bird, Landowners Clash," *Blade Tribute*, February 4, 1988.

10. Ibid.

11. E.g., San Diego Association of Governments, "CSMP Task Force Meeting Notes," March 20, 1990.

9. Endangered Rats and Endangered Homeowners: The Affordable Housing/ Species Clash in Riverside County

1. See Regional Environmental Consultants, *Short-Term Habitat Conservation Plan for the Stephens' Kangaroo Rat*, prepared for Riverside County Planning Department, September 1989.

2. Ibid. p. xiv.

3. Ibid. p. xvii. "Implementation Agreement," August 1, 1990.

4. Dangermond and Associates, *Multiple Species Habitat Conservation Plan*, for

Riverside County, California, with Regional Environmental Consultants, January 1991, draft.

5. Riverside Parks and Open Space District, "Status of the Draft: Multiple Species Habitat Conservation Strategy," July 1991, p. 1.

6. Advisory Commission on Regulatory Barriers to Affordable Housing, *Not in My Backyard: Removing Barriers to Affordable Housing* (Washington, D.C., 1991).

10. Preserving the Desert Tortoise: The Clark County Habitat Conservation Plan

1. "Determination of Threatened Status for the Mojave Population of the Desert Tortoise," *Federal Register*, April 2, 1990.

2. "Assessment of Las Vegas Valley 'Commenced' Parcels," Fish and Wildlife Service, 1990, p. 1.

3. Regional Environmental Consultants, "Short-Term Habitat Conservation Plan for the Desert Tortoise in Las Vegas Valley, Clark County, Nevada" (San Diego, Calif., 1990).

4. Ibid.

11. Preserving the Kit Fox and Other Flora and Fauna of the San Joaquin Valley: The Bakersfield and Kern County Habitat Conservation Plans

1. Thomas Reid Associates, *Metropolitan Bakersfield Habitat Conservation Plan and Environmental Impact Report*, prepared for Metropolitan Bakersfield Habitat Conservation Plan Steering Committee, September 1990; see also USFWS, *San Joaquin Kit Fox Recovery Plan*, 1983, Portland.

2. See Jim Carnal, "Native Kit Fox Gains Ally," *Bakersfield Californian*, January 7, 1989.

3. Reid Associates, *Metropolitan*, p. iii.

4. Dames and Moore, *Endangered Species Element, Kern County General Plan*, preliminary draft, July 1991.

12. The Promise of Regional, Multi-species Approaches: The Balcones Canyonlands Conservation Plan

1. E.g., Biological Advisory Team, *Comprehensive Report of the Biological Advisory Team of the Austin Regional Habitat Conservation Plan*, January 1990.

2. See *Balcones Canyonlands Conservation Plan*, prepared for the BCCP Executive Committee, final draft, February 1992.

3. Seth Searcy and Kent Butler, "Memo to Executive Committee, Balcones Canyonlands Habitat Conservation Plan, Synopsis of Local Bill Authorizing Enforcement and Financing of the BCHCP," October 12, 1990; Seth Searcy, "Memo to Executive Committee, Balcones Canyonlands Habitat Conservation Plan, Draft Interlocal Contract Creating the Balcones Canyonlands Habitat Conservation Authority," August 24, 1990.

4. Michelle Kay, "Proposed Habitat's Final Cost, Who Will Bear It Undetermined," *Austin American-Statesman*, August 25, 1991.

5. Ibid.

6. George W. Gau and James E. Javrett, *Economic Impact Study: Balcones Canyonlands Conservation Plan*, preliminary draft, June 5, 1992, pp. 1–12.

7. Ibid.

8. Kay, "Proposed Habitat's Final Cost."

9. Michelle Kay, "Conservation Crossroads: Preserve Proposal Forks Paths to Future," *Austin American-Statesman*, August 25, 1991.

10. Balcones Canyonlands HCP Executive Committee, *Balcones Canyonlands Habitat Conservation Plan*, 1991, pp. 7–11.

11. City of Austin, *Austin Tomorrow Comprehensive Plan*, Department of Planning, 1980.

12. Kent S. Butler and Dowall Myers, "Boomtime in Austin, Texas: Negotiated Growth Management," *Journal of the American Planning Association* 50, no. 4, (1984): 447–458.

13. Evaluating the Success of Habitat Conservation Efforts: Lessons Learned and Recommendations for the Future

1. For a more detailed review of the case see Timothy Beatley, *Land Development and Endangered Species: The Coachella Valley Fringe-toed Lizard Habitat Conservation Plan*, prepared for the National Fish and Wildlife Foundation, February 1990.

2. See Thomas Reid and Dennis Murphy, "The Endangered Mission Blue Butterfly," in Bruce Wilcox, Peter Brussard, and Bruce Mascot, eds., *The Management of Viable Populations: Theory, Application and Case Studies* (Stanford, Calif.: Center for Conservation Biology, Stanford University, 1986).

3. See Cameron Barrows, "1989 Monitoring Report: Coachella Valley Fringe-toed Lizard," Southern California Area Manager, TNC.

4. Richard E. Webster, "Habitat Conservation Plans under the Endangered Species Act," *San Diego Law Review*, vol. 24 (1987).

5. See Coachella Valley HCP Steering Committee, *Coachella Valley Fringe-toed Lizard Habitat Conservation Plan* (Riverside, Calif., 1985), section 7.

6. See San Diego Association of Governments, *Comprehensive Species Management Plan for the Least Bell's Vireo*, 1989, pp. 67–88.

7. See *Balcones Canyonlands Conservation Plan*, final draft, February 1992.

8. See Dames and Moore, *Endangered Species Element, Kern County General Plan*, Kern County, Calif.

9. See J. Michael Scott et al., "Species Richness: A Geographical Approach to Protecting Future Biological Diversity," *BioScience*, vol. 37 (December 1987); J. Michael Scott et al., "Beyond Endangered Species: An Integrated Conservation Strategy for the Preservation of Biological Diversity," *Endangered Species UPDATE*, vol. 5 (1989).

10. For a review of these issues see James R. Udall, "Launching the Ark," *Sierra*, September/October 1991; William Stolzenburg, "The Fragment Connection," *Nature Conservancy*, July/August 1991; Larry Harris and Peter Gallagher, "New Initiatives for Wildlife Conservation: The Need for Movement Corridors," in *Preserving Communities and Corridors* (Washington, D.C.: Defenders of Wildlife, 1989).

11. For discussions of these concepts see Douglas H. Chadwick, "The Biodiversity Challenge," *Defenders* 65, no. 3 (1990): 19–34.

12. See John DeGrove, *Land, Growth and Politics* (Chicago: APA Planners Press, 1987).

13. See Dames and Moore, *Endangered Species Element*.

14. For example see *Room Enough: Housing and Open Space in the Bay Area* (San Francisco: People for Open Space, 1983).

15. Riverside County Planning Department, biological background report on Stephens' Kangaroo Rat, 1989.

16. See Robert L. Carlton, "Property Rights and Incentives in the Preservation of Species," in Bryan G. Norton, ed., *The Preservation of Species: The Value of Diversity* (Princeton, N.J.: Princeton University Press, 1986).

17. For a review of these programs see Timothy Beatley, David Brower, and LouAnn Brower, *Managing Growth: Small Communities and Rural Areas* (Chapel Hill, N.C.: UNC Center for Urban and Regional Studies, 1988).

18. See Regional Environmental Consultants, "Short-Term Habitat Conservation Plan."

19. George W. Gan and James E. Jarrett, *Economic Impact Study: Balcones Canyonlands Conservation Plan*, preliminary draft, June 5, 1992.

20. See Timothy Beatley, David J. Brower, and Lou Ann Brower, *Managing Growth: Small Towns and Rural Communities*, prepared for the State of Maine, Office of State Planning, 1988; Luther Propst et al., *Successful Communities* (Washington, D.C.: Conservation Foundation, 1990); Samual Stokes et al., *Saving America's Countryside: A Guide to Rural Conservation* (Baltimore: Johns Hopkins University Press, 1989); Robert Coughlin and John Keene, *The Protection of Farmland: A Reference Guidebook for State and Local Governments* (Washington, D.C.: National Agricultural Lands Study, 1981).

Index